M 1: 333

Innovative Austrian Architecture
Ramesh Kumar Biswas (Ed.)

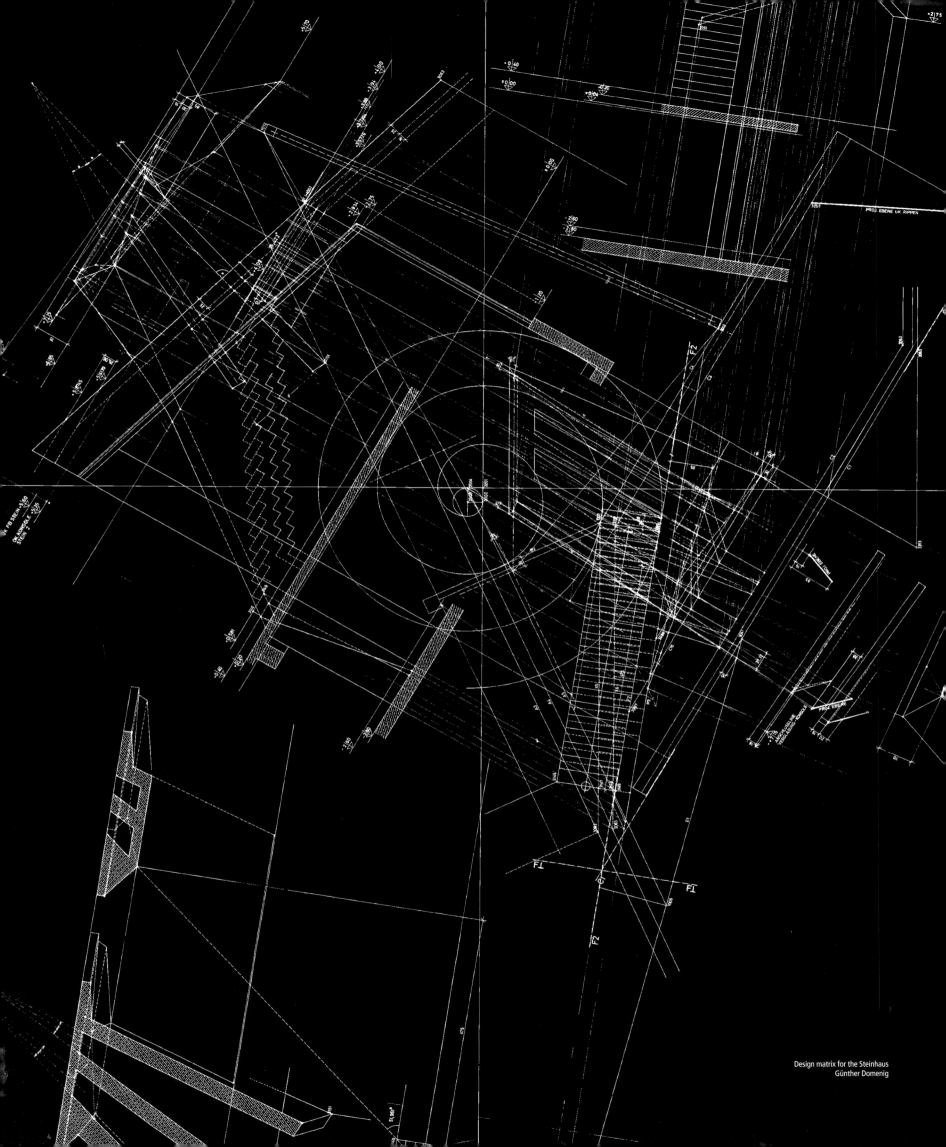

Design matrix for the Steinhaus
Günther Domenig

WORK ON PHILOSOPHY -

LIKE MOST WORK ON ARCHITECTURE -

IS ACTUALLY WORK ON ONESELF.

ON ONE'S OWN CONVICTIONS.

ON THE WAY ONE SEES THINGS.

AND WHAT ONE DEMANDS OF THEM.

LUDWIG WITTGENSTEIN

This book was published in January 1996. It accompanied an international

exhibition on the same theme to be displayed in 15 countries beginning in 1996,

commissioned and sponsored by the Cultural Division of the

Austrian Federal Ministry of Foreign Affairs

Head of the Cultural Division

Peter Marboe

Head of the Exhibition Department

Barbara Lee-Störck

© Springer-Verlag WienNewYork and contributors 1996

ISBN 3-211-82728-5

Typeset in Frutiger by Adrian Frutiger, Matrix by Zuzanna Licko, Gill Sans by Eric Gill, FF Meta by Erik Spikermann,

FF Scala by Martin Majoor, Bodoni by Chauncey H. Griffith Printed on KNP-Leykam Magnomatt 150 gm

Kodak material was used.

We would like to express our thanks to

Federal Ministry for Transport and Public Enterprises

Federal Ministry of Commerce

Niederösterreichische Landesregierung

Wiener Verkehrsbetriebe

Österreichische Postsparkasse

Landeshauptstadt Linz

Funder Industrie GmbH

KNP-Leykam

Österreichische Beamtenversicherung

Vorarlberger Landesregierung

Kärntner Landesregierung

Wüstenrot

Holzbauwerke Kaufmann

SEG Stadterneuerungs & Eigentumswohnungs GmbH

Stadt Wien

Stadt Krems

Stadt Graz

PETER ALLISON was born in 1944 in Blackpool. He trained at the Architectural Association and Cornell University. Assistant at Milton Keynes and with O.M. Ungers in Ithaca and Cologne. He has taught at the University of California at Los Angeles and the AA, and has recently been a visiting professor in Graz and Hanoi. Frequently publishes architectural criticism and essays. Currently teaching at South Bank University, London.

RAMESH KUMAR BISWAS was born in 1957 in Madras. Of Malaysian origin, he studied architecture in New Delhi and urban design in Edinburgh. Doctoral research on urban ecology. He has worked in Kuala Lumpur, Helsinki and Vienna, where he has his own design practice since 1991. His concepts and designs for exhibitions for major museums in Europe have been published widely. He has lectured in numerous universities in Asia, Europe and Africa, was Visiting Professor at the ENPC, Paris, in 1985, and now lectures at the Academy of Fine Arts, Vienna and tutors design studio at the Technical University of Vienna. Consultant to international organizations on habitat issues. Publications and books on cultural phenomenology and society include "Magical Hands - Art and Everyday Culture of India", Vienna 1993.

Editor
Ramesh Kumar Biswas

MATTHIAS BOECKL was born in 1962 in Vienna. He studied art history at the University of Vienna. Subsequent to his doctorate in 1989, he has been teaching and researching history of architecture at the University of Applied Arts in Vienna. He has edited or authored numerous books, exhibitions, essays and articles on Modernism, including "Visionäre und Vertriebene", a major work on Austrian traces in modern American architecture.

Graphic and book design
FINE LINE, Vienna
Erich Monitzer with Regina Rowland
and Karen Schmitzberger

WALTER M. CHRAMOSTA was born in 1956 in Vienna. He studied architecture and civil engineering in Vienna and writes as a critic for newspapers and magazines. Juror in architectural competitions and curator of exhibitions. Books include "Autochthonous Architecture in Tirol" with Kenneth Frampton, Hall in Tirol 1992.

OTTO KAPFINGER was born in 1949 in St. Pölten. He studied architecture at the Technical University in Vienna. In 1970 he founded the avant-garde group Missing Link with Angela Hareiter and Adolf Krischanitz. He has published several hundred essays in books and journals, most notably in the daily newspaper "Die Presse" and in the architectural journal "Umbau" which he co-founded in 1979. He has taught at the University of Applied Arts in Vienna and curated many exhibitions on 20th century architecture in Austria.

Translations and sub-editing
Chris Clouter, Susan Tapply and
Ramesh Kumar Biswas

SIEGFRIED MATTL was born in 1954 in Mürzzuschlag. He studied history and political science at the University of Vienna, where he completed his doctorate on agricultural policy, and where he now teaches at the Institute of Contemporary History. He is a researcher at the Ludwig Boltzmann Institute of History and Society, and has been awarded an Austrian State Prize for his research. He has edited books and curated exhibitions on the history and phenomena of the 20th century, recently focussing on technology and urbanism. He is working with Ramesh Kumar Biswas on a major exhibition and book on the phenomenology of food, "Food of the Gods". In 1995 he co-curated the architecture festival "80 Days of Vienna".

KATERINA RUEDI was born in 1957 in Brno. She studied at the Architectural Association and the Bartlett in London. She has taught at the AA, the Bartlett and Kingston University, where she runs the postgraduate diploma course in architecture. She has worked for architects in Europe and is in private practice in London. Her work has been exhibited in the UK, Germany and Canada, and published in the AA Files, Daidalos and a/r/c. Her collection of essays, "Against the Grain: Architecture, Culture, Criticism", is due to be published soon.

Curation, coordination
project conception and exhibition design
Ramesh Kumar Biswas

YORGOS SIMEOFORIDIS was born in 1955 in Athens. He studied in Rome, Florence and London. He has taught history and theory at the Graduate School of the Architectural Association and the Graduate School of Fine Arts, University of Pennsylvania. Editor of the international review "Tefchos", consultant to the European Secretariat of EUROPAN, editor of several books, organiser and curator of exhibitions, producer of videos on architecture, he has published and lectured extensively in Europe. In 1994 he founded the Centre for Architectural Research based in Athens.

MICHAEL SORKIN was born in 1948 in Washington. He studied English at Columbia University and at the University of Chicago, architecture at the Massachusetts Institute of Technology and fine arts at Harvard. He has been Visiting Professor at Yale, Cooper Union, the Southern California Institute of Architecture, the AA and the University of Illinois among others, and is currently Professor of Urbanism at the Academy of Fine Arts in Vienna. Design practice in New York since 1977 with current projects in Leipzig, Vienna, Mexico City and Arizona. Exhibitions of his work and exhibitions designed by him have been shown widely in the US. Architectural critic for the Village Voice from 1978-89. Publications in the major architectural journals. Books include "Variations on a Theme Park", NY 1991 and "Exquisite Corpse", London 1991.

The editor wishes to thank Prof. Friedrich Achleitner, Peter Allison,
Prof. Peter Blundell-Jones, Prof. Iain Boyd-Whyte, Walter M. Chramosta,
Roger Connah, Otto Kapfinger, Yorgos Simeoforidis,
Akira Suzuki and Prof. Hiroyuki Suzuki for advice
on the selection of projects and other assistance.

HIROYUKI SUZUKI was born in 1945 in Tokyo. He graduated from the University of Tokyo and completed his doctorate in 1975 at the Courtauld Institute of Art, University of London. He has been Visiting Professor at Harvard and Professor at the University of Tokyo since 1990. His best known book is "Contemporary Architecture of Japan", co-authored with Reyner Banham.

BRUNO ZEVI was born in 1918 in Rome. He is a renowned writer on 20th century architecture. He returned to Italy after his education at Harvard and did his doctorate in Rome before published his first books: "Verso un'architettura organica" (Towards an Organic Architecture), 1945, Saper vedre l'architettura (Knowing how to see architecture), 1948 and "Storia dell'architettura moderna", 1950 and "Architettura e storiografia", 1951. In 1946 he co-founded the journal "Attualità, Architettura, Abitazione, Arte" which later circulated internationally as "L'architettura". Professor of Architectural History in Rome and Venice, practising architect, editor and writer in Rome. Several dozen significant articles and books, including "Architecture as Space", "The Modern Language of Architecture" and an autobiography, "Zevi su Zevi".

Project descriptions by Ramesh Kumar Biswas

INFORMATION ON THE MAIN PROJECTS:
Project type
Name of building, location, year of completion
Name of architect, year of birth
Name of structural engineer
Names of those who worked on the project
Total floor area in square metres
Total building costs in Austrian shillings (10 ATS = 1 US$)
Original place names and orthography have been used except
for Österreich (Austria) and Wien (Vienna).
Footnotes on page 220

TECHNO-WALTZ

M 1:**33**3 INNOVATIVE AUSTRIAN ARCHITECTURE   8

This book looks at Austrian architecture at the end of the 20th century. It documents the important currents and events that have survived fashion to make a permanent impression. For a relatively small country, Austria has had a tremendous influence on the development of modern architecture, beginning with the achievements of the giants Otto Wagner and Adolf Loos at the turn of the century and carrying on through the proponents of the Modern Movement in the interwar years to the inventive and refreshing work in the 80s and 90s. A few Austrian architects have continued to astonish and inspire their fellows in other countries to this day. I hope the projects and analytical essays in this book will go a long way towards helping to understand why.

Marshall McLuhan's hoary global village is also a global school of architecture. A building is scarcely completed in one corner of the world before its innovatory features have acquired a common visual currency in the other three. Austria has without a doubt produced some exceptional buildings. Their presentation is a valid excercise, which, however, must be seen and justified in a global context. The recognition of uniqueness has little to do with patriotism or uncritical praise, as this book will show. A review of work in the context of its place of origin is a useful way to clarify and restate achievements and failures. It is a pause between the endless moving picture frames. It helps the actors and the observers, inside and outside the place, to take stock of developments, to reflect, to analyse. It is a positive look at the role aesthetic and economic criteria play in the development of national consciousness. It places architecture "in the order of things".

With architects all over the world plugged into satellites and subscribing to the same glossy magazines, is it possible at all today to talk about a national architecture? More importantly, in the face of the ugly side of nationalism, is it desirable? Despite its dangerous re-emergence, nationalism is at the same time being undermined in everyday life. The constantly shifting power base of the international economic structure has been accentuated by the data highway. The informational city experiences changes beyond the control of conventional systems, as Manuel Castells points out.[2] National cultures are dynamically related to global space. Borders between the inside and outside of buildings, which formerly defined not only limits and enclosure but also exclusion and isolation, were dissolved by Richard Neutra and his contemporaries in the 20s. In the same way national boundaries in architecture have blurred, replacing isolation with exchange. The Old German words for dwelling and being have the same roots; therefore to dwell in a house is to inhabit the world. Nevertheless, every place still has its own special qualities which cannot be denied and which should be protected against MacDonaldisation.

The ancient Roman concept that every independent being (even a place) has a genius, a guardian spirit, is reflected in the genius loci (the spirit of place). This spirit is not bound by political maps but created by the landscape, the climate, the histories and the peoples. This mountain-bound, landlocked country forces its own particular world-view on its inhabitants. Claude Levi-Strauss's study of societies indicates that a definite standard or signature is used by each society.[3] Christian Norberg-Schulz writes that beyond the functionalism that is the universal rationale for Modernism, there are functions specific to different groups.[4] He also maintains that man cannot gain a foothold through scientific understanding (function) alone—he needs symbols, meaning, orientation, schemata, a specific atmosphere or character, nothing less than a microcosmos to live—all of these being characteristics of Austrian identity.

It is not easy for a small country, however unique its contribution to civilization may be, to establish its position in a world of great powers and spheres of influence. Austria is seen by many to be part of Germany, or of Eastern Europe, as the fancy may be, and nothing irritates Austrians more than such mistaken assumptions. The unparalleled history of this country—ruled for 600 years by a single family, forming the cradle of 20th century thought

TECHNO-WALTZ
M 1:333
Innovative Austrian Architecture

Ramesh Kumar Biswas

LOCAL AND
GLOBAL MEANING

in the fin de siècle, emerging into a simmering republican freedom by World War I, shaken by political instability and social developments in the interwar years, fettered again by foreign occupation from 1938 to 1945, badly scarred by World War II, occupied by the Allied powers from 1945 until independence in 1955, and blessed by unprecedented growth and wealth thereafter – has left its mark on every aspect of its culture and psyche. A country once at the centre of a fifty million soul monarchy that covered half of Europe and such far-flung lands as Mexico, it was reduced after the war to a tiny core of eight million inhabitants, later to become part of a large entity once again upon joining the European Union in 1995. The population reflects this colourful history, as a glance at the names in Vienna's telephone directory shows. In the light of this history the question of national identity is blurred. It may be more fruitful to look at regional rather than national architectural identity, especially in a country with a strong federal structure, where the building agenda lies in the jurisdiction of the federal states. Kenneth Frampton says of the architecture of the Austrian region Tirol, "...time seems to stand still in the mountains...In this rarified mountain air, a century opens up before us in which while the forms are inflected they are not radically different from what they once were. They provide further proof of the adage that architecture is like an elephant, slow moving, expensive and heavy, and hence generically unsuited to the enervated restlessness of commodity culture and dynamic fashionable change".[5]

The regional approach, however, poses serious problems. There are architects who claim to be regional, to be almost defiantly not international. This defiance can quickly degenerate into a provincial stance unless the local and the global are constantly connected. Vienna itself is the bête noir of provincial architects, even though it is here that they are most likely to realize their work. The admirable generosity of the politically conservative federal state of Steiermark in offering young designers the chance to build their radical propositions is widely known. The reader may have heard of the so-called 'Grazer Schule' which refers to the stream of ideas and projects of varying quality to emerge from the town of Graz and its architecture school in the 70s and 80s. The leading proponents produce exceptional work, but the trouble with labels like this that describe heterogenous activity as a movement is that a lot of mediocre architects jump on to the bandwagon to acquire publicity. Talented young architects in Graz today shudder when they hear the name 'Graz School' and firmly disassociate their work from this name tag and its older practitioners. With all due respect to the enthusiastic activities of architects and students in Graz, one cannot oversee the fact that the Graz School was a creation of its patron, the state government, and that it collapsed as soon as certain progressive bureaucrats were removed and policies were changed. A smaller but more sound anti-establishment group operates in the westernmost state of Vorarlberg, where a synthesis is being sought between modern expression and the materials and traditions of the land. In neighbouring Tirol, architects are most often seen on the high road to Vienna. The centre absorbs the periphery of the country, while the periphery of the city swallows its centre. I have documented signs of life and quality outside the metropolis, but ultimately regionalism as a definition is more stifling than liberating.

I also did not seriously consider grouping projects according to style, that home-within-a-home, though those who were once among the most influential Brutalists, Eclecticists, Post-Modernists, Deconstructivists or other stylists-of-the-year would probably scream in protest now at being branded with such descriptions. This is why it is not schools, styles, regions or the oeuvre of individual architects but outstanding buildings in the selected functional categories, regardless of the fame or the obscurity of the architect, that were the basis of choice. This also reflects the multivalence of architectural attitudes in Austria. The inclusion or exclusion of individual names was not an issue, for while there may be a number of competent, prolific and successful yet uninteresting architects not included in a review of good work, this could just as well be the case in any other country. It is coincidence, but perhaps no accident, that some architects appear twice and have even more works that could have been included, and many others not at all – it is after all the buildings that have been selected for their quality. The final choice lies with the readers, who can use their eyes like television remote-control units – the time they spend looking at each project draws their own subjective judgements into a dialogue with ours.

Otto Wagner's Hands
crayon on paper, Vienna 1910, Egon Schiele
Courtesy: the Z·V Austrian Architecture Assosiation

REGIONALISM

A phenomenon that does vary from country to country is the architectural culture. Architecture has been a dominant component of cultural life in Austria in this century, and the pace of its development always a tangible part of the public realm. How many countries can speak of regular and detailed reviews of new buildings in daily newspapers and weekly magazines, of heated debates in the letters columns, of regular exhibitions, talks, events, television documentaries and even architecture festivals? There are signature campaigns and demonstrations on the streets for and against certain projects. There are 'architecture centres' in Vienna and some of the federal capitals, not to mention the traditional cafés which cater to a regular 'scene' that, to Christopher Alexander's astonished exhilaration, "meets and discusses architecture till 2 am on a working day". Members of the scene would, with that typical Austrian brand of cynicism, probably disparage it — not for nothing does the philosopher and mayor of Venice Massimo Cacciari refer to Vienna as the City of Nihilism.[6] But there is considerable hidden pride in their comments. Public interest has a salutory effect on architects, who tend to operate as elites in society. Even if some of the public attitude to modern projects is antipathetic, at least it is not fatalistic or indifferent. People here actually get excited about architecture.

CULTURE

The spirit of innovation is not just a tradition, it is a live issue in Austria. A valid question at the beginning of a project with a clear sense of purpose like this book is to ask if anything in architecture now can really be called innovative. A search in the annals does reveal astonishing parallels. Much of what one sees today seems to be based on the avant-garde of the early 20th century. Rem Koolhaas has remarked, "It's typical now to find that there is almost nothing you can like wholeheartedly. You either have to wear your critical apparatus, and then almost everything is unbearable. Or you have to swallow it."[7] But if one can put cynicism aside for a moment, modern architecture constantly demonstrates its progressive and creative nature anew. Not everything may be brand new today, and masterpieces are few and far between. The complex whole is rarely transported to higher planes, but certain aspects may move it beyond the commonplace. Projects that attracted our attention were innovative in an architectonic or technical way. Design, spatial quality, ecological sensitivity, and the enrichment of the urban sphere were additional criteria. Ingenuity and originality also influenced the choice, as did sudden insight and creativity. Although bold departure from well-trodden paths was striking, restrained and hard-won achievements under difficult conditions were also honoured. Selective observation involves a transformation of expectations. The object is not seen as new because of any particular stylistic or technical contrivance, but as its transformation through another way of seeing. "The feeling of the mind at work most strikingly shines forth in two complementary aspects of utopian life: the use of science and technology and the style of architecture."[8] Let us not nurture any illusions. More than ninety per cent of buildings in Austria, as indeed elsewhere, are not the work of architects. Of those that are, only an equally small proportion may be considered good. This country is not a high-tech Futureland any more than it is a twee collection of wooden huts up in the mountains. Austria as a whole is no more a haven of excellence in architecture than anywhere else, but its output of brilliant work is disproportionately creative and innovative for a small country. This was confirmed by colleagues I consulted in other parts of the world on the state of Austrian architecture and its international influence, in order to avoid the pitfall of provincial self-praise. Even though it was risky to collect the opinions of architectural critics and architects from different countries before making the final selection of projects for this book, there was unexpected consensus among them.

INNOVATION

The international panel of scholars who pre-selected the projects were unusually unified in agreement about those which should be included - and those which should not. One or two of the projects did not appeal to everyone's aesthetic codes and perception of beauty, but were included because of their pioneering nature and influence on the debate. We were suspended between feeling and intellect. The buildings here did not just meet objective criteria, they also touched us emotionally, the quintessential quality of all good architecture. It is what Walter Gropius (surprises never cease) referred to when he founded the Bauhaus in 1919: "What is architecture? The crystalline expression of man's noblest thoughts, his ardour, his humanity, his faith, his religion!.. Build in fantasy without regard for technical difficulties. To have the gift of imagination is more impor-

CHOICE

tant than all technology, which always adapts itself to man's creative will."[9]

The most obvious novelties are those which involve technological innovation, new materials, applications and methods of construction. This so very sensual and tactile aspect of building naturally fascinates all architects, and is an important part of the many facets of the profession that make it so pleasurable. But innovation begins to be exciting when materialistic concerns are subordinate to artistic concerns, though the very best of engineering feats really demonstrate a synthesis of both. Perhaps the reason why the turn-of-the-century hero Otto Wagner is still held in such high regard by contemporary architects of differing ideological disposition is that he was one of the few figures who could combine vast commercial building volumes with artistic quality.

PROCESS AND CONTEXT

Architecture does not have the acontextual freedom of music to experiment. It is most often than not a prisoner of the compulsions of the industrial, financial and organizational systems that it operates in. Those works that escape the system are all the more worthy of regard, like symphonies in a cacophony of commercial jingles. At their best they signal creation and conviction, to a certain degree unrelated to their functions, and have the character of a manifesto like much of early Modernism. When the idea and the process are innovative, it is not always immediately evident in the finished product. Subtlety is a valuable quality, especially in the context of a small country that can only excel with rare and non-populist standpoints. Deleuze and Guattari express the simultaneous dilemma and opportunity of innovation in their book on Kafka, "How many styles or genres or movements, even very small ones, have only one single dream: to offer themselves as a sort of state language, an official language. Create the opposite dream: know how to create a becoming minor."[10]

While ideas and concepts are in the forefront of innovation, this book deals primarily with their translation into actual buildings. There are several good reasons for this. The sheer number of interesting but unrealized projects in Austria would require several books of their own, and, much as I would like to do so, I do not have the time to make a list. Major projects are often discussed, opposed and delayed until they die a natural death; all the more reason to admire those that have actually been built against all odds.

This relatively slow process of democratic decision-making in Austria and its neighbouring countries, unheard of in booming Asian economies, also slows down the period of realization of a project. This may well be no wholly bad thing, as it results in a constant refinement of the design, time to consider. Faits accomplis are not as frequent as in fast-building economies. The original idea has to stand the test of time, even before it has been built. Public and media interference means blockage, but also grants time to reconsider. An example of this process is the prize-winning design of the international competition for the museum quarter in Vienna. The plans have been truncated and delayed so long that no one is enthusiastic about them any more. Soon it will be time to hold a new competition to find a more contemporary design.

While 'architecture on paper' is often influential, identifying path-breaking ideas is always easier in retrospect than at the time of conception. The inclusion of student projects, possible indicators of future directions, would also have been problematic due to the epigonous nature of 'master classes'. The intention behind restricting the choice to built projects was not a narrowing down, but an opening up, an opening wide of one's eyes to the incredible possibilities of architecture. It would truly be difficult to believe that these dynamic designs, these idiosyncracies, such twists and folds, such crystaline forms and fractured planes were possible to build if it were not for photographic evidence. It is easy today to collage ideas into graphically interesting works, but the act of building is more often than not the test of the validity of an idea. It separates the wheat from the chaff.

TIME AND TRIAL

Whereas Alvar Aalto believed that a building can only be judged when it has been standing for fifty years, it would be interesting to look at some of the buildings in this book in ten years' time to see if these directions have been developed further, to see whether these promising buds have blossomed or withered. Styles are changing rapidly and certain recent projects which are on the crest of a wave may well crash down to mingle with the sea. By the same token, one or two of the unknown projects that are now on the drawing boards may be widely-discussed buildings in five year's time, but will have to wait until they are built to prove themselves. The very nature of being up to date implies the danger of being out of date immediately thereafter. Short-lived modes cannot be tested for their validity, but architecture, thankfully, does not always need to provide ultimate answers. After Karl Popper, hypotheses are called not true but fruitful. That is why actual buildings are more fruitful - they are often the last stage of a thought process, the ripe fruit as it were.

Of course it is not just the spectacular acrobatics that interest us, not just the highly publicised highlights on the star circuit, but also more quiet, scholarly work. Certain well-known projects have been excluded because their showmanship is what Charles Jencks calls 'white noise', "extreme and violent complications...which destroy narrative and organisation by absolute saturation... a glut of information".[11] Pyrotechnics sometimes replace conceptual thought. Belief and passion in one's work does not necessarily have to be flown out on a pole. We differentiate between work that is challenging, and buildings that would probably deserve a new, politically correct description as being 'architecturally challenged'.

Other work which is a reduction to the essentials, simplicity without boredom, has been included even though the dearth of information that it communicates makes it unpopular. The minimalist projects do recall the essence of architecture, but they also point out a great deficit. With the exception of a few early Modernists, Austrian architects have rarely been concerned about socio-cultural aspects. The utopias and dreams of a just society haunt the imagination but are not reflected in the work. Social concerns are obviously not accorded high priority in a very rich country with only eight million inhabitants. The few exceptions are certain housing schemes where user participation was either voluntary or mandatory, some of which unfortunately turned out to be battle-fields rather than grounds of consensus. Criticism that Austrian architects are more concerned with aesthetics and technology than innovation and diversity of function and use is to a great extent justified. Manfredo Tafuri describes this, admittedly worldwide, phenomenon,"The decline of the social utopia sanctioned ideology's surrender to the politics of things brought about by the laws of profit. Architectural, artistic, and urban ideology was left with the utopia of form."[12] A telling sign is that architects in Vienna rarely live in the buildings they design, preferring 19th century apartments in the city centre. Of the projects in this book, only two have their designers living or working in them. The other area where a deficit is strongly felt today is in the spiritual dimension - there is little to match the grand Gothic cathedrals and simple village chapels of the past that elevated the spirit above the concerns of everyday life. This is probably a mirror of modern society, which has lost deep belief to replace it by eclecticism of desire. Having established the importance of identity in Austrian architecture and its innovative nature, one is faced with the problem of propagating it. Should one add to the flood of information, should one spread the message? And if so, how? In the age of the video clip ephemeral images seem more real than actual events. Football fans in the stadium prefer to watch the match on their pocket TVs with its freezes and delayed action shots rather than on the field in front of them. During the recent Rolling Stones Voodoo Lounge tour the crowds faced the huge video wall, not the tiny stage on the side where the group actually was. Photographs of buildings are taken to enhance their qualities or to lend them qualities they do not really possess. Architecture once demanded physical presence, that of the observer and that of the building. Journeys to buildings and cities of magnificence were traditional paths of pilgrimage for those who explored cultures. The work put into producing, building, had to be matched by the effort invested in travel; this was the appropriate oblation. Today buildings are brought to the observer: books, magazines, exhibitions and videos replace the direct experience, indeed, they enhance it. Is it because today's buildings are not worthy of the effort? Or is it the uncontrollable inherent dynamics of the media, which interpose themselves by force, as their name demands, between the observer and the observed? "For one thing, because of the absolute barrage of images to which we are subjected, we become blunted. Remember that a hundred years ago there were relatively few images, and people living in a more simplified environment, a farm environment, encounter very few images and they see those quite clearly. A farmer really sees his cows, he really sees what's in front of him quite clearly. But if you are absolutely bombarded with images from passing trucks and cars and televisions and newspapers, you become blunted and this makes a permanent haze in front of your eyes, you can't see anything."[13] The haze can be overcome if the flow of information is not considered an item for consumption, but a challenge to the reader and the

UTOPIA

IMAGE AND REALITY

COMMUNICATIONS PARADIGM

viewer to participate in an interactive process, to take up and respond to what we are presenting here. In Partage des femmes Eugénie Lemoine-Luccioni speaks of "the intimate bond that ties a woman to her objects."[14] Without her objects, the woman seems lost. But her objects inhabit an interior — the house in which they are collected must be inhabitable, not visible from without. The act of seeing a house was very different in principle from the act of inhabiting it. What is actually taking place now is no less than a paradigm shift in this relationship. With the transition from the older production model (exemplified by Prometheus, to use Michel Serres' analogy[15]) to the new communications model (represented by Hermes), the notions of rationality and individual are preserved and somewhat expanded. Communicative rationality is by no means confined to the earlier idea of an objectifying, individualistic, instrumental reason. It has come to mean a performative discursive process of intersubjective argumentation. We have come back to the book. The challenge is to unite perceptions on different levels, for, as Andrea Branzi says, "In our time, the project is faced at birth with a reality so complex and articulate that it has become unfathomable."[16]

BACK TO THE BOOK

Using secondary media to understand architecture is similar to what Hannah Arendt calls the transition from nous (the capacity of contemplation, whose chief characteristic is that its content cannot be rendered in speech) to logos (reasoning with words).[17] It is possible that the new paradigm entails nothing more than a metamorphosis from the older technological aspiration to a more creative intersubjectivity, that is, from a new classicism to a new Romanticism. If this is the case we have not bypassed the hackneyed oscillation between scientific and aesthetic values which has bedevilled the development of theory in this century. The new paradigm has to justify its existence without renouncing either the notion of rationality or that of the subject. The shift is from productive activity (the Greek poiesis, in this case, the act of building) to communicative interaction (the Greek praxis). Praxis here is writing, reading and discussing architecture, examining models and drawings, viewing still and moving pictures. Earlier we dealt with the reflectively objectified knowledge of the paradigm of consciousness. What we now have is participatory re-examination and reconstruction of knowledge. It exists in the performative attitude of discursive argumentation in the new communications paradigm. As validity claims raised in discourse are fallible, revisable and criticizable, there is always the possibility of correcting errors. By opting for fallibility in the context of change, we have come a long way indeed from the domain of Plato's philosopher-king, whose ideas correspond perfectly to reality. Notwithstanding the many problematic aspects of the global village we are living in, one advantage is certainly that discoveries no longer need occur to people so far apart that they are unaware of each other's work. Experiments and mistakes need not necessarily be repeated. Exchange, inspiration and synthesis are possible as long as the creative act is not exhausted with looking. The sharing of insights and difficulties is a book's contribution to an ongoing debate. History does not make one particularly optimistic on this count, but failing to use the new communications paradigm to avoid repeating misconceptions would surely, given the pace of development today, destroy the basis of existence on this planet.

The book attempts to transmit the essence of the design with the same unique strength of feeling that the buildings themselves radiate - the idea, the main lines, the intention, the direction, the transparency or lightness, rythm or transformation have been taken up in the layout. Far from the direct, banal, supposedly objective 'frontal nude' transfer of information, we celebrate subjectivity. Fragments have been bitten out of carefully composed commissioned photographs and juxtaposed with other fragments that they are metaphorically related to, like a glass roof and the sky it reflects. Hierarchies are reverted. Even the cover with the imprint and contents on the outside reflects one of the features of the Modernist project: the reversal of the conventional interior and exterior. Just as there are "buildings which no longer want to be buildings"[18], the book is trying to escape the parameters of the page.

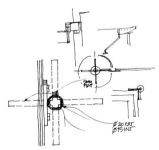

M 1:333

**Design sketches for the exhibition
Innovative Austrian Architecture**
Vienna 1995, Ramesh Kumar Biswas

And yes, the strange title. It is simply a scale frequently used for publishing architectural drawings, the only common denominator of the diverse projects. Readers of the book can judge the size of the buildings by referring to familiar elements like doors and stairways. The scale 1:333 was used in the accompanying exhibition to facilitate quick comparision. Long after I decided on the title, I learnt that Le Corbusier did all his own working models in the unusual scale of 1:33, something he did not explain but which affords me quiet and amused satisfaction.

014/015

Next page
Major banking hall of the Postal Savings Bank PSK
Vienna 1906, Otto Wagner

HISTORICAL REVIEW

THE VIEW FROM OUTSIDE   18

OF FATHERS AND SONS   22

How can one compile a review of good architecture? I can begin to answer the question by stating how I personally judge a building or a neighbourhood, a city or a landscape or a regional plan. I adopt seven criteria, extracted from historical experience, to examine the quality of any architectural or urban work. Of course, you are free to refuse these criteria a priori. Or you could test them and then refute all or parts of these linguistic invariants. I can promise you at least one thing: they are not boring or pedantic. You will have fun using them to evaluate buildings by Hollein, Domenig, Himmelblau or even Hundertwasser, for that matter. In all probability you will find that about 50% of all buildings do not respect any of these seven principles, that 30% accept one or two of them, 15% four of them, 3% five or six, and perhaps no building respects all seven. Here are the criteria I submit:

1. Listing contents and functions. The use of listing as a design methodology, without applying a synthesis either a priori or a posteriori, is a lesson we have been aware of since William Morris elaborated on the theme in 1859. Modern architecture was born of Morris's rejection of all past styles, building types and formalistic attitudes. Each element had to be reinvented, had to acquire its own unrepeatable meaning in a manner not unlike new words being used at random in a non-pattern, without sentences or even speech. Let us look, even if only superficially, at any one of the selected buildings. Is it honest? Are its volumes derived from the spaces it contains, from its uses, or do they reflect the classical idolatry of the unitary and finished form? Has it analysed its own ingredients or has it preferred the escape of an easy synthesis? Let us examine the windows: do their different sizes and shapes show how much light is needed inside, or are they uniform, standard, repetitive, totally indifferent to the inhabitants' behaviour? In other terms, do the single words pronounced by the architect have any factual semantic value, or are they contained in ready-made phrases, at the risk of being meaningless? How many of the innovative Austrian architects meet Morris's criteria, 137 years after they were established?

2. Asymmetry and dissonance. If it was Morris who gave us the notion of difference or variety, enabling us to analyse and register building content and functions, it was the Viennese composer Arnold Schönberg who explained dissonance as a principle common to modern art from literature to music. Both Art Nouveau and Rationalism explored dissonance. Each element of the building should communicate its independence to the external world. Therefore: is the building symmetrical? Forget it. The architect was so lazy that he only drew half of it. Are the various facades identical? Forget it. With differences in orientation, light and views it is not appropriate to have identical facades. The first principle underlines the differences caused by changing contents and functions. These differences can be simply registered, as they were from the Arts & Crafts architects up to Charles Rennie Macintosh, or made creative with dissonance, as illustrated by both Art Nouveau and Bauhaus. Moreover, a symmetrical building is closed in on itself and self-sufficient. It does not have any dialogue with its surroundings; it is awfully selfish. Do you see any selfish buildings around you?

3. Anti-perspective tri-dimensionality. Let us be frank: Satan is in the box. Is it a boxy building, working from the outside towards the inside, instead of from the inside towards the outside? Dismiss it. You know that the codified Renaissance-perspective, with its single, immobile point of view of the box, is obsolete. Such static vision became unbearable to the cubist architect who sought a modern, dynamic viewpoint. Cubism made this viewpoint move, externally as well as internally. So we can accept a three-dimensional object only if it is not boxlike. This has been demonstrated by the Expressionists, from Gaudí to Mendelsohn, who crossed the limits set by the Renaissance.

4. Four-dimensional decomposition. This is the principle formulated by the Dutch 'De Stijl' group back in 1917 in order to give a new syntax to the cubist language. They stated that in order to conquer the box, the third dimension has to be eliminated. Volumetric envelopes must be decomposed into two-dimensional slabs, so that they can be reassembled later in such a way as to form a four-dimensional object, not a new box. Is there any sign of this

THE VIEW FROM OUTSIDE

Bruno Zevi

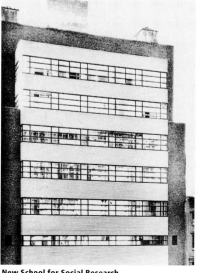

New School for Social Research
New York 1931, Joseph Urban

design technique in the building in question? Do you get the impression that its architect knows something about 'De Stijl', a fundamental precedent of contemporary Deconstructivism?

5. Structural involvement of architecture. There should no longer be any separation of engineering structure and architectural form. Does the building you are looking at reflect the consciousness that the 19th century schism between technology and art has finally been overcome? Is the architect aware that the new consciousness applies not just to High Tech showcases, not just to stadiums and bridges, but to all buildings?

6. Space in time. Architecture is space to live in. But space may be static or monumental, a series of rooms apparently self-sufficient, with no fluency between them; boxes of voids, one after the other or one over another. Frank Lloyd Wright manipulated space in time better than Michelangelo, Borromini, Neumann and Gaudí. Is this spirit of spatial conception present in the building in front of you?

7. Reintegration of building, city and landscape. There is a season for decomposition (see the fourth principle above) and a season for reintegration. The latter is the moment when the building has to deal with its context, with its urban texture and territory, with its ecological imperatives. Be careful, however: architecture should not simply reflect its context; rather, it should significantly create its context. If 'Falling Water' had been designed merely to be in harmony with its context, it would have simply ended up as an awful hut.

By monitoring our check-list of architectural errors, we open the way to the direct experience of art. Having thus clearly expressed my opinion on the qualities of the buildings illustrated in this book, I should perhaps touch on certain specific aspects of Austrian architecture so that the reader can identify my critical approach.

The modern movement in Austria, after Otto Wagner's prelude, is based on the splendidly contradictory dualism of Josef-Maria Olbrich/Adolf Loos: ornament is, respectively, either a joy or a crime. This dualism has been stimulating the debate for decades. If an Austrian wants to be parochial, he may substitute Josef Hoffmann for Olbrich; the conflict will remain, but it might be less obvious.

I do not believe that Austrian quality, and Viennese quality in particular, can be mechanically exported. I maintain that Clemens Holzmeister and many others lost tension while living abroad. However, it is true that Hoffmann's masterpiece, the Palais Stoclet, is in Brussels, Rudolph Schindler did great things in California and Richard Neutra built at least three wonderful houses. Other examples come to mind. Bernard Rudofsky, Joseph Urban and Victor Gruen deserve to be mentioned: the first for the villas designed with Luigi Cosenza near Napoli and later in Brazil, but particularly for his glorious book 'Architecture without Architects'; the second for the New School for Social Research, a jewel in downtown Manhattan, built in 1931; the third for the invention of the American shopping centre. I have heard of Austrian gifts to America, and indeed Neutra's Lovell Health House in Los Angeles is still, after 67 years, a celebrated gift. But let us not forget what Austria gave many other countries, including Israel and Italy. In the first two decades of this century every valuable building in Rome that was vaguely Secessionist, refined, articulated, having a generous well designed garden in the courtyard, was attributed to Hoffmann's influence, and people called it 'Austrian'.

The work of at least two personalities requires a deeper knowledge and a more inspired interpretation than has been published so far: Rudolph Schindler and Friedrich Kiesler. The former has yet to be revealed by a great critic. As for the latter, perhaps the next big exhibition in Paris will solve the problem.

Austrian architects did assimilate almost all of the main aesthetic currents, but one of these has largely been undervalued: the organic trend of Frank Lloyd Wright and his school, which includes Bruce Goff. Architects from Holland, Germany and, briefly, even Italy were more interested in the work of the Taliesin's genius than were architects from Austria. The battle between Cubism and Expressionism is fundamental to the structure of the Modern Movement, but Austria, like France

Lovell Beach House Interior
Newport Beach 1926, Rudolph M. Schindler

and Italy, preferred Cubism. In the long run, this resulted in linguistic impoverishment. Even today, this development determines that we see only one dominant theme and those who rebel against it. We feel the lack of a true alternative, though we may recognize the potential for one. Our task now should be to overcome the century-long Mannerist pendulum swinging between Cubist and Expressionist, abstract and organic, classical and romantic, rational and emotional. Post-Modernism ended in a shameful fiasco, as it deserved to. I am glad to note that Austria only contributed very modestly to this idiotic horror. Fortunately, the Krier brothers were born in Luxembourg, so they are not Austria's fault. As regards the Italian situation, I do wish that Aldo Rossi and Co. were at least based in San Marino.

Schindler/Chace House, Los Angeles 1922, Rudolph M. Schindler

I do not believe that we are in a crisis now; as a historian, I know that we always were, or considered we were. I do not agree that we are lacking a set of values by which to judge what is valid and what is not valid in contemporary architecture. It is fashionable to pretend to be impotent – but actually, in spite of our best intentions, we are not. Where are we now? In the midst of a rather positive and productive season, I feel. The gloomy 80s are far behind us, but even then I could have indicated a hundred frankly modern buildings of excellent quality, which is more than I could do for the fifteenth or sixteenth century.

It would seem that on the whole one can find all the good wares on the Austrian market, except for the two Franks: Lloyd Wright, the poet of fluent space; and Owen Gehry, the poet of cheapscape.

Kaufmann Desert House, Palm Springs 1946, Richard Neutra

Urban Renewal project
Fort Worth 1956, Victor Gruen

Lovell Health House
Los Angeles 1929, Richard Neutra

Lovell Beach House
Newport Beach 1926, Rudolph M. Schindler

In the city where Sigmund Freud once worked, father-son relationships are particularly significant. This is why architectural historian Friedrich Achleitner ironically described the architectural scene in Austria as a constant and almost compulsive clash between the pupil and the teacher, an incessant father-son relationship, burdened with all its associated crises. Between 1900 and 1920 Austrian architecture was in fact dominated directly, and indirectly through his pupils, by Otto Wagner, in the interwar period by Adolf Loos, Josef Hoffmann, Josef Frank and Peter Behrens, and in the postwar period by Clemens Holzmeister. Achleitner's interpretation cannot be dismissed out of hand. It depicts a continuity that reaches beyond 1918, 1934, and 1945, crucial years in contemporary history, and this father-son attitude has affected Austrian architecture much more than any international event.

This whole orientation, of a 'father following' architecture with actual and imagined patriarchs could be a good way of explaining developments. However, there are important individual events less central and outside this tradition which should not be left out of a survey of the innovative side of Austrian architecture. Examples from the patriarchal tradition, some of the parallel developments and their relationships to general history are presented here.

OTTO WAGNER, THE FATHER OF MODERN ARCHITECTURE. Otto Wagner (1841-1918) counts as a central figure in Austria's architectural scene through his buildings and the legendary training given at his school, not just during his lifetime but also during the interwar years. In the 1920s it was the Wagner School which stood for advanced architecture per se in Austria and the succession states. As 'father of modernism' in Austria, 'universalist' as regards the state's aims (although the Habsburgs had, on the whole, a decidedly anti-modern attitude), and, as he said of himself, a radical rationalist compared to the romantic and historical architectural styles of the period, Wagner almost single-handedly led the change from historicism to the new architecture.

Wagner was not only a social and artistic example of the modern movement. His life, and the way he emerged from being a dry entrepreneur of the Gründerzeit (Founder's Era) who not only designed but also speculated in houses by financing and selling them, to the idealist 'builder artist' was a symbol of the victory of modernism. The trigger, driving force and main motive of Wagner's doctrine was technology. His understanding of modern building techniques, such as iron construction and semi-industrial manufactured facade elements, was at the same time traditional and avant-garde. Developing Gottfried Semper's theories further, Wagner picks out as a central theme, and made lasting and visible, the relationship between surface and structure. Like Auguste Perret in Paris, he tried to use the new technologies to combine classical qualities, like axiality and the hierarchy of storeys and material, with the modern concern for clarity, direct circulation, and functionalism in his buildings.

Examples of these principles are seen in the Postsparkasse (1903-06, extended 1910-1912). The initial concept was for one of the classic monumental Ringstrasse buildings, in the traditional, palatial pattern and loosely neo-Renaissance, but Wagner changed this plan by his consequent use of the latest technology and form. The result was a symbol of the modern world. In the last two decades of the monarchy it was this subtle balance between tradition and change, borne by the self-confidence of a representative of the Gründerzeit and corresponding positioning in the international spectrum (Wagner's pupils had to study the works of Frank Lloyd Wright for example), that created a powerful base for a whole generation of architects and left its mark on the interwar period.

OTHER MODERNIST TRENDS BEFORE 1918. Alongside Wagner's classical Modernism there were other varieties of modern architecture. Wagner's ideas had developed from a loosely Renaissance style and peaked with the demands of the ever-growing metropolis, for which Wagner produced an almost complete infrastructure from the city transport system via the postal savings bank to the psychiatric hospital. In the spectrum of variety at hand before 1918 Wagner stands alongside the Art Nouveau-Romanticism of Friedrich Ohmann and Josef Urban, the English country house style (and, from 1910, the neo-classicism) of Josef Hoffmann, the 'state pragmatism' of Ludwig

Of Fathers and Sons
Innovative Austrian Architecture
1900-1970

Matthias Boeckl

Baumann and Adolf Loos' critical attitude to culture. These five architects are representative of the pre-1918 approach.

To raise the question of innovation in Austrian architecture before 1918 also raises the problem of regionalism. The Danube monarchy had two other centres besides Vienna: Prague and Budapest, the capitals of the succession states Czechoslovakia and Hungary. Artists like Alfons Mucha and Wagner's pupils Jan Kotera and Josef Plecnik for Czechoslovakia and Slovenia, and Hungary's Ödön Lechner and the duo Böhm & Hegedüs developed their own original national Modernism. The degree to which the umbilical cord should be severed, and the distance from Vienna and thus from Wagner's rationalism, which, particularly in Hungary, was countered by a national Romanticism, was a political question which eclipsed the purely artistic aspects of the problem.

Events within the borders of the later republic were strongly influenced by Vienna. The most important developments came from architects who had been students of Professors Ferstel and Krauss at the Technical University in Vienna, or of Wagner and Ohmann at the Academy of Fine Arts. Their positions vacillated between Wagner's Rationalism, National Romanticism and Secession, as can be seen in the works of Mauriz Balzarek in Oberösterreich and Franz Baumgartner in Kärnten. The western part of the monarchy, Salzburg, Tirol and Vorarlberg, were still mainly under the influence of the Munich School.

ANGLO-AMERICAN INSPIRATION-ADOLF LOOS, JOSEF HOFFMANN, RUDOLPH M. SCHINDLER AND JOSEPH URBAN. While Otto Wagner mainly developed his rational doctrine from the Mediterranean tradition, it was the new geo-political situation and Anglo-American culture which influenced young architects in Austria and resulted in the most innovative architecture. Adolf Loos lived in Philadelphia and Chicago from 1893-96. This, and Josef Hoffmann's enthusiasm for English country houses, a synonym for an elegant life-style in Europe at the turn of the century, gave rise to the most important impulses which, along with Wagner, dominated the Modernist position before 1918.

Both Adolf Loos and Josef Hoffmann were born in 1870 in what before the birth of the Czechoslovak Republic in 1918 was the crown territory Moravia. They used the Anglo-American stimulus in contrasting ways. Loos took up the practical side oriented towards the suitability of the material and direct fulfillment of purpose and adapted this for Vienna. Josef Hoffmann was influenced more by the elegant and the traditional aspects, which, with his restless urge to design, he then proceeded to graft onto the Wiener Secession.

Both approaches were in their own way successful and gave rise to schools of architecture. By establishing the Secession in 1897 along with others such as Josef Olbrich, Koloman Moser, Gustav Klimt and setting up the 'Wiener Werkstätte' in 1903, Josef Hoffmann institutionalised the internationally effective trend of young art as a revolutionary but nevertheless luxurious answer to the conservative Gründerzeit period. Loos remained a loner. A pupil of Hasenauer and Wagner, after 1899 Hoffmann was also able as a teacher at Vienna's School for Arts and Crafts (Kunstgewerbeschule) to commit an official institution to the aims of the noble crafts. The public effect Loos at this time as a culture critic in daily newspapers (where he attacked the Secession with great vigour) was developed later in his private Loos School.

Before 1918, the major architectural results of these two antipodes were the 'Loos house' on Vienna's Michaelerplatz (1910-12), and Josef Hoffmann's Palais Stoclet in Brussels (1904-06). The motifs for the Loos house come from the classical period around 1800, just as was suitable for the client, the exclusive fashion designers Goldmann & Salatsch, but this conflicted with the ruling taste for neo-Baroque architecture. Josef Hoffmann on the other hand was able to erect the Stoclet Palace, with its English country house style geometrically adapted to suit Secessionist ideals, without having to face any furor. With Gustav Klimt among those who designed its interior, this has become the most significant major work of Viennese Art Nouveau.

Loos's and Hoffmann's approaches, supplemented by those of Josef Frank and Oskar Strand, created a spring board for the more important architectural trends in the interwar period. World War

Nordkettenbahn funicular railway
Seegrube, Innsbruck 1928, Franz Baumann

I also brought about fundamental changes in architecture. The year of the deaths of Otto Wagner, Gustav Klimt and other heroes of Modernism, 1918 was also the year of changes that prevented the return of some young architects who had gone abroad before 1914 looking for better working conditions. The US was a favourite destination for emigrants.

Prominent representatives of these 'first wave' emigrants were Paul Theodor Frankl, Josef Urban and Rudolph Schindler. They took up three different positions within the spectrum of Viennese art at the turn of the century and added their individual approaches to the emerging North American Modernism. Josef Urban's sets for the opera houses in Boston and New York meant that the most opulent variant of the Viennese interior design had gained acceptance. He developed a comparatively simpler architectural language, more along continental European lines, after 1929. From 1925 Paul Theodore Frankl was one of the pioneers of Art Deco design, while Rudolph M. Schindler, a pupil of Wagner, Loos and Frank Lloyd Wright, established his own specific Modernism on the west coast, exploiting local conditions in a spontaneous and undogmatic manner. Another pupil of Loos, Richard Neutra, who in 1919 like Schindler had decided he had no future as an architect in Austria, became Schindler's partner in 1924. With the help of his client Dr. Philip Lovell, Neutra became the American hero of the 'International Style' established by Philip Johnson and Henry-Russell Hitchcock in 1932.

SOCIAL INNOVATION: PUBLIC AND PRIVATE HOUSING IN VIENNA 1924-34. Those who stayed in Austria after 1918 had to accustom themselves to a radically changed state of affairs. This in turn lead to a remarkable wealth of innovative solutions to the pressing social and economic problems of the interwar period. Vienna had previously been the capital city of an empire with a population of more than 50 million. Now capital of a shrunken republic of only 6 million, it was regarded by the provinces as a hydrocephalous head. These provinces began developing their own identities and regional trends for the first time.

The most significant architectural achievements in Vienna were in housing. A city of 2 million, it was itself given the status of a province soon after 1918. It was then able to make decisions independent of Lower Austria, the province of which it had previously been the capital. Between 1924 and 1934 Vienna's council carried out a massive program to provide more than 60,000 homes by constructing what was to become known internationally as 'Gemeindebau'. Something previously unknown in Europe, this programmme was of considerable benefit to the homeless families of workers and refugees, the architects, and the building and construction trade. Nearly all of Vienna's architects were involved. Of these, pupils of the Wagner School dominated by their sheer numbers. The most outstanding were Hermann Aichinger, Karl Ehn, Franz and Hubert Gessner, Alfons Hetmanek, Franz Kaym, Ernst Lichtblau, Rudolf Perco and Heinrich Schmid.

In Vienna, apart from the Wagner School, the ideas of individuals like Oskar Strnad, Josef Frank, Peter Behrens, Clemens Holzmeister and pupils of their schools were the most important in the interwar period. Heinrich Tessenov at Vienna's Kunstgewerbeschule provided a significant interlude until 1919. A climate stimulating high levels of architectural achievement in social housing was caused by contrasting concepts of the best solution for social housing. Adolf Loos and Josef Frank were among those who supported the concept of terraced houses which gave their inhabitants greater self-sufficiency and individual choice of lay-out, while the city's social democratic administration favoured multi-storey superblocks. Both socially oriented approaches were to take over from the densely built private block developments of the Gründerzeit and provide light, airy, healthy homes amid green spaces with adequate utilities. The shortage of land and the ideological differences of orientation between the supporters of the garden city and the multi-storey, meant that the interwar period saw the erection of far more social housing in the form of superblocks than as terraced housing estates.

Vienna's social housing projects of the interwar period are highly significant in the history of architecture in the 20th century. It was a vast building programme that united the conflicting interests of an advanced architectural language, the necessary acceptance and identification of the inhabitants, economic viability and job creation. Those architects who could not realise their imaginative ideals with their concepts of a truly modern architecture could at least earn a living from council commissions.

At the international level, there were also pioneers in the building of private homes, the main purporters being Adolf Loos, Josef Frank and their circles. Two key buildings reflect the most important achievements: the Moller house by Adolf Loos (1927-28), and Josef Frank's Beer house (1930), both in Vienna. They represent an urbane and luxurious modern Viennese style of home decor, original, open reactions to international stimuli and with their own place in the spectrum of international modernism. The Moller house was the first time that Adolf Loos reached perfect functionality in spatial planning (the 'Raumplan'). All the rooms in the house were designed to have varying heights depending on what they were to be used for, and that within the rigid limitations of the cube. The rooms were also placed in a spiral around a centre so as to make the best possible use of the volume available. Tasteful furnishings in the English style gave this three-dimensionally developed and innovative 'Raumplan' a further elegant note.

Before World War I, Josef Frank, Oskar Strnad and Oskar Wlach had been constructing and exhibiting new types of dwellings to provide for the psychological needs of those who would use them. Frank's Beer house was a climax in this philosophy of the house as a path and a place. The main emphasis of this concept with its orientation towards being a positive psychological experience for the occupants was an intricately conceived path leading through light and dark, high and low ceilinged rooms and various different levels. The consequent opening into the garden which was to be seen as part of the house itself meant that this style of home decor had, through the use of a simple method, a rich architectural complexity and provided security for its inhabitants. This artistic level has hardly ever been achieved since.

REGIONAL AND INTERNATIONAL: THE SITUATION IN THE PROVINCES, THE VIENNESE 'WERKBUNDSIEDLUNG' AND THE SECOND WAVE OF EMIGRATION. The architectural innovations in the provinces were tied up with and dependent on the political situation in the 1920s and 1930s. There were not only social problems, there was also the matter of the cultural identity of the young republic. Fortunately, regional idiosyncrasies could be tied to the national policy of developing tourism. In this way it was possible for a cultural development of modernism and international tourism together with local tradition to lead to a completely new field of purpose and to very ambitious architecture. The best examples of this development are Innsbruck's 'Nordkettenbahn' (funicular) by Franz Baumann (1927-28) and Salzburg's Festival Theatre, by

Clemens Holzmeister (1926).

The funicular opened up an area of spectacular mountain landscape to tourism, the first time this had been done mechanically on such a large scale. Its three station buildings are strongly express-ive reactions to the terrain and to their surroundings and use none of the preconceived urbane or later pseudo-alpine forms. Such examples of independent new answers for buildings for tourist centres in alpine regions became more common in the works of Baumann and Lois Welzenbacher, whose Park Hotel in Hall in Tirol (1930-31) is another example. Salzburg's Festival Theatre on the other hand is an attempt to develop an adapted form of Modernism through the use of Baroque motifs and a certain degree of monumentality. The aims were to become more international, to have state representation in cultural matters and to provide a catalyst for the tourist industry. With Holzmeister, this trend came to dominate the Modernist movement and was, after 1934, a concept supported by the government of the corporate state.

The urban antithesis to this concept was not so much the block dwellings in the city of Vienna, although they also made conscious use of traditional motifs, but the Viennese 'Werkbund-siedlung' coordinated by Josef Frank, Austria's only member of the CIAM. It was erected between 1930-32. Numerous prominent foreign architects and practically all the important contemporary Austrian architects took part in the project. It is one of the most significant in the history of architecture in the interwar period. Simple, architecturally advanced single-family and terraced houses were presented in a large model housing estate. It is indicative of the cultural situation of this period that half of the architects who participated in the 'Werkbund' estate project were driven out of the country after 1938 when Austria became a part of Hitler's Germany.

The interwar period saw a new wave of emigration by architects, particularly to the US. Friedrich Kiesler thought he had better chances of realising his constructive visions in America than in Austria. He went to New York in 1926. Richard Neutra left as early as 1919 to work with Mendelsohn in Berlin, then moved on to Frank Lloyd Wright's office in 1924. Bernard Rudofsky went to Italy in 1931 and from there to Brazil and the US. Josef Frank, a prominent Social Democrat, went to Sweden in 1934.

FROM THE CORPORATE STATE TO RECONSTRUCTION - THE PATH AWAY FROM THE CON-FLICT BETWEEN MODERNISM AND FASCISM. Austria's cultural constitution today is closely connected to developments in the interwar years, particularly those of 1934. After Hitler rose to power in 1933, Austria came under considerable pressure due to the conflict between those who wanted a merger with Greater Germany and those who wanted to further the independent

Crematorium
Vienna 1898, Clemens Holzmeister

Secession art gallery
Vienna 1898, Josef - Maria Olbrich

democratic republic. The conservative Christian regime of the corporate state, led first by Engelbert Dolfuss and after 1934 by Kurt Schuschnigg, tried to solve this problem by propagating the Catholic tradition and in hoping for a guarantee of Austria's existence from Mussolini's Italy. Both ideas turned out to be chimeras. Austria was a country made up not only of rural Catholics; it also had an urban, industrial and intellectual tradition - and Mussolini was unable to avoid forming an alliance with Hitler. The corporate state's resistance to Hitler's Germany then collapsed, and in March 1938 Austria became a part of Germany. The long list of architects who at that point in time had to leave Austria for 'racial' or political reasons, or who were killed, represented a major part of the country's cultural elite, and they were lost to Austria for ever.

The seeds of reconstruction after liberation in 1945, and also of today's cultural constitution, lay in the internal make-up of the corporate state period. Clemens Holzmeister and Josef Hoffmann predominated in government commissions and carried out nearly all the prestigious works of the corporate state. The only political monument of this period which is still appreciated is the war memorial in Vienna's triumphal arch by Rudolf Wondracek, a pupil of the Wagner School (and a friend of the émigré Rudolph M. Schindler). The guidelines were now formulated by the conservatives, who held the relevant government posts after 1945. Despite the repressive cultural climate and the clear preference for the conservative, the trend towards modern architecture were able to continue, since the state's idea of culture was not homogenous and did offer numerous niches.

The National Socialist era was a period of hibernation. By 1945, the only architects left over from the rich interwar scene were those who had not been forced into emigration or been killed by the Nazis. Among those who had left were many pupils of the Loos and Wagner Schools. They were not brought back, although they would have been prepared to help with the reconstruction of a democratic Austria. Clemens Holzmeister's circle was thus the main source of innovation in the 1950s. He had returned from exile in Turkey where he had erected numerous government buildings in Ankara. The main direction of architectural innovation now was the development of clarity and elegance derived from the technical possibilities of steel and concrete given to the International Style re-imported from America. Max Fellerer, Eugen Wörle, Erich Boltenstern, Franz Schuster, Oswald Haerdtl, Roland Rainer and the young Karl Schwanzer, who made a lasting impression with his Austrian pavilion for the World Exhibition in Brussels in 1958, were among those who carried the ideals of the interwar period into the 1950s. They also set the stage for the revolution of the 1960's, a revolution sparked off by the friction of younger architects with these 'carriers of tradition'.

FROM RECONSTRUCTION TO POST MODERNISM - THE DEVELOPMENTS FROM THE 1950s TO THE 1970s. The restricted situation of the postwar period, when all available energy had to

Hagenbund Exhibition Hall
Vienna 1902, Joseph Urban

Minor banking hall , Postal Savings Bank
Vienna 1906, Otto Wagner

be concentrated on the political and economic reconstruction of the country, did not allow for any experiments in housing or monumental building. What did happen though, was that the Catholic church opened up. The church had been sceptical about Modernism and had had an unfortunately close relationship with the authoritarian corporate state in the 1930s. In its search for a new way, its new openness and its use of committed individuals, it was the church that brought about Austria's reemergence into the contemporary architectural scene - at a high international level. The first timid attempt was the parish church of Salzburg-Parsch (1953-56). It was built by three Holzmeister pupils, Wilhelm Holzbauer, Friedrich Kurrent and Johannes Spalt, from 'Arbeitsgruppe 4'. The result was a clear area, flooded with light, perfect in detail and with the altar as the centre.

Ottokar Uhl, J.G. Gsteu, Josef Lackner, Günther Domenig and Eilfried Huth were among those who could now progress, applying the dynamics of advanced architecture to church building. Their main architectural theme was the central position of the altar. They used the new technologies, modular arrangements, and, later on, the free development of volume to space (Domenig, church in Oberwart). This, too, led to international interest. The fine sacral architecture of the German Rudolf Schwarz and the module-based concepts of Walter Gropius' former partner Konrad Wachsmann, who in the early 1950s taught young architects at Salzburg's Summer Academy, were important stimuli during this phase.

Palmenhaus Conservatory
Vienna 1906, Friedrich Ohmann

Palais Stoclet
Brussels 1911, Josef Hoffmann

Palais Stoclet
Brussels 1911, Josef Hoffmann

House in the Werkbund-Siedlung
Vienna 1932, Hans Vetter

Moller House
Vienna 1928, Adolf Loos

Moller House
Vienna 1928, Adolf Loos

House on the Michaelerplatz
Vienna 1911, Adolf Loos

Leisure park, changing rooms
Vienna 1950, Max Fellerer, Eugen Wörle

Museum of Modern Art
Brussels 1958, transferred to Vienna 1962, Karl Schwanzer

This orientation towards American architecture, itself formed by Europeans who had emigrated, resulted in a movement initiated in the 1960s by Wilhelm Holzbauer and Hans Hollein. They introduced new technologies and new semantics. After trials in experimental exhibitions and small commissions for shops, these early manifestations of Post-Modernism quickly gained international recognition. Gustav Peichl's studios for the Austrian Broadcasting Company (ORF) in the provinces transposed this techno-semantic trend into monumental building. Hans Hollein and Wilhelm Holzbauer, both Holzmeister's pupils, worked mainly in Holland and Germany. They only received large commissions in Austria in the late 1970s and the 1980s. Parallel to this, groups of young architects in Graz and Vienna experimented with Pop Art, mega-technology, sociology and in other fields, through which they were able to become part of the international scene.

Looking back over the first seventy years of modern architecture in Austria, one can see that despite many catastrophes in recent history which set back developments by decades, the creative and innovative potential in Austria has always been strong enough to add to the fundamental principles of the indigenous tradition and the individual's ability to adapt international trends of a liberal and humane Modernism. Vienna has established its own independent position among the other European centres of Modernism such as Paris, Berlin, Prague and Milan and is part of Modernism's field of energy.

Grossglockner Alpine Road
Kärnten 1935, Franz Wallach
Monument to its builders 1936,
Clemens Holzmeister

INTERVENTIONS
in old buildings

A CERTAIN LACK OF RESPECT   34

EXHIBITION STRUCTURE HÜTTENBERG   42

MUSEUM RENEWAL HALLEIN   46

CONFERENCE CENTER SEGGAU   48

MUSEUM RENEWAL VIENNA   50

PENTHOUSE ADDITION VIENNA   52

ATTIC CONVERSION VIENNA   54

Expansion of the Jewish Museum
Vienna 1995, Project
Eichinger or Knechtl

KIX bar
Vienna 1988, Oskar Putz

Sport centre conversion
Graz 1993
Alfred Bramberger

Boutique Knize
next to Adolf Loos's Boutique Knize
Vienna 1994, Paolo Piva

"YOU GENTLEMEN PERHAPS THINK I AM MAD? ALLOW ME TO DEFEND MYSELF. I AGREE THAT MAN IS PREEMINENTLY A CREATIVE ANIMAL, PREDESTINED TO CONSCIOUSLY STRIVE TOWARD A GOAL, AND TO ENGAGE IN ENGINEERING, THAT IS, ETERNALLY AND INCESSANTLY, TO BUILD NEW ROADS, WHEREVER THEY MAY LEAD. MAN LOVES TO CREATE ROADS, THAT IS BEYOND DISPUTE. BUT MAY IT NOT BE THAT HE IS INSTINCTIVELY AFRAID OF ATTAINING HIS GOAL AND COMPLETING THE EDIFICE HE IS CONSTRUCTING? HOW DO YOU KNOW, PERHAPS HE ONLY LIKES THAT EDIFICE FROM A DISTANCE AND NOT AT ALL AT CLOSE RANGE, PERHAPS HE ONLY LIKES TO BUILD IT, AND DOES NOT WANT TO LIVE IN IT." FYODOR DOSTOEVSKY [1]

The history of architecture has a curious way of springing surprises on us. The dominant positivist model of the natural sciences of the last century finally led to the neo-Kantian reaction, whereby the gulf between fact and value, knowledge and meaning — between the natural and the human sciences — was clearly established. This corresponded to the rationalist period of architecture that governed ideology until the 80s, and still dominates practice. By a profound irony, the latest developments in the fields of thermodynamics, biology, cybernetics and information theory have dramatically reversed these roles. The attention in these areas is rapidly shifting from order to disorder, stability to instability, unity to diversity, equilibrium to dis-equilibrium, universals to particulars and atemporality to temporality (or irreversibility). Architectural and urban ensembles are also increasingly subject to violent and disturbing interference, uncommented upon except when it is a deliberate act of design. In the context of interventions in historic architecture, it is time itself, its subjective historical form, its culturally specific interpretation as continuum, and its scientific application in evolution, that needs to be understood so that it can guide us in the search for a combinatorial architecture of montage. The montage implies that a series of separate fragments are placed next to each other.

Rising populations, the sustainable use of raw materials and energy combined with financial and ecological imperatives are forcing the question of how to deal with the existing stock of old buildings to become one of the great challenges of the future. However, it is not these pragmatic aspects that dominate the debate, but cultural and psychological questions. A building is not a product but a chain of events that continue to happen even after it has been built. A building survives its creator; it has to answer different questions and meet changing needs. It has to look out for itself, and its ability to do this depends on its inherent strengths as well as its flexibility. One has to look at the destiny of the building and that of the idea, because establishing an idea is more difficult than building a long-lasting edifice. Sometimes the building outlives the idea; in our fast-changing world it is rarely the other way round. The transformability of the building has to match that of the idea. Carl Pruscha considers invention to be no more than a process that begins with a 'philosophical archeology' and continues with the reinterpretation of that which is already known to history, not the specific result of one's egoistic endeavours or invention. Though few of his projects are in old buildings, they emanate an air of archaic and long-living vitality. The processivity of design involves the collage and combination of ideas from the past and present, which Günther Domenig describes as a path, the end of which cannot be seen; as a process which pushes the architect to the limits of his physical, mental, psychological and financial abilities. Domenig's interventions in historic buildings or urban contexts, such as his bank in the Favoritenstrasse in Vienna, have always maintained the distinction between new and old, which guarantees that their interaction is full of excitement.

Very often a building that is meant to last forever has to be given a new content. In order to ensure its long-term validity it has to be provoked and interfered with rather than be cocooned and mothballed in a state of hibernation. Like every ecological system, it needs small disturbances to keep it alive and developing, external inputs and influences that maintain the process of evolution instead of stagnation and eventual extinction. "The fascinating secret of a well-functioning organism seems to lie not in its overall unity but in its structure, maintained in health by the life-preserving mechanism of division operating through myriads of cell-splittings and rejuvenations under the smooth skin of an apparently unchanging body." [2]

A CERTAIN LACK OF RESPECT
The Re-interpretation of Time

Ramesh Kumar Biswas

In addition, we could examine the biological concept of ontogenesis that describes the development of a living being from the ovum onwards. Overlaying this is the extraordinary phenomenon described in Haeckel's Law, where each individual ontogenesis briefly traverses momentous stages of its evolutionary history. Every human embryo thus passes through the fiscian, amphibious, reptile and mammal stages of evolution in the womb: it briefly has a tendency to develop gills and different circulatory systems, for example. The biological metaphor has its limits when applied to buildings, but why shouldn't we apply this process to a building in the search for its definite, final form? There is a saying that a town without old buildings is like a man without a memory. Undoubtedly the presence of old buildings relates the general public in a very visible way to their culture, it anchors them in their history. But I also believe that a town without new buildings is like a man without imagination. Countries with little built history to show, or others with little that has survived, seem to have an uncomplicated attitude towards new buildings. An extreme case is the country I come from, Malaysia, where whole streets in old towns are demolished without sentiment, to be replaced by totally unsuitable new monofunctional commercial buildings. This may have to do with an understanding of history or an attitude to time itself that is completely different: think of the Ise shrine in Japan. Living in Malaysia and seeing the daily destruction of one's heritage would turn anyone into a conservationist. Living in Austria, on the other hand, would turn one into a burning advocate of anything modern. Virulent opposition is common here to practically any overtly contemporary building in historic centres, whereas no one seems to bother about what is built outside central locations. Most of the public and the press find it easier to accept new buildings disguised as old; sentimental pathos which results in the most terrible forms of kitsch. Whereas the reconstruction of St. Stephen's Cathedral in Vienna after extensive bomb damage during the last days of World War II was justified by the cathedral's eminent position as a national symbol, the argument in favour of inserting a true copy in a historic setting fails in the face of the change in the mode of production from hand made to industrially prefabricated mass production. The State Opera in Vienna, also severely damaged during the war, was reconstructed in its full acoustic and functional imperfection in spite of earnest pleas to change the auditorium inside to allow for better sight and sound. Combined with the economies of space that rule building today (lower floor to floor heights and smaller common areas), these changed parameters result in buildings that are nothing more than a parody of the historic edifices they seek to emulate. The lack of authenticity is the result of the basic irreconstructibility of historic processes.

The difficulty seems to lie in a purely visual judgement of transformations, whereas it is the hybrid relationships of spaces, functions and economies that are determinant. Harmony and unity take on complex dimensions and can no longer be defined in purely visual terms. More than aesthetic considerations, it is the conservation of resources, the adaptation of spaces to match uses that demand additive transformation, an incremental process of the addition of new parts.

Equifinality is, however, too simple to be a goal, it is multifinality that creates the necessary flexibility. While there is no need for an ultimate metalanguage to disprove Gödel's theorem,[3] the fact that architectural idiom is not an exact copy of reality will only arouse anxiety in an age where there is an artificial schism between past and present, I and others, self and world. "What is denounced as 'utopian' is no longer that which has 'no place' and cannot have any place in the historical universe, but rather that which is blocked from coming about by the power of established societies."[4] The deeply conservative attitude towards architecture dominant in Austria, that manifests itself so often in a regressive nostalgia, has many roots. Every architecture is as adequate to its socio-cultural reality as it needs to be. To begin with, the greater part of the population, including most of those who now live in cities, has a rural (which often means anti-urban) background. To add to that, most Austrians (especially architects) grow up, live and work in old buildings. There is no escaping the weight of history, and modern architecture has to measure up to it—an unfair demand given the completely different conditions of production, political decision making and resources available. Even those architects who react against history are not acting in a vacuum. You cannot forget forgetting history.

Sigmund Freud
by his couch, Vienna 1930s

In the 20s, the writer Hugo von Hofmannsthal dealt with the theme of things and time passing, posing the problem of the past. How can one face this fading away? How can one look at it without becoming nostalgic? How should one face change and the refusal to change? When the ever lasting validities of past values are evoked, everything is left still, like in a station with a train that does not depart. In that immobility everything is waiting for the signal - to start all over again, to go where it was thought the world would go decades ago.

The urge to restore buildings to their imagined original state, to recreate urban ensembles and to resurrect a lost unity in the city reflects a deep-seated need for harmony. A nation which has experienced many conflicts this century seems to repress conflicts in architecture. The conflict between new and old is not seen as a constructive challenge that should be met with integrity, not with the bland conformity of faithful restoration or with the cheap provocation of pseudo-deconstructivist pyrotechnics. There seems to be a subconscious level of prejudice which does not tolerate an idealised harmony being disturbed by unfamiliar or new elements. Oblivion and memory, hope and regret are inner conflicts of society and the individual. Most of us consider ourselves progressive or even radical on certain issues, while being deeply conservative on others. This kind of conflict is difficult enough to resolve on a personal level. Why should it be easier when projected onto the built environment?

Sigmund Freud, who opened up the modern mind as modern architecture opened up space, wrote that "what is forgotten is not erased but repressed, its traces in the memory are fresh but isolated through occupation by antithetical thoughts."[5] Layering and separation are both complementary and highly complicated attributes of man and his shelter. Otto Kapfinger maintains that the psychological analysis of the blockages in the human mind is similar to that of the petrified memory of the urban corpus.[6] Rediscovering life's dynamic is acknowledging the multiplicity of existence, the variety of its modes of being, and its contradictions that are to be systematized in a building. This is the task of fully exhausting the meaning of multiplicity, of mastering its particular value so that the synthesis can be realized concretely and not mythically. Georg Simmel writes in his essay on "Fashion": "The way in which it is given to us to comprehend the phenomena of life causes us to perceive a plurality of forces at every point of existence."[7] Tensions, antagonisms, the plurality of forces, the incessant transformation of directions uproot the idea of a stable home but create new places to dwell. A striking example of this ability to create a new place with a little disrespect for the old is Sepp Müller's recent renovation of the Austrian Museum of Applied Arts (MAK), a nineteenth century building housing decorative arts, which was basically turned upside down and inside out, then dusted and reorganized to allow more light and transparency. Most of the collection which once filled the overcrowded rooms, difficult to peruse, was exiled to the basement but is accessible for study, while a few selected pieces were highlighted in novel exhibition-type displays designed by contemporary artists. Since then it has become one of the most delightful museums to visit, a place where the younger generation likes to spend time. The older generation, on the other hand, bemoans the disappearance of all the objects that could be compared with each other as in an antique dealer's shop, and protests the insertion of alien elements in a familiar building. This example is symptomatic of the conflicts discussed earlier in this essay. What is overseen is that such a transformation actually guarantees the extended use of a building and prevents it from becoming obsolete at a particular moment.

"Everything is pregnant with its contrary."[8] At the centre of Adolf Loos's work we see the development through differences which composes contradictions and gives form to their dissonance. This

includes the ability to be cut up, dismounted and recomposed, totally at the disposure of the project. According to his logic, the project, freed from continuum, becomes the new subject, the substance of this uprooting power. Confrontational design was also seen in Artecs' exhibition installation in the interior of Fischer von Erlach's Imperial Stables and in Adolf Krischanitz's container-like steel art hall placed temporarily in front of Olbrich's Seccession. Cities and places are the result of a constant creative altercation between cultural and economic forces in a particular situation. Kapfinger points out that the phrase 'organically grown city' creates the illusion of a natural born entity that regulates itself in complete autarchy, and ignores the fact that all architectural and urban development is a disunified product of ever new conflicts between political, economic, functional and aesthetic interests. It is only the rate of change that varies, not the existence of change itself. In spite of the difficulties described above, vistors from other parts of the European continent are surprised at the number of Austrian architects who seriously try to integrate the resonance of memory in today's culture, and the quantity of work that has actually been realized. There seems to be a strong urge for innovation in Austria, which competes with the strong conservatism. Synthetic, a word with negative associations, can be applied to invented styles of architecture propagated universally and forced on people regardless of place or history; synthesis, a positive word, refers to a sensitive and complex solution to the conflict. Going beyond this, one recognizes that the finiteness of mind does not always allow progress toward the ultimate synthesis. The introduction of similarity instead of identity, of relation instead of opposition, marks the crumbling of structures in the deconstructionist spirit. In this aesthetically-minded pluralism courting multi-levelled relations, both the search for origins and teleology need to be discarded.

Great innovations in architecture are seldom realized on a tabula rasa. The beginnings of an architectural career are rarely found in large new buildings. Small renovations, interventions in the existing fabric of a building or a street are usually beginners' commissions for young designers, mainly because cautious clients with larger projects prefer to invest their money in tested architects. But it is also the great numbers of old buildings with their constantly changing users that account for the many commissions in this field. Renovations are not usually considered as prestigious as new buildings although they are often more complicated and labour-intensive. This gives young designers their first opportunity to start a dialogue with the architectural history of which their own education is a product. Wolfgang Feyferlik's insertion of a complete new house within the envelope of an old one and Riegler/Riewe's cultural centre intervention in an old cinema in Steinach without touching the facades embody dignified yet fresh solutions. With Austria's over-whelming historical background, it is not surprising that many architects' first commissions, starting with Adolf Loos, are small renovations, mainly shops, restaurants and bars at street level in historic buildings. Some of these redesigns of the past three decades have been widely published, notably the interiors and facades by Hans Hollein, Boris Podrecca, Paolo Piva, Carl Pruscha and Eichinger/Knechtl. In a jewellery-box city like Vienna these tiny jewel-like projects have a dispro-portionately large influence on general aesthetics. Though these projects may mimic attributes of history, Post-Modernism, with its superficial and eclectic thievery, is an inappropriate label for describing the density of these small Viennese insertions that often condensed the character of detail of a whole palace into a single doorway. That explains why designers who started their careers with such projects to move on to bigger things on the basis of their success with small renovations, continue to work on this scale.

The nature of this dialectic is the germ of the development of architecture: whereas some architects try to fit in as inconspicuously as possible, others introduce elements of contradiction and tension to the existing fabric. This tension may be short-lived or lasting, it may be negative or positive, but in any case it takes architecture a step forward. What is needed, and found in the best interventions, is a certain lack of respect, a demystification. An architect who questions an old building instead of merely accepting it takes issue with traditional habits, but he has to investigate and then demonstrate a deeper understanding of the building than one who merely restores it without questioning. This 'lack of respect' is a useful way to demystify a building before changing it. PAUHOF's work, notably their house in Gramastetten and their exhibition installations, usually contains this tenet; as does the montage technique used by Alfred Bramberger in his modern sports centre in five 19th century sport halls and the superimposition of a grid on an urban square on the Tummelplatz, both in Graz. The desanctification of a building is a necessary first step to its transformation. Not surprisingly, the 'deconstructionist' solution of post-structuralist thought has been to renounce all claims to truth and morality, in the liberating form of an aesthetic 'otherness' vis-a-vis the constraining rationality of the Enlightenment. The strategy lies in adopting a deliberate, playful style both in life and art, while at the same time maintaining a radical plurality of immanent architecture, which strenuously repudiates all tentatives towards a transcendental principle of universalization.

"The insatiable builders, slaves of Hephaestus, who have torn all place away from space and all time away from indifferent duration, have completed their work."

It is true that many new buildings and interventions in old buildings have often failed the test of creating consonance and a new lease of life for them, so that general public resistance to modern architecture cannot be dismissed solely by reference to conservative taste. Only a handful of talented architects have sincerely approached the problem with sensitivity. The different expressions range from the Post-Modern shops for Schullin and the Haas Haus by Hans Hollein, to the Deconstructivist attic renovation and the graphic designer's atelier by Coop Himmelblau. They vary from the subtle enhancement of the existing fabric found in Hermann Czech's restaurants in MAK and in the Hotel Schwarzenberg, Oskar Putz's Kix bar or Konrad Frey's Seggau Castle renovation, to the glossy elegance of Paolo Piva's Schullin watch shop and Knize boutique, Boris Podrecca's Palmers shop or Hollein's early Retti candle shop. They range from Frey's high tech expressions of the exhibition centre in Mürzzuschlag or the Scala restaurant and the ironically named Hobby Room (their own studio) by Driendl/Steixner, to the calculated Minimalism of Adolf Krischanitz's exhibition centre in Krems or Eichinger/Knechtl's bars, offices and Jewish Museum renovation. Each of these approaches initially faced resistance from the building industry, only to be embraced

House
Gramastetten 1995, PAUHOF - Pautzenberger & Hofstätter

Intervention in an urban square
Tummelplatz, Graz 1994, Alfred Bramberger

by it thereafter in the production of third rate versions of these styles. Just as big business in the US has appropriated and perverted the aims and forms of Modernism, the building industry in the 80s adopted Hollein's Post-Modern motifs to decorate its otherwise monotonous sheds. Now that high tech is in fashion, the industry can leave out the decoration and cover the land with these cheap, simple, industrial sheds with a clear conscience and the pride of being up to date.

The high cost of building curtails the artistic freedom of the architect. Artists may do sketches, water colours or sculptures for themselves, whereas architects depend on commissions from the public sphere. The fact that buildings are always in the public sphere severely limits the private nature of architecture. A new field of activity was opened up in this century to the architect who wanted to go beyond the visionary sketch. I am referring to exhibition design. New developments in architecture since the industrial revolution have often been presented for the first time in designs for exhibitions. From Paxton's Crystal Palace through Aalto's and Mies' exhibitions in the 30s to Hollein's ice-breaking installations in the Venice Biennale, the large exhibition has become an important and rewarding field for the visionary architect. This is where an architect can realize and prove his concepts of space and design. Materials, forms and colours can be tried out with effect, but without the high costs of permanent buildings. The temporary nature of an exhibition and the wish to attract attention through it mean that the client can be tolerant and encouraging of revolutionary design. A similar field of activity is that of set design for stage and screen. The Austrian exile Fritz Lang's unforgettable set for "Metropolis" (1926) is the archetypal example. Public reaction, the effects of an experimental design, can be seen at little cost. Large buildings always involve compromise with the powers that be.

There is no doubt that the new form of large-scale expensive staged exhibitions in Europe and Japan was strongly influenced by Hollein's exhibitions, not just by his designs but also by his skill in presenting the connections and interdependencies of events and ideas. Based on his early interest in exhibiting phenomena rather than mere objects, his 1985 show on turn-of-the-century Vienna "Dream and Reality" for the Historical Museum of the City of Vienna in the Künstlerhaus was a milestone in exhibition design. Spaces were dedicated to major figures of the time and reflected the essence of their work. Themes were more important than actual exhibits. The huge, dark Sigmund Freud room had absolutely nothing in it except a surrealistically illuminated miniature model of Freud's couch in one corner at eye level, to signify that Freud's impact was not material but in the realm of the mind. Boris Podrecca does not combine the role of the curator and the designer, but he shows a similar 'lack of respect' for the dusty scholarly chronological display techniques familiar from exhibitions by ivory-tower academics. He works primarily as a designer with objects

Office renovation "Hobby room"
Vienna 1995, Georg Driendl • Gerhard Steixner

Office renovation
Vienna 1994, Eichinger or Knechtl

Boutique Ioham
Graz 1990, Claudio Silvestrin

preselected by the curators, but he applies the strength of his metaphorical associations to produce dramatic spaces, such as that in the 1989 exhibition on the life and times of Count Bismarck in the Martin Gropius building in Berlin. A huge mysterious wrapped statue of Bismarck in the central hall was the focus of different themes radiating from it. Both Hollein and Podrecca tend to create their own exhibition architecture within the existing structure, a valid though somewhat indirect approach to a dialogue with it.

Some of the competent exhibition architects in Vienna fall into the trap of 'total design' as once practiced by the members of the Wiener Werkstätte—every bolt and screw, every glass case is specially designed and constructed. They tend to regard the exhibits as sacred, and create beautiful forms around them without questioning the interpretation of history offered by the specialist academics. They lack the necessary 'lack of respect', which can also be shown in other ways. The exhibition "Magical Hands" on Indian art and culture, in Schallaburg Castle in 1993, gave this author as curator and designer the opportunity to combine antique high art and contemporary kitsch thematically for the first time, to explain the continuum of Indian culture. This erosion of barriers was contrary to the usual scholarly isolation of eras and styles out of their context. Displays and spaces conveyed the quintessence of the stages of life visually, acoustically and olfactorily, as did the presence of master craftsmen, story-tellers and dancers. The processivity of time was represented multi-dimensionally: money-making, for example, by the riches of an urban palace, not reconstructed but alienated into its component parts to convey the impression of a whole; eroticism with the play of the erosion of borders between the private and the public. The exhibition installations bridged what had seemed to be an insurmountable aesthetic gap between the unified character of

Set from the film "Metropolis"
1926, Fritz Lang

Exhibition "Dream and Reality"
Vienna 1985, Hans Hollein

Exhibition "Dream and Reality"
Vienna 1985, Hans Hollein

Exhibition "Magical Hands"
Schallaburg 1993, Ramesh Kumar Biswas

Exhibition "Magical Hands"
(top3) Schallaburg 1993, Ramesh Kumar Biswas

Exhibition of their own work
Architecture Foundation, Brussels 1995, PAUHOF

Exhibition "Bismarck"
Berlin 1990, Boris Podrecca

the 15th century Renaissance castle and the diversity of Indian iconic and bazaar images. In this case the building was not concealed by the designed exhibition spaces, which related similar craft techniques in their different temporal contexts to those of the castle. An audacious approach was taken to combine the images, without the respect convention usually gives them.

With Günther Domenig's 1995 exhibition in Hüttenberg, a new structure placed on top of the ruins of an early industrial blast-furnace, we have come the full circle. The juxtaposition of the geological formation of the region that later determined its industrial archeology, the modern steel construction that is ultimately its yield, and the original site, is a dialogue between the origins of the industrial age and the products that overlay the origins. The steel structure is an outcome of the brick kiln which it now supersedes and dominates. The content and design of the exhibition and the building that envelopes it are conceived as a whole consisting of parts that are in confrontation with each other. The tension that arises from this confrontation was created by a lack of respect for conservatorial parameters which creates the excitement characteristic of the best interventions of the new in the old.

Time is the only critic without ambition. All these interventions will in turn be tested and re-interpreted by it. Interiors are ripped out and changed ever more frequently to satisfy the flux in fashion and taste, new owners and new uses. This means that time as we know it is being replaced by a multiplicity of times connected through both the unchanged and the transformed elements of a building. The city is being transformed in a constant montage within and without, in a fascinating process that cannot be frozen in time and judged in isolation.

P.S: A newspaper recently reported that private enterprise cemeteries in the United States are losing money - bodies are not decomposing at the calculated rate for the efficient reuse of burial ground, due to the high amount of preservatives they have stored after decades of absorbing chemically processed foodstuffs. Vienna's huge Central Cemetery has a pragmatic approach whose functional principle could be applied to the transformation of old buildings - plots are 'rented' for ten years. Should the bereaved not continue to pay the rent, the space is vacated for another paying guest.

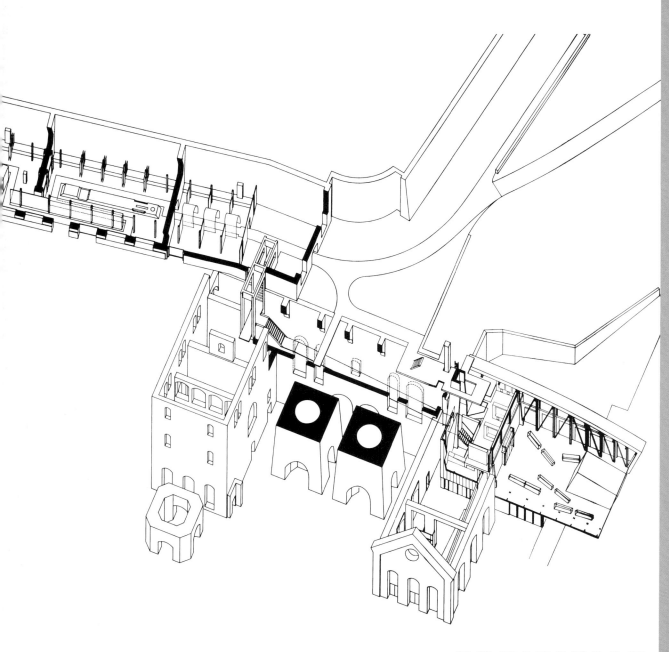

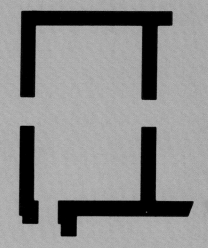

EXHIBITION STRUCTURE

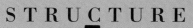

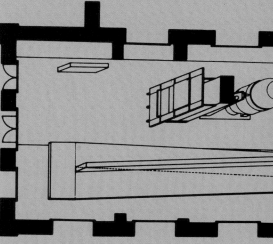

EXHIBITION STRUCTURE
Hüttenberg, Kärnten 1995
Architect and exhibition designer: Günther Domenig b. 1934
Engineer: Albert Tripolt
Project team: N. Müller, D. Fritz, J. Rögener, E. Herz, P. Liaunig, C. Andrews
Area: 2300m²
Cost: 42 million ATS

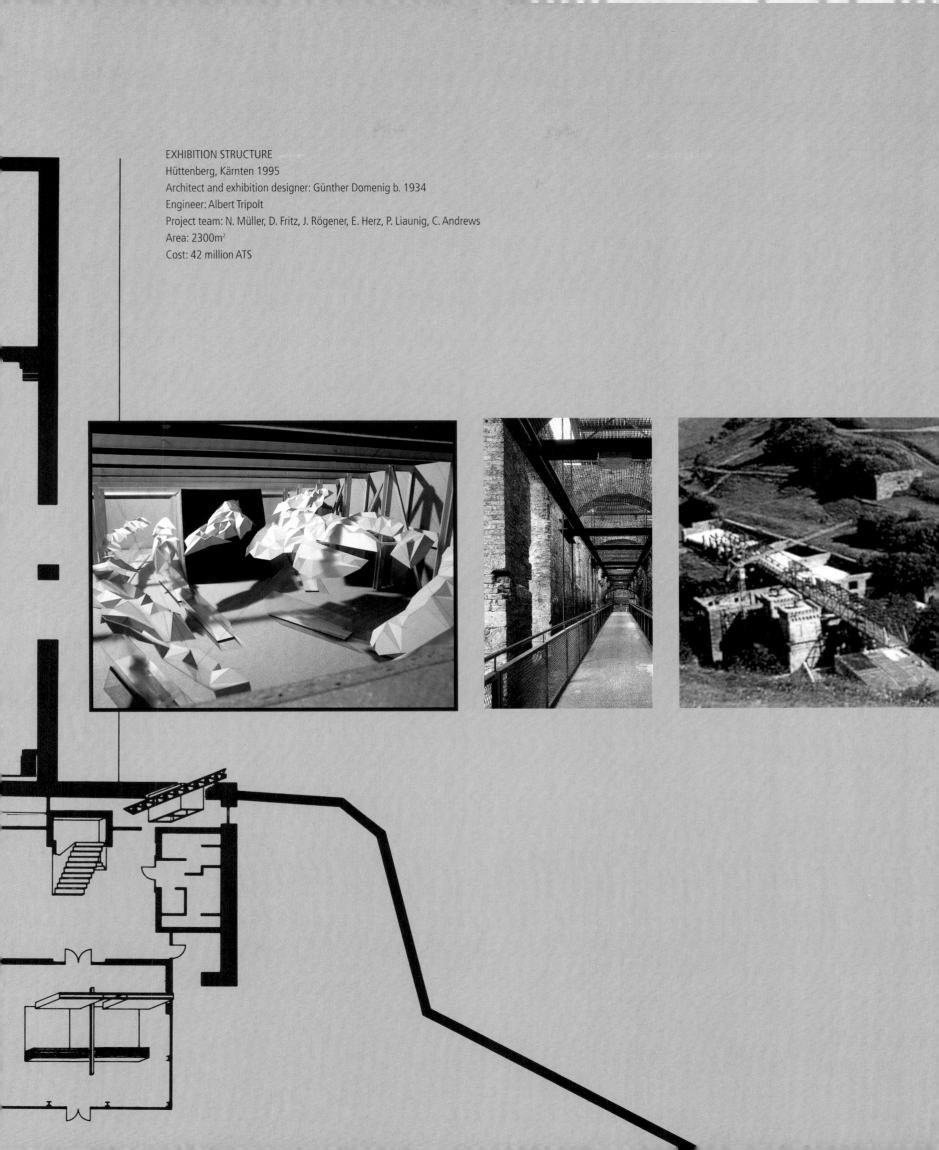

The iron ore extraction and smelting works in Hüttenberg were closed down at the beginning of this century, leaving the colossal kilns as a monument to the early industrial age. It became an open air industrial archeology museum in 1980. Ten years later it was decided to hold an exhibition on the mining and industrial history of the southern state of Kärnten. The project suffered long delays and financial cuts, but the final realization in 1995 has lost none of the power and plastic expression of the first sketches. The need was to create weather-proof spaces to protect the exhibition without

EXHIBITION STRUCTURE

concealing the actual ruin which is itself the biggest and most important exhibit. The appropriate industrial metaphor of the steel, zinc sheet and glass insertion seems to float above and weave between the huge brick 'cathedrals' of the kilns, the structural connections between the two honest and visible to the last detail. Glazed apertures in floors and ceilings in the new exhibition areas allow unexpected views of the historic structures, enhancing the experience of seeing them. Domenig has created an unusually restrained and impressive layering and articulation of the two eras that coexist in this complex.

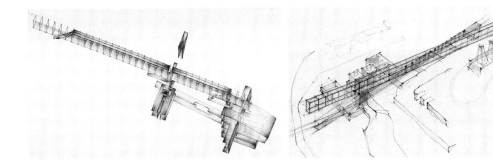

The reorganisation of an existing museum on Celtic history in the centre of an old town offered the opportunity to create a new entrance hall between the two oldest buildings in the town, directly accessible from the square. Minor additions over the years were removed to create a naturally lit lobby that extends the entire height of the two old buildings The basement contains a Celtic grave as well as technical installations. The grand staircase seems to float freely in the room, the lift and the other facilities in the lobby wing serve various levels of the museum culminating in a terrace overlooking the river. Space is determined by new concrete walls which are connected with stainless steel plates to the old walls to replace the stability offered by floors that were removed. The strength of the space is that of a medieval environment of heavy walls enhanced by the atypical introduction of natural light.

The design ties in with the restructuring of the museum and the restoration of the city theatre nearby. The difficult parameters of urban place, conservation and modern museum organization have been successfully unified in this scholarly and concentrated design.

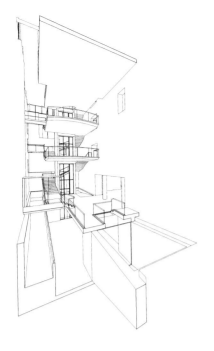

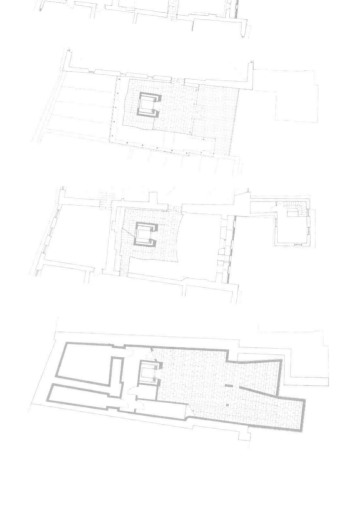

MUSEUM
RENEWAL

MUSEUM OF CELTIC HISTORY
Hallein, Salzburg 1994
Architect: Heinz Tesar b. 1939
Engineer: Bernd Ferstel
Project team: K. Langer, S.Ertl, M. Donay
Area: 3.900m^2
Cost: 25 million ATS

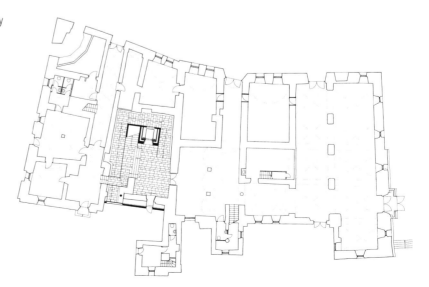

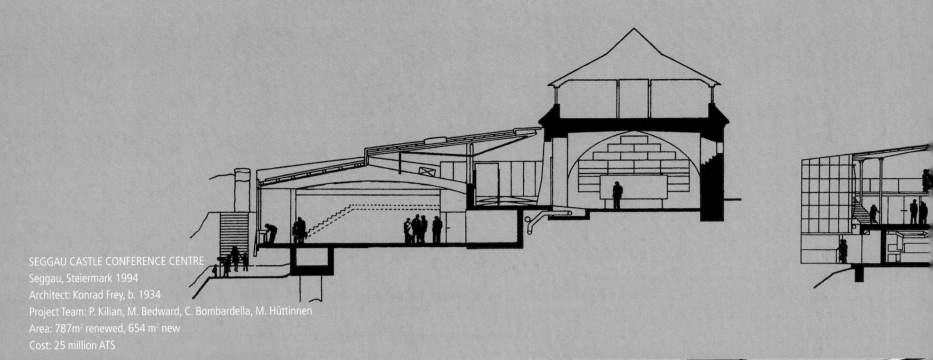

SEGGAU CASTLE CONFERENCE CENTRE
Seggau, Steiermark 1994
Architect: Konrad Frey, b. 1934
Project Team: P. Kilian, M. Bedward, C. Bombardella, M. Hüttinnen
Area: 787m² renewed, 654 m² new
Cost: 25 million ATS

CONFERENCE CENTRE

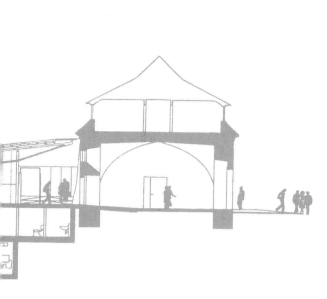

The church-owned 18th century castle with a 2000 year old Roman core and an extension built in the 1960s was no longer capable of meeting the needs of the conference and educational centre it houses. A courageous intervention that does not try to be spectacular at any cost. The new elements, additive in nature, do not try to blur the edges between new and old, but to focus on them, thus gifting the older part with even greater identity and appreciation than it had before. The new entrance foyer and the intermediary zone make the entire complex more comprehensible and usable, giving it a fulcrum. Accessibility for handicapped persons, a difficult task in historic buildings, was improved during the renovation. The existing slope of the site was used to add service rooms under grade. Technical installations have been integrated in an intelligent way. Natural light has been increased in the interior and dead areas surrounding the buildings converted to usable space for open air events, bringing the old and the new buildings to life. The conscious contrasts and oppositions combine to make this a scholarly, refined work which amounts to more than a mere adaptation.

The Austrian Museum of Applied Arts with its legendary collection of furniture, textiles, glassware, porcelain and other handcrafted wares of the Baroque, Biedermeier and Jugendstil periods, was founded in 1864 and was a dusty collection of overfilled storerooms until a radical operation converted the whole building from the basement to the attic. The insertion of a 3400m2 storage unit under the existing buildings freed them of objects and allowed their restoration and upgrading to be carried out. New interventions such as a connecting tract between the two old buildings, technical improvements, renovated offices, vistor's flats, a shop and a restaurant improved the functioning of the museum. The most interesting innovation, however, lay in the museum's new philosophy of interpreting traditional craft in the light of conteporary art and vice versa. To this end, renowned artists were invited to design the new galleries for specific antique collections. As a result, only a few representative pieces of the collections were displayed to dramatic effect, the rest being accessible to the interested public in the store rooms. Though some critics consider that that it is no longer a museum but a collection of exhibitions, the fact is that it has become a delightful and exciting institution, one of the few large museums in the world where one can spend lots of time with little fatigue and much enjoyment.

MUSEUM RENEWAL
MAK (Museum of Applied Arts), Stubenring, Vienna I 1993
Architect: Sepp Müller b. 1927
Engineer: Wolf-Dietrich Ziesel
Project team: I. Bitzios, J. Dika, M. Embacher, W. Glatzner, S. Jelic, A. Nikowitz, K. Schefferhof
Special galleries and installations:
Donald Judd, James Wines (SITE), P.Noever, etc
Area: 20.000 m²
Cost: 265 million ATS

050/051

MUSEUM RENEWAL

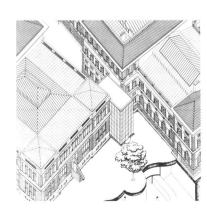

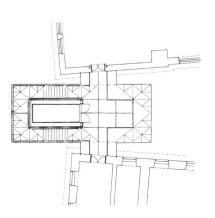

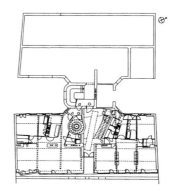

PENTHOUSE ADDITION
Sailergasse, Vienna I, 1995
Architect: Rüdiger Lainer
Project team: S. Bidwell, K. Krummlauf, B. Moos,
S. Sangha, H. Schild, A. Stryjewska
Engineers: Helmuth Locher, Gerhard Wagner
Area: 540 m²
Cost: 16 million ATS

PENTHOUSE

ADDITION

The ironically named 'neutral zone' (Vienna's inner city centre around St. Stephen's cathedral) is practically a jealously guarded reservation for the historic styles it contains - all renovated attics are forced by the conservationist authorities to adopt 'traditional' attic windows, resulting in claustrophobically dark interiors. This penthouse, that adds five units of flexible space for offices or flats, divided by removeable sliding walls, on two floors on top of a 19th century building, ignores all conventional rules.

The flat roof replaces a similarly functional sloping roof and creates a maximum of useable and agreeable space. Economical flat folded steel plates as permanent shuttering for in-situ concrete floors are carried by a light prefab steel skeleton to reduce loads on the building below. Full-length glazed walls are silicon-sealed in a slender stainless steel frame construction, with openeable doors that act as windows, reversing the attic/window relationship. Visual privacy is ensured by translucent external

fabric blinds operated by solar sensors to control solar gain by day, and by floodlighting the blinds externally at night, which also lightens and extends the space from the interior. It is an open bird's nest, whose residents experience the unchanging historic buildings and the changing sky directly. Yet it is valid primarily as a one-off breakaway from the corset of unimaginative regulations and clichées, not as a generally applicable commercial solution which would render historic centres unrecognizeable.

ATTIC

CONVERSION

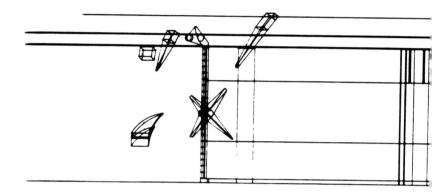

The conversion of this attic into a large meeting room and offices for lawyers working on the lower floors of the same building offered Coop Himmelblau one of their first major opportunities to translate their drawings, generated with explosive heat and light, into reality. The two architects, who had been working obsessively with the concepts of wings and flight, say tongue-in-cheek that the fact that this project was to be built at a height of 21m above the Falcon Street made it an exception. The tradition of private builders of introducing prominent features on their buildings which then contribute to the streetscape has been continued here, albeit with totally different means. Instead of turrets or bay windows in appropriate materials, proportions and colours, the architects have spanned the project with a 'visual

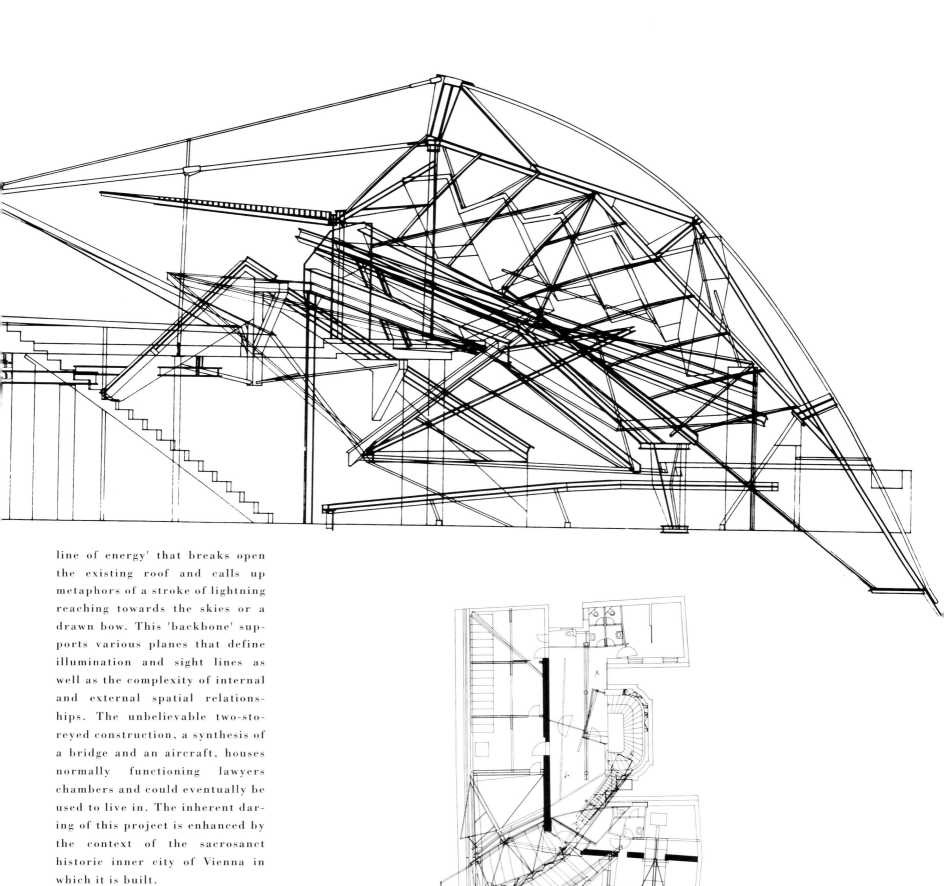

line of energy' that breaks open the existing roof and calls up metaphors of a stroke of lightning reaching towards the skies or a drawn bow. This 'backbone' supports various planes that define illumination and sight lines as well as the complexity of internal and external spatial relationships. The unbelievable two-storeyed construction, a synthesis of a bridge and an aircraft, houses normally functioning lawyers chambers and could eventually be used to live in. The inherent daring of this project is enhanced by the context of the sacrosanct historic inner city of Vienna in which it is built.

ATTIC CONVERSION, Falkestrasse, Vienna I 1988, Architects: Coop Himmelblau (Wolf Prix

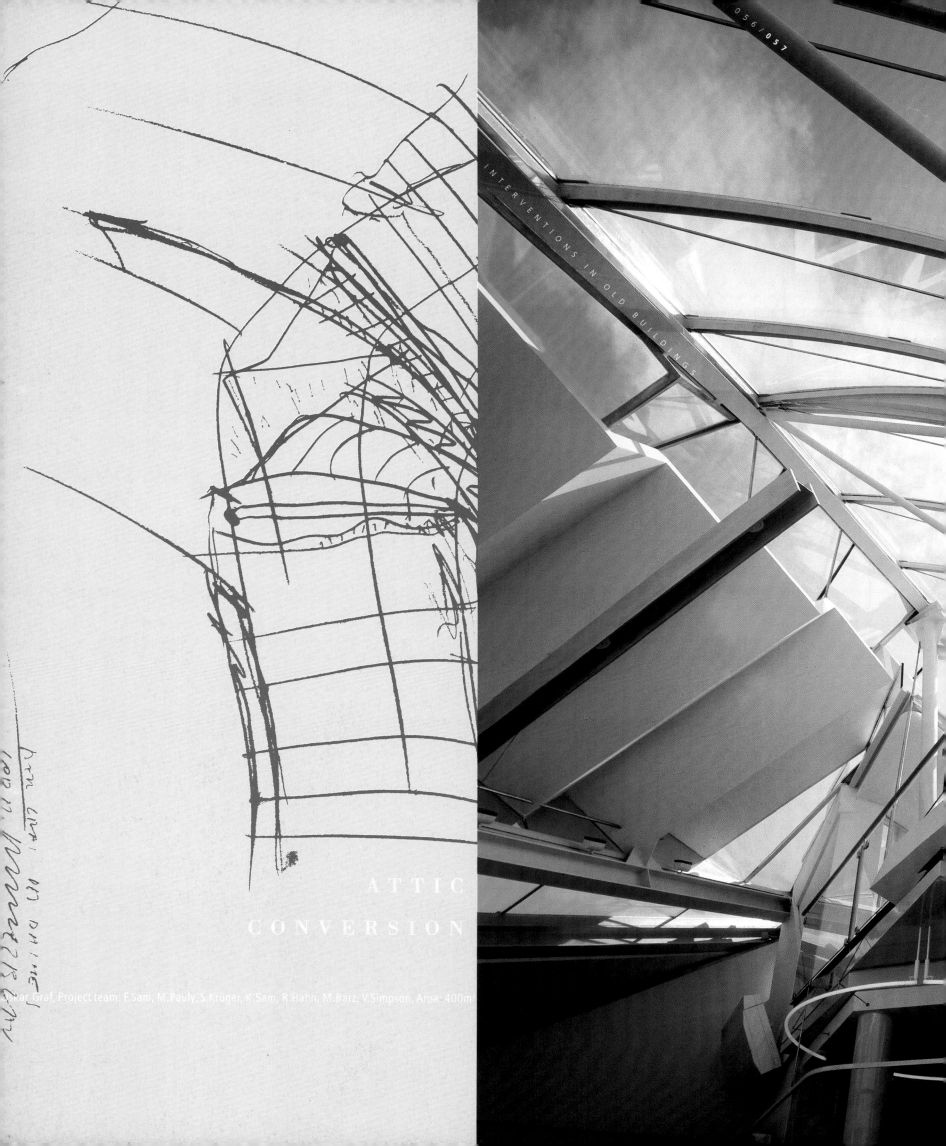

INTERVENTIONS IN OLD BUILDINGS

ATTIC
CONVERSION

Oskar Graf, Project team: F.Sam, M.Pauly, S.Krüger, K.Sam, R.Hahn, M.Barz, V.Simpson, Area: 400m²

INTERNATIONAL CONTEXT

MINIMALISM   62

INNOCENTS ABROAD   68

THE VALIDITY OF THE MODEL   78

VOLCANO MUSEUM AUVERGNE   82

MUSEUM PAVILION GRONINGEN   84

PHOSPHATE ELIMINATION PLANT BERLIN   86

Influences on minimalism in Austria
Untitled, Detail, 1973, Donald Judd

Incomplete Open Cubes
Detail, 1974, Sol Lewitt

Despite connections with several other movements, including Konkrete Kunst and certain aspects of Constructivism, the development of Minimalism in New York in the 1960s was notable for the creation of a major body of work whose material and formal characteristics were markedly different from anything previously known. Its larger purpose was to redefine the nature of artistic activity and its success in this respect is shown by the number of other radical movements which can trace their origins back to Minimalism, including Process and Conceptual art, Performance and Body art as well as more recent Installation work. Although they shared several concerns, the immediate effect of Minimalism on architectural design was virtually non-existent even if some of its later derivatives have played a significant role in some schools of architecture. In these circumstances, a particularly surprising aspect of the New Minimalism which is currently practised by a number of younger architects in Austria and Switzerland is the manner in which many of the original inventions of Minimalism have been given a new validity, and a different identity, through their incorporation in the architecture of a different culture.

In its quest to redefine the role of art following the excesses of Abstract Expressionism, a large part of Minimalisms's output was comprised of a new type of object which was intended to be displayed in galleries but did not fulfil the expectations which might otherwise be considered normal in such an environment. In place of more traditional materials and a corresponding emphasis on the details and finish of individual artists, the new works were often constructed of everyday materials with no applied finish or painted a single colour. To further reduce the possibility of secondary readings interfering with a direct perception of the scale and form of each work, constructional detail of any kind was largely avoided by assembling a number of standard elements, usually on a grid and with no intermediary fixings. As a number of well known works by Andre, Judd and LeWitt demonstrate, the immediate effect of such decisions is to throw into sharp contrast the simple physicality of each work and a perception of its complex role in the extended physical environment of which it is part.

Examples of recent Austrian buildings which go to some lengths to avoid conventional expectations are not hard to find but one which combines common materials with a complex programme, so that one acts as a foil to the other, is Das Paradies at Vorderberg near Villach, the workplace and garden of Cornelius Kolig, an artist who makes extensive use of his own faeces. Located within a larger walled garden, a long central courtyard is enclosed on either side by identical buildings devoted to the display of two of the central themes in Kolig's work, metabolism and female sexuality. To the south two larger volumes, a generous storage facility and the Sixtina whose gently vaulted space is used for concerts and the simultaneous presentation of various forms of artwork. To the north a number of smaller constructions clustered around a semi-circular court serve a variety of more domestic purposes. All of these buildings are constructed of concrete blocks with corrugated metallic roofing, each simple volume with its own distinctive proportions. The larger ensemble is composed on additive basis with a series of external spaces which support a number of characteristic smells and sounds, based largely on plant and animal life, at different times of the year. The complexity of the overall programme allied to the simplicity of the constructional means, are essential aspects of the New Minimalism.

Another famous confrontation between an ambitious programme and everyday construction occurs in the Kunsthalle in Vienna by Adolf Krischanitz. At first conceived, the Kunsthalle was originally constructed for an exhibition on the subject of Art and Nature which was staged inside the Imperial Riding School. The rectangular steel enclosure of the first project was designed to fit precisely within the cross-section of this magnificent Baroque interior and to provide a neutral enclosure for the Art and Architecture exhibits which would have otherwise been lost in the larger space. In order to meet a pressing need for a contemporary exhibition space prior to the completion of the prize-winning proposal for the development of the Messepalast for this purpose, Krischanitz's design was re-erected on a traffic island immediately opposite Olbrich's Secession Building and within sight of the church of St Charles Borromeo. In each of its two locations of date, the apparent

MINIMALISM

Peter Allison

simplicity of the construction of the Kunsthalle has served as a highly effective foil to the elaborate readings provided by its immediate neighbours. By appearing to lack conventional architectural purpose, it has on each occasion made a subtle and successful contribution to the larger organisation of which it has been part.

If one material in particular has become synonymous with the New Minimalism, it is surely reinforced concrete. Although concrete continues in widespread use for its structural and fire-resistant properties, its use for internal and external enclosure is far less common following the popular reaction to earlier generations of Modernist buildings. In contrast, several recent buildings have sought to capitalise on the versatility of concrete by using it for a variety of purposes within a single design. In the low cost housing at Graz Strassgang by Florian Riegler and Roger Riewe, where the floors and all cross walls giving the basic layout of each unit are in insitu concrete, the solid sections of the external walls are constructed of precast panels of similar dimensions to the shorter transverse fins. A particular complete demonstration of the all round versatility of concrete is to be found in the Kunsthalle at Krems, also by Krischanitz, in which two exhibition spaces together with a new circulation system have been inserted within the courtyard of an old building using insitu and precast concrete for all the major elements. The language of concrete is the language of this design as neatly summarised in the elegantly monolithic enclosures which tie the new ramp into the original building at ground and first floor levels.

In the 1960s there was considerable controversy surrounding the use of applied colour which, when it was used, was almost always intended to unite the different elements of a work within a single form. Of Austrian architects, Krischanitz has been conspicuous in his investigation of the role of colour and there have been traces of a similar controversy over his Neue Welt Kindergarten which, in collaboration with the painter Helmut Federle, is finished externally with a black insulating render. Working with a different painter, Oskar Putz, Krischanitz's use of colour on the detached blocks along the eastern edge of the social housing at Pilotengasse is also interesting. Externally these blocks were intended to bring together a range of features or cliches from everyday domestic architecture and the application, with some exceptions, of a single colour selected from a slightly garish range was intended to counteract any tendency towards fragmentation and leaves instead a series of 'elephant like' presences. In the Kunsthalle at Krems the subtle tones of the interior concrete work are matched where necessary by luminous shades of grey.

In the absence of applied colour, the self-colour of materials and their ability to respond in a precise way to shifts in lighting as they occur are of considerable importance. In this respect, the close-grained textures which are characteristic of many mass-produced materials, especially those available in sheet and board form, are particularly important as they were in New York in the 1960s. An especially important area of innovation in classical Minimalism was that of composition and here too a tendency to invert previous practice is discernible. The complex hierarchical relationships found in earlier types of Modernism, in which a subtle balance was maintained between major and minor elements, was replaced by a movement towards 'non-relational' compositions in which the possibility of separate figure-ground readings, within a single work, was severely reduced or avoided altogether. In Frank Stella's paintings of 1960 and 1961, flat stripes in black enamel or metallic paint to avoid the rich associations which normally attach themselves to the use of artists' oils progressively repeat the shape of the canvas towards its centre. On completion, this progression may also be read in reverse so that through the use of a single component — the stripe — the shape of the canvas becomes the composition and vice versa. At a banal level, this kind of reversible relationship might be claimed for many groups of buildings on their respective sites but an instance in which it clearly informs the spatial reality of the entire project is that of the social housing at Pilotengasse completed on a joint basis by Herzog and de Meuron of Basel, Otto Steidle of Munich and Krischanitz. Located on the eastern edge of Vienna and conceived of by the designers in terms of "a dialogue between the centre and the periphery", a series of blocks with slightly staggered ends form gentle arcs to either side of the site's long axis. True to their intentions, and due primarily to the use of a single element whose general function is not dissimilar to that

Untitled, cardboard and plastic
Vienna 1987, Heimo Zobernig

of the stripe, the designers at Pilotengasse have established the same reversible relationship between edge and centre which is the basis of Stella's innovatory paintings. Within this rich context each practice was then free to design a series of house types on a more independent basis.

In non-relational compositions the role of secondary elements is always subsidiary to the identity and character of the whole as in the modular works of Carl Andre. As Andre's work also illustrates, this principle readily combines with an emphasis on shape. Of recent Austrian work, several projects by ARTEC, the Vienna-based practice of Bettina Götz and Richard Manahl, have systematically explored the linkage between shape as a compositional goal in a specific context and the satisfaction of planning and constructional requirements on a modular basis. In their office building for the Heinrich Manahl Company at Bings in Vorarlberg the enclosed volume of the upper storey extension encased in large aluminium shingles is contrasted with the scale and framed construction of the internal spaces. And in the social housing at Bärnbach in Styria, the overall identity of each building is established by a gently triangulated roof, which at one end wraps around the main access stair, whilst the detailed requirements of the programme are accommodated within a repetitive bay system with a number of distinct variations.

In the quest for non-hierarchical relationships, the use of modules led directly to the investigation of "systematic order", specifically in Andre's work but most famously in Sol LeWitt's Incomplete Open Cubes of 1974. In this sculpture, each of the 122 different structures included in the form of a cube as defined by its edges is represented in separate three-dimensional figures laid out side by side in grid formation. The crucial aspect of this work is not that most of the interesting possibilities are shown but that all possibilities are included quite regardless of their individual interest or lack of it. In architecture, using mobile elements such as screens and panels, it is possible within a single proposal to create the potential for a complete range of distinct possibilities without their needing to exist at the same time. The most complete demonstration of this principle is provided by the layout of the smaller and the larger flat types in Riegler Riewe's Strassgang building. As designed, the kitchens and bathrooms lie alongside parallel circulation spaces in the centre of the section so that the bays to each side may be progressively opened up or closed down, using sliding panels on the cross section and folding screens on the long section. On this basis, it is possible to create a single continuous space, several closed ones or any option between the two extremes. The element of personal choice is also reflected on the exterior where storey-height panels of perforated nylon to the west and expanded galvanised steel to the each slide on continuous rails to provide privacy or protection from the sun, as required. As the panels which compose the exterior are of almost identical dimensions regardless of whether they are solid or transparent, static or mobile, Strassgang's unadorned rectangular volume appears to be largely composed of a single module repeated in a limited number of materials. Not surprisingly, the craft element receives little emphasis beyond the concerns of professional responsibility so that, at a number of different levels, this building provides a direct architectural equivalent to several of the basic inventions of classic Minimalism forty years ago.

Minimalism was also responsible for a serious reassessment of the role of the gallery space in relation to the display of art. In both mixed and one-person exhibitions, the characteristics of particular spaces and their architecture were seen as important contributors to the occasion and were therefore seldom modified or disguised in any way. Whilst Minimalist works always maintain a degree of independence from their surroundings and from other works, many were conceived of partly in terms of an exploration and clarification of particular settings. In order to achieve this

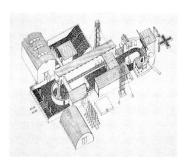

'Das Paradies', Vorderberg
Work in progress, Cornelius Kolig

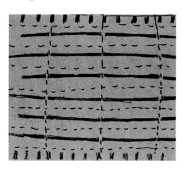

Housing, Pilotengasse
Vienna 1991, Jacques Herzog/Pierre deMueron, Adolf Krischanitz, Otto Steidle

end, their collective layout was always open in character, encouraging a continuity of perception, and generally avoided the possibility of hierarchical readings between different works which might also have detracted from an awareness and appreciation of the environment in total.

In architecture such preoccupations translate into an interest in the basic dimensions of a site combined with a desire to reveal its inherent qualities in relation to the specific context. A somewhat extreme case is Riegler/Riewe's design for the Information and Electronics Institute at the Technical University in Graz where the buildings are organised as a series of parallel blocks whose overall length is precisely that of the entire site. Although these blocks might be read as a series of continuous and unmodulated walls, the parallel open spaces between them combined with several transverse routes and landscaped courtyards ensure a continuous awareness of the immediate surroundings. Krischanitz's proposal for the development of several blocks of the city between the United Nations Offices in Vienna and the Danube is also particularly interesting because of the systematic investigation of different forms of block and their incorporation within a continuous grid.

The directness and clarity of Minimalist art created new responsibilities for its audience. Lacking conventional detail, the physical reality of such art could be seen and understood relatively quickly although its exact significance might be more difficult to discern. In scale, most Minimalist works lacked identifiable references to the human body but it is clear from their size and character that they are intended to share the same space as the viewer without the need for intermediate conventions. Such art confounds expectation by deflecting attention away from an appreciation of the artistic sensibility of the author, as reflected in its detail, and towards an understanding of the work as a totality within a larger world of production and reflection.

As an experience, most Minimalist work makes a very clear distinction between what is solid and what is space, as in one of Judd's box-like construction. The possibility of choosing between these alternate readings and of moving freely between them only serves to heighten awareness of the different sets of conventions which apply to each. Such distinctions are commonplace in architecture except that in the New Minimalism they become the theme itself rather than providing the basis for the development of other intentions. Part of the drama of the Neue Welt Kindergarten is that, with its black render and tinted glass, the exterior reads as a continuous solid whilst the interior, with a parallel continuity of surface, presents nothing but a sequence of spaces. A similar intention is demonstrated in Riegler/Riewe's work by their tendency to place an enclosed rectangular volume next to an open rectangular volume of identical or similar dimensions in such a way that the use of one depends on the use of the other. At a large scale, this may be seen in the section of their proposal for the Information and Electronics Institute in Graz and, at a small scale, in the design of the check in counters at the airport in Graz.

In asserting the distinction between the creation of free space and the supportive but independent role of the enclosing fabric, the New Minimalism directs attention to the activities of a building's occupants and the expectation that these will be organised on the basis of self-determination as circumstances develop. Through the omission of various types of expressive form and detail, such as those which are often incorporated in the design of roofs, the responsibility for the definition of a building's identity in use is left firmly with the occupants. Developments of this kind can be controversial, especially for those who are not directly involved. The social housing at Strassgang is thought by some to look spartan and unsympathetic on the outside and yet combines low cost with the possibility of real personal choice in the use and definition of space. Similarly, the black

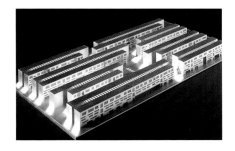

Information Science Institute
Graz 1996, Florian Riegler - Roger Riewe

exterior and exposed concrete of the Neue Welt Kindergarten are supposed to be inappropriate to a building for young children but in use it is clear that these very features provide a much appreciated back-drop to the daily activities of teachers and children in and around their new building in its parkland setting in the Prater.

Although there is now a distinct possibility that, in common with other innovatory movements, the New Minimalism is about to enter a period of general acceptance and progressive trivialisation, there is still a shortage of good examples on the ground. A less complete demonstration of similar intentions may, however, be seen in the work of certain designers whose main intentions may lie in other directions. In Driendl and Steixner's prototypical Standard Solar house, the constructional organisation of the bedroom wing, together with the use of materials in standard sized sheets, has direct connections with Minimalism. As part of their emphasis on urban design, several of Pauhoff's proposals include elements with distinctly Minimalist characteristics. In a recent exhibition at the Architecture Foundation in Brussels, they included a large scale realisation of the type of space which appears in an elevated position in their project for the Austrian pavilion as Seville: entitled Angst Zwei, it took the form of a large box viewed through an open side with floor, walls and roof of equal thickness and clad all over in panels of black rubber-an architectural equivalent to Judd's boxes. In different ways, Anna Popelka and Heidulf Gerngross have developed proposals for social housing which make a clear distinction between the abstract geometry of their overall organisation and the individualistic manner in which they may be occupied. In Gerngross' recently completed project at Wiethestrasse in the east of Vienna houses with identical sections are used side-by-side in one terrace and end-to-end in its neighbour so that each terrace is confronted with the alternative view of its own organisation.

As examples in Austria show, the New Minimalism can take quite different forms in different hands and this possibility is also demonstrated in Switzerland where two of the most significant practices doing similar work are Herzog and de Meuron and Peter Märkli. Of their recent buildings, Herzog and de Meuron's Railway Depot in Basle with its big boned structure and use of common materials, rather than the more special ones which they sometimes employ to great effect, is particularly Minimalist in character. By way of contrast, Märkli has just finished the modestly scaled house at Grabs with its remarkable cut-back section and cantilevered canopy which, thanks to reinforced concrete, can be presented as an example of complete normality.

Untitled installation
Jöss 1990, Heimo Zobernig

Housing Wiethestrasse
Vienna 1995, Anna Popelka & Heidulf Gerngross

In cultural terms, the re-emergence of Minimalism in the architecture of Switzerland and Austria forty years after its initial development may seem to be a surprising phenomenon. But the history of architecture in both countries includes several important figures and a related tradition who attached considerable importance to the different but complementary roles played by built fabric and enclosed space within a single design. Their work is recognisable by simplicity of physical definition and rich variety in use: two of the qualities which are often evident in the drawings of Josef Frank (1885-1967). Several designs by Ernst Plischke (1903-1994), including the Frey House of 1973 in Graz, also share many connections with the new work whilst in Switzerland the sculpture and architecture of Max Bill (1908-1995) provide a major source of inspiration.

Both countries enjoy considerable prosperity and as a consequence are able to provide good support for both architecture and the visual arts in general. In a film made for Herzog and de Meuron's retrospective exhibition at the Pompidou Centre, Jacques Herzog admitted that for them "art is an elixir" and they have often collaborated with artists such as Helmut Federle and Rémy Zaugg. An important figure in Vienna is Peter Pakesch whose gallery showed the work of Minimalists such as Sol LeWitt as well as the Contextual Art of Heimo Zobernig, G. Günter Förg and others which often made direct and real connections with architecture and buildings. Adolf Krischanitz was also responsible for a programme of public exhibitions exploring similar themes during his time as Director of the Secession from 1991 to 1995. And since 1993, under the direction of Edelbert Köb, the Kunsthaus at Bregenz has published a series of studies on the New Minimalism including Roland Gnaiger's prismatic school at Warth.

Apart from physical similarities, the other main connection between Minimalism and the New Minimalism in architecture is that both represent a reformist view in relation to their immediate context. In New York, the situation in which Abstract Expressionism took centre stage was seen as decadent due to the exhaustion of the visual language on which it was based whilst the New Minimalism is clearly a reaction against much of the architectural output of the 1980s which for a variety of reasons put an excessively heavy emphasis on elaboration and display. Compared with the architecture of the 1980s which appeared to advertise a society in which everyone's position was already known and fixed, the New Minimalism can be seen as promoting a more open view in which the identity of individuals and institutions is not the subject of caricature in the design of individual buildings.

Kunstraum Wien, exhibition space
Vienna 1993, ARTEC - Bettina Götz, Richard Manahl

Housing
Bärnbach 1994, ARTEC - Bettina Götz, Richard Manahl

Neue Welt School
Vienna 1994, Adolf Krischanitz

There is a certain school of thought which says that much that began in Vienna as a nice, small idea was then taken up and blown out of proportion elsewhere, only to wreak havoc all over the world. Proponents of this sarcastic view refer to Freud's psychoanalysis, to the invention of the internal combustion engine used in automobiles, and to the Karl Marx Hof as examples. It is true that the Karl Marx Hof, a large but pleasant 1920s public housing scheme built to assuage the terrible housing conditions of the working classes and provide them with better communal facilities, did become a prototype for the vastly inferior and dreaded mass housing schemes being built everywhere to this day. Yet the bottom line of a century of international influence of and on Austrian architecture is not absolutely negative.

The interplay of global and local experiences is part of a broad extension of thought reaching beyond national borders, touching other cultural evolutions and intellectual endeavours and returning to enrich the local situation. Civilizations do not flourish when isolated and spared contamination, but when they intermingle and exchange ideas and know-ledge, and when they extend beyond exchange to produce transformation. Internal context-ualization inevitably implies a close analysis of external contextualization, for today no architect is an island. Common as it may appear now for architects to build in places other than their country of origin, there are differences in the way they do it. Large multi-national offices resemble contractors and builders' firms more than what one normally associates with an architectural practice. Pinstriped managers wielding mobile phones are far removed from the self-image of the artist-architect. It is therefore refreshing to see the handful of slightly chaotic, bohemian Austrian architects, who, in spite of their awful accents and terrible foreign-language skills, manage to communicate their concepts, receive commissions and influence developments abroad in a measure strikingly disproportionate to the tiny size and the minor global economic influence of their country. Not all the work they have done outside Austria can claim to be an unqualified success, as we shall see. However,

the word 'innocent' is meant positively in this context - it is the force of ideas and quality of work of individual architects that stand alone and are more convincing than a network of inter-dependencies based on contracts to architectural firms associated with major economic powers. The different phases of Austrian architecture have never developed in isolation. The work of Austrian architects has always been tied to their connections with other countries, and has often been a two-way process. The Viennese is often described as part immigrant emeritus and part potential emigrant. This internationalism is not due to their being particularly cosmopolitan —more often than not it has been forced on them. Under the monarchy, with its conservative taste, it was easier for unconventional architects to realize their work outside the capital. In peripheral regions, progressive industrialists and rich patrons commissioned figures like Adolf Loos and Ernst Plischke to translate their ideas into reality. Josef Hoffmann was one of those who were renowned for their Gesamtkunstwerke (total design works that embraced every detail of the building down to its furnishings and cutlery) all over the continent, and which brought him commissions such as the Palais Stoclet in Brussels. At the turn of the century, Otto Wagner was the most significant figure, as much due to his teaching position and his publications (Moderne Architektur, published in 1895) as to his buildings. His students Pavel Janak and Jan Kotera in Prague, Istvan Benko-Medgyaszay in Budapest, Josef Plecnik in Ljubljana and Prague, Josef Maria Olbrich in Darmstadt and Rudolph Schindler in California, disseminated his architectural and urban design concepts through exceptionally beautiful buildings. Antonio Sant'Elia was one of the Italian Futurists strongly influenced by Wagner's thought.

During the interwar years, many Modernist architects left Austria to join the pioneering new Bauhaus in Germany and to participate in the social building programme of the Weimar Republic. Here we come to another of those originally brilliant Viennese inventions that now, in a distorted form, plague the world. Margarete Schütte-Lihotsky, approaching her hundredth year of age in 1995, developed a rational, ergonomic kitchen in the 20s for new

INNOCENTS ABROA

Ramesh Kumar Bisw

council housing, meant initially to free the working woman from the slavery of the old-fashioned, labour-intensive kitchens of the past. Her good intentions were perverted when the scale and the motives were deformed. Her Frankfurt Kitchen was readily snapped up by industry and developed into the mass-produced fitted kitchen we now know, with its standard sizes — the very opposite of an ergonomic design flexible enough to suit different people. Women were chained to their little cell of a kitchen, cut off from the rest of the family. The quality of cuisine suffered and the standardized kitchens were brought into step with the standard packages of the food industry and the kitchen appliances of the consumer industry.

In the 1920s, Kemal Attaturk's modernization and secularization progamme led him to seek Central European architects to build symbols of his vision of a westernized Turkey in the new capital of Ankara. Clemens Holzmeister, a very influential architect and Austrian State Counsellor for the Arts, won one of the competitions held at the time and was later given direct commissions for several monumental governmental edifices, including the Turkish President's Palace. One may well ask whether Ankara, built mainly by Western architects, had the same effect as Chandigarh, which discredited indigenous architecture in favour of the Western model for generations, until its 'rediscovery' in recent years. When the Nazis invaded Austria in 1938, Holzmeister happened to be in Hungary. As he was on the most wanted list of officials from the deposed government and would have been arrested and deported to a concentration camp, he fled to Turkey, where he remained until 1945. Upon his return, he built several modernist classics and headed a master school for architecture in Vienna, which became the incubation cell for most of the prominent members of the older generation of architects today, Hollein and Holzbauer being among them. Others emigrated earlier and for many different reasons. The most famous, Richard Neutra, who left Austria for Switzerland and the US in 1919, and Rudolf Schindler, who emigrated to the US in 1914, can be mentioned as one of those pioneers who changed the relationship of architecture to its environment by redefining and reversing the relationship between the inside of a building and its surroundings.

The International Style, whenever used in Austria, was usually a formalist application without many of its social and technical concepts. In the early 1930s, the rise of National Socialism made it clear to far-sighted architects that they had no future in Austria. This was not merely due to the fear of anti-Semitism, which would have affected all the Jewish architects, but also due to the much larger cultural question of the acceptance of modern architecture. The authoritarian regime of the Nazis, headed by the weekend artist and would-be architect Adolf Hitler, decided on two appropriate styles: a monstrous neo-classical monumentalism for public buildings and a conservative regional Tirolean style for housing. Modernism had no place in this scheme. Modernist architects were suspected of being left-wing and anti-state - which many of them actually were. Some, like the communist Herbert Eichholzer, were killed by the Nazis; many others fled to England and the United States in 1938.

According to the critic Friedrich Achleitner, the tragedy of Vienna's loss of its entire intellectual and progressive architectural potential within the space of five years was not so much the end of the progress of Modernism but the end of progressive criticism of Modernism.[1] The Viennese exiles, such as Schindler and Frank, Kiesler, Rudofsky, Neutra and Gruen, did not accept the International Style wholeheartedly as a universal formal style to be aped. Not surprisingly, few of the Viennese were in the exclusive group created by Philip Johnson and Henry Russell Hitchcock, whereas the German exiles Walter Gropius and Marcel Breuer were the champions of this cause. Adolf Loos's earlier criticism of styles was reflected in Josef Frank's statement, "The goal of modern architecture is greater freedom. The more scientific modern approach has made for greater variety and greater individuality among works of architecture, engineering and decoration. We shall therefore never again have a style in the old sense. Attempts to create one today, whether modern or modernized historical, have a reactionary and totalitarian effect."[2]

Matthias Boeckl points out that the Viennese were critical of dogma and rationalism, and open to a broad cultural, anthropological and psycho-physiological interpretation of habitat. Their

House Dr. Oro
Posillipo, Italy 1937, Bernard Rudofsky and Luigi Cosenza

undogmatic, liberal and humane stand rejected the monumental, banal and commercial distortion of the Modernist ideal. America at that time offered political refugees a freedom that was narrowly defined by capitalist ideology, and left them to their own devices. It hollowed out the content of the new buildings and reduced the shell to suit its own values and priorities, which had no place for the development of the artistic avant-garde.

The American system, with its simultaneous naivety and belief that everything was possible, forced many of the sensitive Viennese exiles into other fields or early retirement. Those few who offered resistance to the American ethic, like Bernard Rudofsky, or those who were adaptable enough to deny this part of themselves, like Richard Neutra and Victor Gruen, were highly successful.[3] Gruen continued his Viennese political theatre performances on Broadway, where he soon became well known in emigrant circles, receiving his first commissions to design shops from emigrant businessmen. His work for Ludwig Lederer, for example, culminated in the design of a chain of shoe shops all over the country, which increased his fame and led to his first suburban shopping mall for Cyril Magnin, outside Detroit. Here is yet another well-meant invention by a Viennese that is now strangling cities everywhere. This model was so successful that Victor Gruen Associates became one of the largest architectural firms in the US, with Cesar Pelli as a partner. Gruen attempted to make up for the loss of vibrant American inner-city areas by creating pedestrianized shopping malls - for all those pedestrians who could reach them by car - with a few social and cultural facilities. This attempt boomeranged when the malls multiplied in number and scale, killing off street life in the city itself, atomising existing urban structures and hastening the ubiquity of the car. Popular as they are, they have become the bane of urbanity in five continents - yet another well-intentioned Austrian invention that suffered from the wrong scale and fundamental misapplication.

Two Austrian-born architects who left the country in the 30s, Bernard Rudofsky and Christopher Alexander, are less famous for their buildings as for their writings and almost missionary activities. They acted as the conscience of generations of architects the world over who had ignored traditions of building and living in favour of the Modernist ideology. When asked the question, "Don't you have any roots?" Rudofsky replied, "I don't believe everyone needs roots. Like certain tropical plants, aerial roots are good enough for me." An answer that goes a long way towards understanding the extraordinary life of a true cosmopolitan whose curriculum vitae contains two decades described as "Travel in four continents." It began in 1905 in Mähren in the Austro-Hungarian Empire and led later to the capital, Vienna, and from there to Italy in 1930, where his "Villa Oro" in Napoli brought him the praise of Gio Ponti and an editorship in Domus. He moved on to Brazil, where he built courtyard houses which re-interpreted the traditional patio, and from there on to New York when he stopped building because, as he said, "I didn't want to sacrifice my talents to a so-called 'career'." Rudofsky gave up building because his doubts about the dogmas of contemporary architecture forced him into a public polemic against them. What is more, his accurately targeted attacks were no longer solely directed against modern architecture. Instead, he became increasingly concerned with the complex expressions of culture in man's daily life: the tools he uses, the clothes he wears. About his first exhibition in the Museum of Modern Art in New York entitled "Are Clothes Modern?" he said, "I admire women who do not need a tailor all their lives because they know how to transform uncut cloth into clothes." He also respected traditional Asian ways of building, socializing, playing and eating, as well as Asian cuisine. To eat with one's fingers, he said, was the civilized way - only barbarians used metal knives, forks and spoons to cut and transport food to their lips. He didn't explain things, he presented them in a way that challenged one to explain them to oneself.

Lobby, Parliament
Ankara 1938-63, Clemens Holzmeister

Parliament
Ankara 1938-63, Clemens Holzmeister

He questioned the right of the West to appropriate the terms 'civilized' and 'cultured' for itself. In fact, he dismissed Western designers as illiterate slaves of fashion. His exhibitions "The Kimono Mind" (1965) and "Now I Lay Me down to Eat" (1980) showed his respect for Asian culture and tradition (specifically the Japanese and the Indian), whose simplicity and elegance were the embodiment of style. The exhibition that brought him world-wide fame and which was shown in 84 cities of the world, "Architecture without Architects" (1964-75) displayed anonymous, 'primitive' architecture from mud houses to Bedouin cities, from underground villages to floating colonies. Rudofsky referred to the knowledge of anonymous builders as the greatest source of architectonic inspiration, thereby demolishing in one stroke the work of the sacrosanct stars of modern architecture, as well as the writing of architectural history in toto: "An endless anthology of buildings of and for the privileged, which merely communicate power and riches."[4] Unfortunately, the very cultures he admired in Asia are neglecting their strengths and instead adopting ways of building, clothing and consumption that are gradually resulting in a uniform global cultural and ecological decline. Rudofsky's search for the best in other cultures and the rejection of the worst in them is the exact inverse of what is happening in Asia today.

Christopher Alexander was born in Vienna and left the country for England with his parents in 1938. He abandoned his "futile" studies in Cambridge to go to Harvard, where he began to take an almost anthropological interest in the way people behave and how human needs develop and are satisfied in buildings, culminating in his series of books on pattern languages for building.[5] His aim is to search for a native architecture with a healing vision that transcends the banal, to find a poetic dimension that allows people to feel themselves and the environment they have been alienated from. His constant contact over the decades with Austrian rural architecture as well as with turn-of-the-century design has been a source of inspiration, but he feels that contemporary architects labour under a compulsion to be avant-garde, to be conspicuous at the cost of their pragmatic roots and cultural traditions.

Alexander and Rudofsky were among those Austrians who did not only look westwards. Whereas the work of architects who emigrated to the West is well documented, little information is available on those who went to countries like India, Nepal, or China. These buildings can be seen today, but there is hardly any reliable information on names and dates.[6] Their two and a half-storeyed, flat-roofed bungalows in New Delhi were among the first modernist buildings there and rapidly replaced the Lutyenesque or Indo-Saracenic colonial bungalow as a model for upper and middle class housing areas. As international aid agencies often observe, the sojourn of development workers in Asia often contributes more to their own personal development than to that of their host country. This is obviously also the case with some architects. Anton Schwaighofer, who acknowledges to having learnt much from Asia, built an architecturally interesting, but climatically and socially wholly inappropriate cluster of isolated pavilions scattered over a 'heat and dust' site near Delhi in the 70s for an orphanage. The good physical condition of the complex after so many decades, unusual in new construction in India, is due more to the maintenance by the organization that runs it than to any intrinsic qualities of the design. But there is also positive work that should be mentioned. Roland Hagmüller and Carl Pruscha went to Nepal as advisors to UNESCO to develop plans for the protection and development of the historic towns of the Kathmandu valley. Whereas Hagmüller is still working in Kathmandu and Bhaktapur, mainly on valuable conservation and restoration efforts, Pruscha also built, during his ten years there, new hostels and faculty buildings of incredible beauty and strength . The reverse influence, that of Asia on Austrian

Northland Centre
Detroit 1954, Victor Gruen

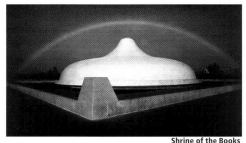

Shrine of the Books
Jerusalem 1965, Friedrich Kiesler and Armand Bartos

architects, is easier to trace. Roland Rainer's regular trips with his students to China and Iran opened the eyes of generations of architects to the wonders of anonymous architecture in Asia. Back in Austria, Pruscha attempts to achieve a synthesis of Eastern and Western ideas, evident in his hamam or Turkish bath in the housing project in the Traviatagasse, as he does not believe in either transplanting purely European architecture to Asia or vice versa. These impressive efforts by individual architects still do not approach a true dialogue or a creative exchange with Asian cultures, with a singular exception. Japan is the only Asian country which has actually developed a strong two-way architectural discourse with Austria. Mutual fascination for each other's historic buildings and contemporary architecture generates much travel between and publication in both countries.

Other important periods of exile were Ernst Plischke's in New Zealand, Walter Loos's in Argentina and that of the few Jewish architects who emigrated to Israel. Friedrich Kiesler's work in Berlin and the US on stage and cinema sets brought him the friendship of Theo van Doesburg, László Moholy-Nagy, El Lissitzky, Salvador Dali, Louis Bunuel, Alexander Calder and most of the major architects of the time. His Shrine of the Books in Jerusalem (with Armand Bartos, 1965) is a powerful expressionistic shell, housing the Dead Sea Scrolls of Qumran that had just been discovered at the time. It is one of those rare buildings that are timeless and spiritual in nature.

In the 70s and 80s, certain major Austrian architects took up commissions and teaching assignments abroad. This was partly possible because of connections established in particular countries earlier when they were students and partly due to international competitions they won and actually executed. The saying, "No one is a prophet in his own land", is certainly true of Austria. Hans Hollein and Coop Himmelblau, for example, the Austrian architects best known abroad, had to establish their reputations elsewhere before they were given major commissions in Austria. Viennese architects acknowledge Hollein's importance only grudgingly, preferring to criticize his glittery postmodern phase in the 1980s which moved with facility between kitsch and excellence. His complete oeuvre, including his early visionary sketches, shows that he is a most versatile and influential figure. One of his projects in the 60s, a proposal for the extension of Vienna University, consisted of a television set which only had to be plugged in, a prophetic symbol of the coming information society and virtual reality. His projects abroad, including the Feigen Gallery in New York (1969), the Olympic Village Media Line in Munich (1972), the City Museum in Mönchengladbach (1982), the Museum for Glass and Ceramics in Teheran (1978), the Museum of Modern Art in Frankfurt (1991), the Banco Santander in Madrid (1993), the Fukuda Motors Building in Tokyo (presently under construction) and many competition entries and unrealized projects have been widely published, and he has been awarded several prizes, including the Pritzker prize. He still has a much greater volume of work abroad than at home, yet he remains very much a Viennese architect. This difficult love-hate relationship is a key to the complexity of his work, and makes it easier to understand the fact that he has maintained his office in Vienna. He left Vienna in the late 1950s to go to Sweden and on to the US, the latter a traditional destination for Austrian architects who wanted to escape the constrictions of urban and political structures. However, unlike others who chose to trek to cities, schools and personalities they found attractive, Hollein deliberately went to the IIT in Chicago to confront

Faculty buildings
University of Kathmandu 1970, Carl Pruscha

Faculty buildings
University of Kathmandu 1970, Carl Pruscha

Ludwig Hilberseimer's theories on urban design with which he disagreed. These fruitful collisions with other ideas in the US strengthened his predilection for stretching the limits of architecture and exploring other related fields. Visionary sketches, the design of objects (furniture, pianos, porcelain, watches, lamps) and events (celebrations, exhibitions) reflect his belief stated in 1972: everything is architecture.

Coop Himmelblau is also well known in every corner of the architectural world. Wolf D. Prix and Helmut Swiczinski, who make up the group today after Michael Holzer left it in 1971, escaped from what they considered the stifling atmosphere of education and the profession in Austria in the 70s to go to the AA in London and to the Southern Californian Institute of Architecture. The totally open structure of Los Angeles suited their conceptual approach and was a refreshing change from the minutely defined and predetermined form of Vienna. They maintain offices in both cities. One cannot fail to notice that in many cases even those who strongly criticize the conservatism and inertia of Vienna obviously appreciate the high quality of life here and are unwilling to cut the umbilical cord.

Until recently Coop Himmelblau were considered far too wild to build in Vienna. This conservatism meant that their winning competition entry for the dramatic conversion of the nineteenth century Ronacher theatre to a multi-media centre in the inner city was abandoned in favour of a conservative restoration of the building. In their frustration they expanded their activities abroad, where they have been given several challenging commissions. Their new museum in Groningen in the Netherlands (1994) is highly controversial. While offering an exciting spatial experience, it is considered by traditional museologists such as Rudi Fuchs to be inappropriate to the collection of old art and prints it was intended to house. Technical problems such as the excessive light, humidity and heat caused by the glass and steel construction are being corrected by new air modulation measures. The aesthetic clash between the deliberately chaotic pavilion wanting itself to be considered a work of art and the works of art displayed within, which it does not suffer readily, is not as easy to resolve. The technical bravado of their recent entry in a limited competition for a United Nations communications centre in Geneva is also based on a difficult visionary translation of a cloud into a structure, "a building that does not want to be a building".

Boris Podrecca, who studied in Vienna, spent his childhood in Yugoslavia and Italy, and has a practical and didactic field of action that stretches into these countries and Germany. His indefatigable work, very Viennese in its conceptualization of a complete project down to the last doorknob, his teaching and his publishing activities have brought him several projects in Vienna recently.

Projects abroad have helped even establishment figures accepted in Vienna to improve their reputations and expand their practices within the country. Gustav Peichl's Kunsthalle, an art exhibition centre in Bonn, and his annexe to the Städel Museum in Frankfurt in the 80s established his command of industrial and structural metaphors. Wilhelm Holzbauer's neo-rationalist aesthetics and his competence in executing large projects have found wide acceptance amongst important clients such as banks, public bodies and universities in and outside the country. Prominent projects

Faculty building
University of Kathmandu 1970, Carl Pruscha

New Eishin University
Tokyo 1987, Christopher Alexander

abroad include the Amsterdam City Hall and Opera and the new faculty buildings for the Goethe University in Frankfurt. Although his pragmatic and functionally neutral spaces, similar in typology to the buildings of the 18th and 19th centuries, which have catered to numerous changes and functions, will probably be in use as long as those were, they do not receive favourable critical judgement because of their large scale and perceived monotony. Earlier, during his stay in the US in the 60s, Holzbauer's conceptual sketches of the urban future aroused much professional interest. Raimund Abraham, who left Graz for New York, has remained faithful to his own fundamental, almost archaic designs, as was most recently illustrated in the winning competition entry for the Austrian Cultural Institute in New York, a skillful and outstanding interpretation of the New York skyscraper.[7]

One of the more peculiar figures on the international scene is the artist Friedensreich Hundertwasser. Despised by architects, he is obviously of some importance, as some of the other essays in this book note. A recent survey in Japan revealed that Hollein was the second-best known European architect there - after Hundertwasser. His work is so widely publicised in the mass media that it is not necessary to illustrate it here. Hundertwasser's valid criticism of soulless assembly-line buildings, expressed in his manifestos in the 50s and 60s,[8] have been converted in his own buildings into a scurrilously kitsch facade decoration that does not improve the quality of living behind it - it is, in other words, the very opposite of innovative. The popularity of this approach, however (his buildings are sprouting up everywhere from Germany to New Zealand), should give architects food for thought on the many failings of modern architecture.

The international architectural debate and the exchange and development of ideas is always considered by the artists involved in it as a two-way process. The establishment unfortunately sees the work of Austrian architects abroad as a kind of export product. There is not half as much enthusiasm about realizing the work of architects from other countries here. Whereas architects from different countries have been building in Germany for many years, there are very few who have built in Austria, even taking into account the relative sizes of the two countries. A strange combination of a superiority and an inferiority complex dominates dealings with other countries. The preconditions for a practicing licence are numerous and difficult to fulfil, something which has often been used to protect the interests of the local members of the profession against competition from abroad (and from younger talent within the country). In spite of Austria having joined the European Union, this practice is generally being continued. The excuse now used for not opening up commissions to foreign architects is the sudden desire to give young local architects the chance

Project for the expansion of Vienna University
Vienna 1966, Hans Hollein

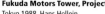

Fukuda Motors Tower, Project
Tokyo 1988, Hans Hollein

Museum Mönchengladbach
Germany 1982, Hans Hollein

to build before inviting others to do so. In essence, this is a commendable motive, but it is equally open to suspicions of protectionism. Very few open international competitions have been held for major projects. The country's reputation was damaged in international professional circles to some extent because two prize winners in the 70s, Alvar Aalto's winning project for the Stadthalle, a multifunctional hall, and Cesar Pelli's project for the new United Nations Centre, were discarded in favour of local solutions.

There seems to have been a more generous attitude in the 20s and 30s. Peter Behrens, Gerrit Rietveld, Hugo Häring and Richard Neutra were some of the dozens of architects based abroad who then acquired commissions in Austria. In contrast to this, no efforts were made to attract the exiles back to rebuild the country after the devastation of World War II. Even Neutra, an established architect, failed in spite of many efforts to acquire a single commission at the time.

The influence of ideas was stronger. Young architects and artists in post-war Austria considered architects of Austrian origin abroad, above all Rudofsky, Kiesler and Schindler, to be symbols of resistance to the International Style, just as the revolutionary London-based groups such as Archigram.

Hans Puchhammer, Hans Hollein, Ottokar Uhl and Gunther Wawrik were among the leading figures who attended the summer academy run by Konrad Wachsmann from the US. Wachsmann introduced technical and modular production criteria to Austrian architecture. To the country's credit, it must be said that several well-known architects, for instance Rob Krier from Luxemburg, Timo Penttilä from Finland, Justus Dahinden from Switzerland, Paolo Piva and Massimiliano Fuksas from Italy and Will Alsop from England, were appointed professors in the three architectural schools in Vienna in the 80s and 90s. The first four were also given commissions to realize large housing projects here. Doors are now opening in Vienna and to a certain extent in the western-most state of Vorarlberg. There is a tendency to invite émigré architects to build here - Raimund Abraham and Mark Mack being among them - but sometimes the criterium of Austrian origin is insufficient by itself. It is not clear why else Harry Seidler, considered in Australia to be a commercially successful but otherwise much deprecated architect, should be commissioned with the planning of a large housing scheme on the banks of the Danube.

Recent interesting plans for projects in Vienna that have been lauded include Jean Nouvel's social housing, conceived as several single-family house types with private gardens and terraces put together in a multi-storeyed building. Zaha Hadid's provocative steel and glass superimposition of apartments, shops, music clubs, restaurants, ateliers and flats embracing an unused part of

Open House, Malibu
USA, Project 1983, Coop Himmelblau - Wolf D. Prix, Helmut Swiczinsky

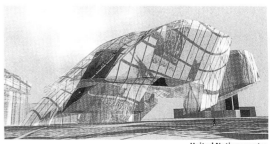

United Nations centre
Competition entry, Geneva 1995, Coop Himmelblau
Wolf D. Prix, Helmut Swiczinsky

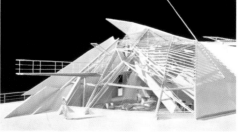

Envelope around the Josef Hoffmann pavilion
Venice Biennale 1995, Coop Himmelblau - Wolf D. Prix, Helmut Swiczinsky

Otto Wagner's protected urban railway viaduct to create a cultural island in an unattractive part of town is bound to ruffle some feathers and bring life into the debate on conservation. The preliminary designs for housing in an urban expansion area by Morphosis, Mack, Abraham, Eric Moss, Michael Sorkin and some local architects form a breathtaking collection of sculptural forms. One suspects, though, that the urge by some to play centre stage has prevented a coordinated or coherent urban ensemble, the American architects having approached the question of building on the periphery in a comparably uncomplicated way. Projects to convert the four huge cylindrical 19th century gasometers for commercial, residential and cultural use by Nouvel and Moss are scheduled to be realised in the next few years, opening perspectives for new ways to deal with early industrial heritage.

Art exhibition centre Kunsthalle
Bonn 1992, Gustav Peichl

Sketch for the Fukuda Motors Tower in Tokyo
1988, Hans Hollein

Merely inviting architects from abroad to build here is not going to guarantee internationalism, of course. It is the travel, publication and debate activated by any good new architecture that leads to fruitful exchange. But cross-pollination leads to unexpected results and conflicts, the creation of extended sensibilities, understanding and respect. Every culture ultimately profits from a fresh breeze from outside, and Austria is no exception. The inhabitants of a mountain-bound landscape must at times escape their confines and raise their sights to an imaginary horizon. The invigoration of one's traditions is enhanced by distance, by exile, alienation and rediscovery.

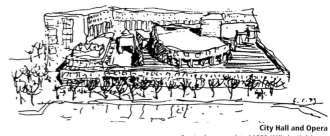

City Hall and Opera
Amsterdam, completed 1986, Wilhelm Holzbauer

Parliament
Ankara, 1938-1963 Clemens Holzmeister

Austrian Cultural Centre
New York, Competition project, 1st prize 1993, Raimund Abraham

Architects have often based their work on a model, an ideology or a world view. Hideto Kishida (1899-1966), who was professor of architectural design at the University of Tokyo from 1929 to 1959, had great influence on the formation of the Modern Movement in Japan. He encouraged and advised young Kunio Maekawa and Kenzo Tange on their work for architectural competitions and projects. Both of them subsequently became central figures in post-war Japanese architecture.

It is well known that both Maekawa and Tange were strongly influenced by Le Corbusier before World War II. Maekawa worked in Le Corbusiers office after graduation.

Their mentor Hideto Kishida, however, regarded Otto Wagner as the most important figure among the pioneering architects of the late nineteenth and the early twentieth centuries. He wrote his first book titled "Otto Wagner" in 1927 to document new directions in European architecture. Although he himself did not study abroad, he was well versed in new trends in the European architectural scene and saw it as his professional obligation to introduce them to Japan. Ever since the Meiji Restoration in 1868 when Japan opened itself to the West, the Japanese have been eager to catch western models to modernize Japan. Westernization was a synonym for modernization. The problem was rather which country was to be chosen as the best possible model.

The first professor of architecture in Japan, Josiah Conder (1852-1920), was invited from London in 1877 to the Imperial College of Engineering in Tokyo. Quite naturally, the first generation of Japanese architects, in the Western sense of the profession, followed the Victorian Gothic line. Government offices, Tokyo Central Station, banks and schools were built in red brick.

Later, architects from other countries were invited to Japan to design buildings of national importance such as the Houses of Parliament and the Supreme Court. Eventually, Japan shifted its model from Britain to Germany. The reason was that many Japanese statesmen regarded Germany as a model for the Japanese political and military system.

Half a century later, when the Modern Movement in architecture emerged, Kishida took Austrian architecture as the model for future Japanese architecture. Kishida placed Otto Wagner in the centre of an ideal modern architecture as he saw it. Kishida agreed with Wagner's declaration of "Architektur zu Baukunst." Kishida realized through Wagner's works that architecture was an abstract art, but he also appreciated Wagner's planning in architecture because the plan was the most important and significant factor in modern architecture.

In Japan, art almost always meant applied art or decorative art. Porcelain, cabinets, lacquerware and Ukiyoe prints were all products of the applied arts. Even buildings were regarded an accumulation of such art. The word "bijutsu" (fine art in Japanese) was not originally a Japanese word either but originated in western languages. It is said to have been coined by Keisuke Otori, a former vassal of the Shogun who rendered service to the Meiji government. So in Japan, the word "fine art" was born in the nineteenth century. Throughout the history of Japanese art, all art has had a tendency to be extremely close to applied art even though that term did not yet exist. It was the reason for the enormous impact of Japanese art at the Vienna World Exposition in 1873. Exhibits were sold off after the exhibition and Viennese collectors and connoisseurs rushed to purchase the Japanese objects. The decorativeness of these pieces and their flatness of composition were among the factors widely appreciated, inevitably these went on to influence the Jugendstil.

It has often been pointed out that the cultures of the latter half of the nineteenth century and of Art Nouveau were essentially urban. The Industrial Revolution concentrated the population into cities and gave rise to new urban cultures. These were not the privilege of the aristocracy or of a handful of elites, but belonged to more anonymous people, those without a personal historical pedigree.

Previous cultures, whether they had been based on Graeco-Roman Classicism or the Gothic, required certain premises and certain sympathy and understanding in order to function. By the late nineteenth century these premises seemed no longer to hold good.

The World Expositions held in Europe began in such an environment. They were attempts to formulate a world order for a time that had

THE VALIDITY OF THE MODEL
IN A PLURALISTIC WORLD

Hiroyuki Suzuki

overflowed the frame of the previous era. The World Expositions were envisaged as microcosms of this expanded world.

Those attempts to build a microcosm with a World Exposition can be regarded as a triumphant declaration of Europe's world conquest. At the same time, they indicate that the whole world could no longer be grasped by the power of Europe alone. Europe had already expanded beyond the pale of its previous cultural territory, and was on the point of losing its identity.

The late nineteenth century expansion of the European sphere gave rise to waves of "modernization" in other Asian countries too. Japan accepted this fact voluntarily under the slogan of "Civilization and Enlightenment." But at the same time these new waves were dangerous and caused external pressures that threatened the original traditions and independence of non-European countries. Modernization was both welcomed and feared. This cultural malaise attacked not only East Asian countries but diffused through many countries more immediately surrounding Europe. Movements intended to reevaluate domestic cultural traditions rose up inside the modernizing milieu of many countries.

The architectural works of Otto Wagner and his successors who produced the fin de siècle arts of Vienna demonstrate how the diffusion of modernization through Eastern Europe coupled expressions of ethnicity with the emergence of avant-gardes.

Otto Wagner, of course, seemed to recognize the crisis of national identity in the modernization process of his country. At the end of his preface to the first edition of "Moderne Architektur", written in 1895, he says; "Naturally the genius loci had to be taken into account, and for this reason predominantly Viennese conditions are considered."

"Genius loci" was a key word for him to save cultural identity in architecture in the modern age. Every place has its own visible and invisible condition and its own historical background. Architecture should reflect genius loci not only to keep identity of the place but also to identity of culture. Otto Wagner understood the true meaning of genius loci because he was Viennese. If he was a Parisian or a Londoner, he would have felt himself in the centre of the modern world. Although Vienna had its own character and historical importance, he knew that Vienna was not the single centre of Europe but one of the centres of Europe. This pluralistic sense of place and culture made possible his insights into the meaning of modernization.

Modernization was a process of turning places into placelessness. Every town and country became more or less the same, and that applied to buildings as well. Viennese architecture, however, flourished at the turn of the century without losing its own cultural character and background. Professor Kishida might have seen this quality in the works of Otto Wagner. Judging from the results, he was right in choosing this model for Japanese architecture. Post war Japanese architecture tried to find a way to create a modern expression of architecture on the basis of its traditional composition.

Viennese, or for that matter Austrian architecture, has always demonstrated that the expression of modernity was compatible with that of national identity. We find examples in the works of Otto Wagner, Adolf Loos and other Austrian architects.

Even today we can clearly find this tradition in surprising forms in recent architectural works in Austria. The bank in the Favoritenstrasse in Vienna by Günther Domenig (1979) distorted not only the structure of building but also the structure of the city. This wierd distorted building ironically clarified the meaning of the structure of an orthogonal city. In this sense, this work reminded us of the genius loci of Vienna. In the case of the social housing in the Löwengasse in Vienna (1986), Hundertwasser freely combined an innocent play of form with the rich decorative tradition of Viennese architecture. No other city would have been able to produce this type of public housing. We also feel a sense of place in Coop Himmelblau's rooftop remodeling (1989). This work was filled with the feeling of a free thinker. It is really just like a bird's nest on top of Viennese architecture. We imagine that only Viennese architecture could afford to allow such a nest on its top. It shows us the strength of the city structure.

The most interesting thing is that these three examples are quite different to each other but all of them express, in their specific ways, the clear sense of place; the sense of Vienna. It is, however,

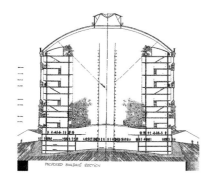

International interventions in Austria
Projects for the convention of the 19th century gas containers
Vienna 1995, Jean Nouvel (top)
Eric Moss (2 below)

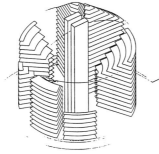

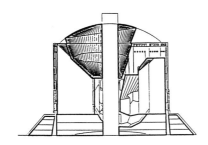

an exceptional phenomenon in today's world.

Half a century after the Second World War, we realize that the Modern Movement in architecture could not find a way to successfully establish an integrity between international expression and the sense of place. We understand the reason to be that modern architecture founded the concept of the "machine" as its model. A machine has the following characteristics:

1 It has a purpose.

2 It has a structure composed solely of purposeful components.

3 It operates universally.

Society itself has changed tremendously since the first half of this century. Cultural influences became global, and the environment is no longer perceived as limitless. In this cultural context, we seem to be caught by the invisibility of the machine model and have not been able to find an alternative model with which to replace the machine. It was Charles Jencks who proposed the notion of Post-Modernism as a reaction to the period. Post-Modernism quickly became adapted to the realms of art, ideology and economics. It is an idea which represents the period when the machine model no longer holds true. The notable point, however, is the fact that this understanding originated from the architectural discourse. The word was invented when architectural expression tried once again to incorporate subjectivity based on historical associations after the long use of the machine model. It is potentially an effort to redefine architecture itself as a model to understand the world. We know that the word "computer architecture" is used to understand the concept of the computer that can no longer be perceived through our physical senses. It may be an effort to define the invisible world of the computer as "architecture" and make it again possible to open the comprehensive field to our perceptions.

**International projects in Austria: SEG Mixed-use building
on Otto Wagner's Stadtbahn urban railway**
Vienna 1995, Zaha Hadid

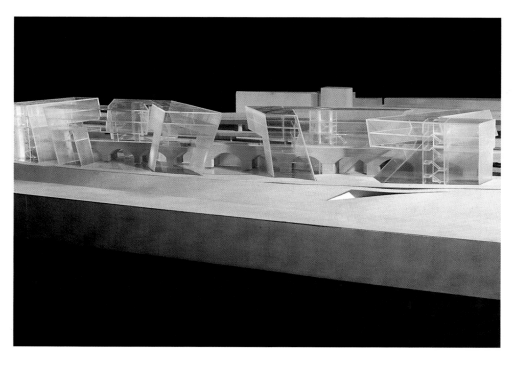

The critical difference between architecture and the machine is that architecture, by definition, creates interior space, which also suggests the state of our social condition. Our culture has explored all areas of the world, and we are at the point when a new world view has to be reconstructed from within. There is no geographical frontier - we can only define our future world by modifying the existing. We are within the globe and we are parts of the global system. The analytical strategy of approaching an object from outside does not work any longer. The viewpoint has be placed within this object itself. In this sense, architecture itself as the new model seems to be quite viable. The other critical point is that architecture has its architectural aspects expressed by words such as expression, association and culture. As opposed to the machine's universality and mass productivity, architecture exists in particularity and singularity. The reason is that architecture occupies a place and embodies the 'genius loci'. This implies another potential for the architecture model. Let us clarify architecture as model:

     1 It has function and structure.

     2 It is a system which accommodates human presence in its interior.

     3 It has particularity and singularity because it occupies a place.

Can we conclude this analysis by saying that architecture itself is the most visible model for the world view at the end of this century? This era was opened when Hans Hollein, again a Viennese architect, paraphrased Joseph Beuys and declared, "Everything is architecture".

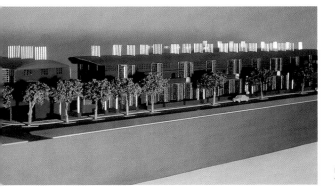

International projects in Austria: SEG Housing
Vienna 1995, Jean Nouvel

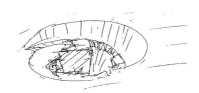

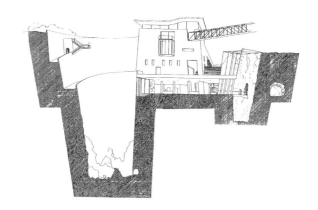

MUSEUM
Volcano Museum, Auvergne, France
Expected completion 1998
Architect: Hans Hollein b.1934
Project team: Atelier 4
Engineer: BET ITC
Area: 16000 m²
Cost: 500 million ATS

THE WINNING PROJECT IN AN INTERNATION-
AL COMPETITION IN 1994, HOLLEIN´S
DESIGN FOR A VOLCANO MUSEUM IS A CULMINATION
OF MANY OF THE CONCEPTS WITH WHICH HE HAS BEEN WORKING IN HIS
CAREER. THE UNDERGROUND CITY, THE ENERGY MUSEUM (WHICH
EXAMINES THE PROBLEM OF PRESENTING PHENOMENA RATHER THAN
OBJECTS), THE THEME OF THE ROTUNDA AND THE UNBUILT PROJECT FOR
THE GUGGENHEIM MUSEUM IN SALZBURG ARE ALL PRECURSORS OF THIS
DESIGN. THE SITE LIES A THOUSAND METRES ABOVE SEA LEVEL AT THE
FOOT OF THE PUY-DE-DOME SURROUNDED BY OTHER DORMANT VOLCA-
NOES, A PRACTICALLY UNINHABITED RESERVE. INFORMATION ON VOLCA-
NOES IS TO BE PRESENTED HERE TO SCIENTISTS AND LAYMEN WITH THE
HELP OF OBJECTS, SIMULATIONS AND OTHER MEDIA. BEYOND THAT THE
AIM IS TO CREATE AN EMOTIONAL AND ATAVISTIC FEEL FOR THIS PRIMAL
PROCESS OF THE EARTH´S FORMATION. IN CONTRAST TO MOST ARCHI-
TECTS AVERSION TO NON-PURISTIC ELEMENTS OF DESIGN, HOLLEIN´S
WELL-KNOWN READINESS TO USE THE TECHNIQUES OF COMMERCIAL DIS-
PLAY, ENTERTAINMENT AND STAGE DESIGN IN A SKILLED MANNER WILL
GO A LONG WAY TOWARDS REALIZING THIS EXPERIENCE. IT IS CONCEIVED
AS A SIGNIFICANT AND MEMORABLE IMAGE OF DESCENT INTO AN ABYSS,
PURGATORY, A WOMB OR CAVE TO ERUPT, EMERGE ONCE AGAIN INTO THE
ATMOSPHERE. ONE PASSES THROUGH A HUGE, OPEN-TO-SKY CONE WITH
A GILDED INSIDE SURFACE AND A FIRE THAT REFLECTS OFF THE GOLD. IT
IS A BUILDING THAT YOU COULD WALK ON AND WALK INTO. THE CIRCU-
LATION IS A SEQUENCE OF DESCENT, PENETRATION INTO UNDERGROUND
ZONES AND CAVERNS, AND FINAL ASCENT INTO A TERRACE RESTAURANT
AREA WITH A PANORAMIC VIEW, A SEQUENCE OF EXTRAORDINARY SPACES
OF THE KIND THAT HOLLEIN MASTERS. SUBTRACTIVE AND ADDITIVE ELE-
MENTS, NATURAL AND MAN-MADE MATERIALS CREATE AN TRULY THREE-
DIMENSIONAL, ATECHTONIC WHOLE.

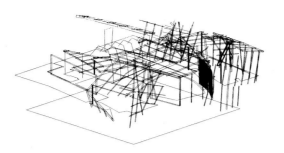

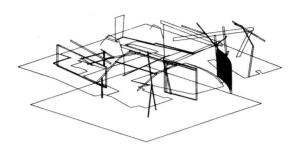

THE MUSEUM ISLAND IN THE DUTCH CITY OF GRONINGEN IS COMPOSED OF FOUR PAVILIONS EACH DESIGNED BY A DIFFERENT ARCHITECT (COOP HIMMELBLAU, ALESSANDRO MENDINI, PHILIPPE STARCK AND MICHELE DE LUCCHI) IN ORDER TO EXPRESS THE DIVERSITY OF THE EXISTING COLLECTION. THE COMPLEX IS TO FULFILL THE ROLE OF A CITY SQUARE WITH DIFFERENT BUILDING TYPOLOGIES. THE ISLAND ACTS SIMULTANEOUSLY AS A PEDESTRIAN AND CYCLISTS BRIDGE CONNECTING THE STATION TO THE INNER CITY. THE COLLECTION OF PRE-1950 ART AND THE PRINT CABINET ARE HOUSED IN COOP´S ROOF PAVILION OF STEEL SANDWICH PLATES SEPARATED BY THIN GLASS STRIPS. THE ARCHITECTONIC DYNAMISM STANDS IN INTERESTING CONTRAST TO THE CONTENTS. THIS IS THE ONLY PAVILION WITH DAYLIGHTING. THE NOVEL SPATIAL EXPERIENCES ARE ENHANCED BY A FOOT BRIDGE THAT PASSES THROUGH THE INTERIOR OF THE PAVILION TO ENABLE SHIFTING VIEWPOINTS OF THE EXHIBITED WORK. THE SURFACE PATTERNS REMINISCENT OF XEROX TRACES REFLECT COOP HIMMELBLAU´S DESIGN PROCESS, WHICH INVOLVES USING DYNAMIC COMBINATIONS OF COLLAGE, ENLARGEMENTS ON PAPER, LIGHT AND SHADOW AND THREE-DIMENSIONAL ELEMENTS.

M U S E U M

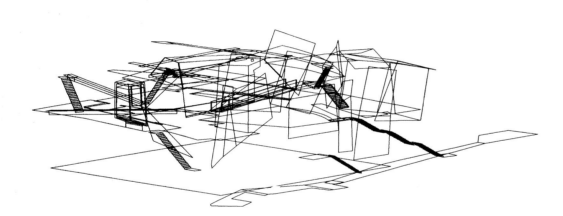

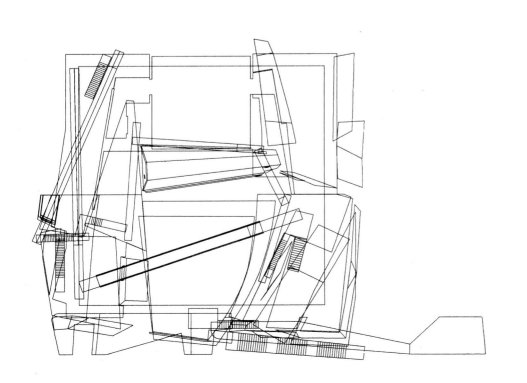

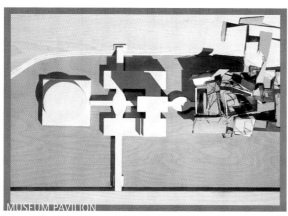

MUSEUM PAVILION
Groningen, Netherlands 1995
Architects: Coop Himmelblau
(Wolf D. Prix b. 1942,
Helmut Swiczinsky b.1944)
Engineers: Wassenaar & Co.
Project Team: K. Schmidbaur
Area: 1000 m²

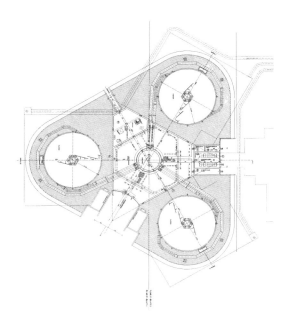

PHOSPHATE ELIMINATION PLANT
Tegel, Berlin 1985
Architect: Gustav Peichl b. 1928
Engineer: Helmuth Marks
Project team: R. Weber, P. Nigst,
F. Fonatti, P. Kugelstätter
Cost: 1500 million ATS

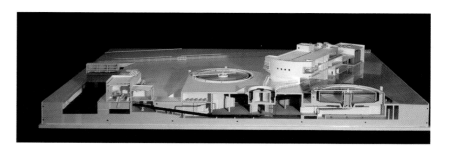

ANONYMOUS ARCHITECTURE, ARCHITECTURE WITHOUT ARCHITECTS, IS NOT RESTRICTED TO ROMANTIC VILLAGES BUT EXTENDS TO A MAJOR PART OF OUR INDUSTRIAL LANDSCAPE. WHAT RAISES THIS BUILDING ABOVE THE LEVEL OF OTHER MORE OR LESS IMPRESSIVE INDUSTRIAL OR TECHNICAL STRUCTURES DESIGNED PURELY TO FULFILL A FUNCTION IS THE CONSCIOUS USE OF ARCHITECTURE TO GIVE IT A SIGNAL STRENGTH. THE STRIKING SYMBOLISM OF THE ECONOMICAL DESIGN ESTABLISHES ITS SIGNIFICANCE AS A CIVIC FACILITY EQUAL TO MANY A MONUMENTAL PUBLIC BUILDING, WITHOUT, HOWEVER, ANY OF THE FRILLS A MONUMENT USES. THE STRONG GEOMETRIC PATTERN THAT STEMS FROM THE ACTUAL CHEMICAL PROCESSES IS CONTINUED IN THE IMMEDIATE GREEN LANDSCAPE IN AN URBAN SETTING, ACHIEVING A TRANSITION BASED ON THE CLEAR PRONOUNCEMENT OF BORDERS. THE TECHNICAL AND THE NATURAL BOTH GAIN BY THEIR CLOSE PROXIMITY AND DEFINE EACH OTHER. THE IMPACT OF THIS BUILDING GOES BEYOND ITS ASSOCIATIONS WITH NAVAL ARCHITECTURE AND REACHES INTO THE VERY ESSENCE OF THE MACHINE, WHICH UNIFIES COMPLEX PROCESSES IN A SEEMINGLY SIMPLE AND OBVIOUS FORM.

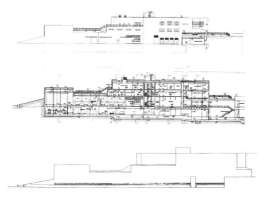

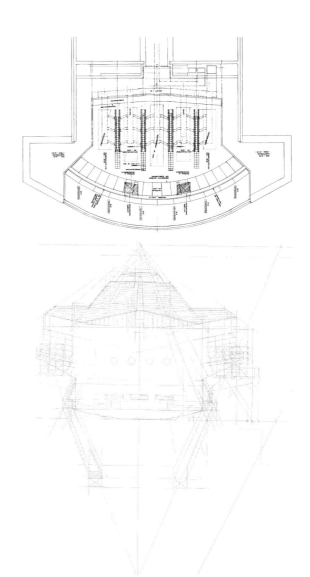

088/089

CULTURAL BUILDINGS

THE CONTEXT OF CULTURE 92

GLASS MUSEUM BÄRNBACH 98

EXHIBITION SPACE KREMS 100

SCHOOL VIENNA 102

SCHOOL WARTH 106

SCHOOL VIENNA 108

KINDERGARTEN VIENNA 112

CHURCH VIENNA 116

CHURCH VIENNA 117

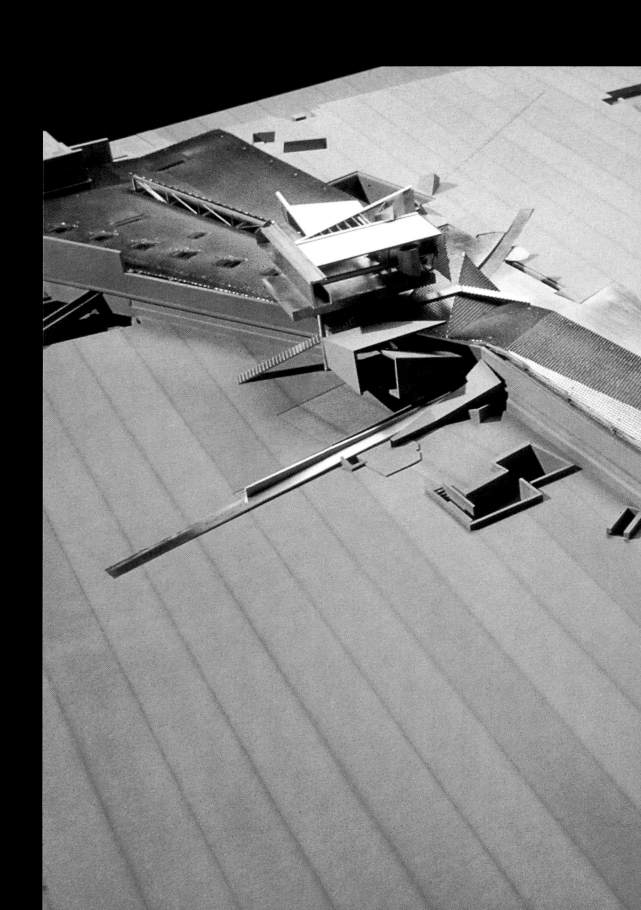

Trigon Museum, Graz
Competition entry 1st prize 1989
Friedrich Schöffauer
Wolfgang Schrom
Wolfgang Tschapeller

Culture involves elements of religion, education and history. The buildings that house them, churches, schools and museums, reflect the condition of the culture in question at the time they were built. At the same time, they influence that condition. Amongst cultural buildings it is the museum that has been at the centre of discourse since the early 80s. Whereas avant-garde groups in the decade before, such as the group Missing Link to which I belonged, questioned the nature of the museum and the museum's presentation of culture, the architects of the 80s seemed unconcerned about the institutional self-definition of the museum. Their efforts were concentrated on the renewal of the total choreographic presentational and communicational aspects of architecture itself. The situation with respect to recent educational and religious building is similar. During the important phase of school and church building in the 50s and 60s the architectural programme was directly based on the fundamental redefinition of pedagogy and liturgy and the built structure was a spatial expression of a revolution within these institutions. Recent schools and churches seem to be purely architectonic in their intentions. Vienna's School Building Programme 2000 forsees the construction of 17 new schools by the end of the century. This programme was initiated to meet the demands of a slight rise in the population, the development of new housing areas, the new limitations on the size of classes to a maximum of 30 children and the provision of more all-day schools. Several talented architects have been given the chance to use their specific vocabulary on a large scale, but they appear to have unquestioningly accepted the current educational system, with the result that the new schools are of a very conventional typology. An example is Helmut Richter's school in the Waidhausenstrasse. A programme of radical transparence has been carried out on a relatively pragmatic plan. What is exceptional here is that in his innovative use of glass and steel technology he has crossed existing barriers. In spite of its breathtakingly crystalline qualities it is structurally extremely isomorphic and homomorphic. In my opinion it is not so much a manifesto for a new school type as a manifesto for technically innovative building as such. It is an exciting structure that just happens to be a school building.

A completely different facet is presented in Rudiger Lainer's school in the Absberggasse. He has used conventional technology to put together a playful montage of an extremely varied polymorphic building. The typology of the classrooms strung along corridors is very conventional compared to the open plan and free-space schools. This has been more than compensated for by the exciting, almost urban spatial sequence of the common areas and circulation on the ground floor. Hermann Czech's pragmatic treatment of the standard rules for school buildings and of the reality of ordinary building techniques, as well as his elaboration of these realities in detail and in the unproblematic employment of the whole is an obscure but hyperreal interpretation of banality. The innovative qualities of this building are very subtle indeed.

Boris Podrecca displays his well-known talent for dealing with very difficult urban situations in his new school. The sensitive insertion of the building into a narrow and unattractive site, the dialectic enrichment and the friction of the confrontation between old and new, and between building and nature is an astonishing synthesis of apparently incompatible contrasts.

The recent projects for new buildings or extensions to schools in the rest of the country are the first since the last big wave of school building in the 70s. Prominent examples include the extension in Blons, Vorarlberg by Bruno Spagolla (1988), in Schlins, Vorarlberg by Markus Koch and Michael Loudon (1990), in Kaindorf, Steiermark by Ernst Giselbrecht (1994), in Mautern, Steiermark by Heinz Wondra (1992), in Bregenz, Vorarlberg by Dietmar Eberle annd Carlo Baumschlager (1994) and in Wels, Oberösterreich by Peter Riepl and Thomas Moser (1994).

The new school in Warth, Vorarlberg by Roland Gnaiger (1994) is a special case. It is less sensational than some of the examples in Vienna and Graz, yet it is definitely the most complex of all. The overlapping of the many aspects, such as the specific programme, the all-encompassing solution of pedagogical, social and aesthetic details and the typology of the one-room school for children of all ages make it unique. The form has evolved directly

THE CHALLENGE OF THE CONTEXT

Otto Kapfinger

'The Thought Laboratory'
Graz 1985, Adolph Kelz

from the local social and topographical conditions. Even the furniture has been developed in cooperation with the staff and the children. The result is a building closely tailored to the site, the climate, the programme, locally used building techniques and the cultural situation of the place. Many individual parts may be conventional, but the whole transcends the commonplace. This architecture is inseparably rooted in its location and its context, yet it has a universal stance.

A much more difficult situation is faced by architects of university buildings. Their realisation is accompanied (or hindered) by extremely restrictive bureaucratic conditions imposed by the centralized national ministry responsible. Nevertheless some remarkable achievements have been made, primarily in the southern province of the Steiermark. The Institute Building III of the University of Graz by Adolph Kelz, Wolfgang Kapfhammer, Johannes Wegan and Gert Kossdorf has a strong plastic character in the functional area around the spine of the generous stair atrium and a shifting perception of the slightly tilted elements. The nearby Legal, Social and Economics Faculty by Günther Domenig and Herman Eisenköck is a convincing balance between structural and repetitive regularity and impulsive spatial freedom. While the public space in the former example is a hidden surprise in the interior of the building, the latter example demonstratively interweaves its three hundred metre long block with circulation routes and transitional areas, with public and semi-public functions and with lines of movement. An example is the indicative projection of the auditoria into the public space that is a pendant to the intrusion of urban space into the building. The dialectic of order and disorder, systematics and sponteneity, openness and introversion is an architectonic interpretation of the polarities of content of the institutions it houses.

New museum building in Austria has been going through stages of development comparable to that of educational buildings. Klaus Kada's Glass Museum in Bärnbach (1988) is unique here. While belonging to the final phase of the museum building boom in western Europe, it shows the temporal displacement apparent in Austria. Without any particularly articulated museological concept, the building reflects the nature of its exhibits in its glass technology in an almost didactic manner.

The best known and most controversial project of recent years is the Museum Quarter, an agglomeration of several museums and exhibition halls on the site of what used to be the imperial stables. The main problem was the insertion of large new building volumes in a sensitive and heterogenous historical ensemble, the most famous element of which was the facade of the stables, designed by Johann Fischer von Erlach. The original project, which was the result of a two stage international competition, has been changed beyond recognition. Its qualities lay in the integration of the completely different geometries of the spacious imperial forum, the densely-knit bourgeois residential quarters behind it and the barrier formed by the dramatic change in level between them. In the long conflict about the content and the form of the project, it still managed to retain the structural differentiation of its different volumes with their technical infrastructure and access despite specific and constant changes being made to its functional programme.

Hans Hollein's museum project (1989) in a cliff overlooking Salzburg was a radically new exploration of this topographically extreme location. An atectonic hollowing out of the rock as a free, three-dimensional multi-directional spatial and circulation system was a negative gestalt of conventional building. This theme and its forms have been developed further in the project for a branch of the Guggenheim Museum in Vienna, and for his winning project for a museum of volcanic history in France. The topographically less spectacular but many layered site for the Trigon museum in Graz was the basis for an even more methodologically complex winning scheme by Friedrich Schöffauer, Wolfgang Schrom and Wolfgang Tschapeller. They carried out an unusual structuralist analysis of the old city walls, dealing with abstract themes such as borders, edges, openings, passages, passe-partouts and brackets. The plan structure they developed looks at the basic questions of topographic siting as well as the imaginary siting on an artistic level. The museum space was redefined as an open and self-regulating place for art and not as a place to conserve art. This as yet unrealised project is one of the few in recent years that goes beyond aesthetics and is an architectonic interpretation of a revolutionary programme of function and content. Swiss architect Peter Zumthor's competition-winning entry for the Kunsthaus (art exhibition hall) in Bregenz, Vorarlberg is currently under construction. At first glance, the design consists of an unproblematic stack of white cubes. In its precise and deliberate modulation of light and in its subtle formation of minimalist wall and floor surfaces it is, however, an artistic statement beyond conventional limits.

Adolf Krischanitz's approach in the Kunsthalle (exhibition hall) in Krems is just as minimalist. The laconically but precisely and intelligently placed new building activates an existing old tract. It creates an ambivalent new inner court and unexpected perspectives. The conversion by Konrad Frey of a desanctified church into the Kunstraum in Mürzzuschlag is equally rigorous in nature but uses other techniques. In spite of its fashionable slopes and angles in the Graz School manner, it has clearly been stringently conceived as a technically ingenious machine-like envelope that penetrates the old building.

The problems that the larger of the projects mentioned here have had to face result from the fact that they were started towards the end of Europe's boom in museum building. Not only do cultural

Kunstraum - Art Centre
Mürzzuschlag 1993, Konrad Frey

School
Vienna 1994, Boris Podrecca

buildings have to overcome resistance from the conservative public, their realization also suffers from the current budget crisis. The very institution of the museum is now being reconsidered and repositioned. Rehabilitated at the beginning of the 80s as a genuine place for art, the museum is now being fundamentally questioned and challenged by other spaces, other media and other cultural audiences. The intense and heated public debate of the last few years about advanced contemporary architecture was ignited by these large buildings for cultural purposes. The paradox is that the art of building is increasingly being subjected to uninformed debate and opposition as well as to arbitrary political, bureaucratic and economic pressures precisely where one would expect the greatest freedom and autonomy to realise a work of art - in the realms of cultural building. Here such buildings are still financed and run by the state, whose democratic decision-making process is often opaque. Private enterprise, with its own motives, has never played a major role in this area and is unlikely to do so in the near future. What we lack is an alternative. True independence of intention and of management of culturally important projects from the administrative or commercial interests of their patrons would encourage a renaissance of the arts and the architecture which houses them.

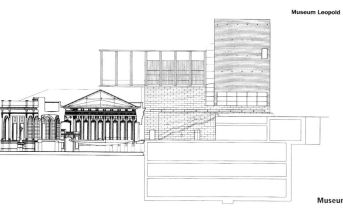

Legal, Social and Economics Faculty
Graz 1995 (under construction), Günther Domenig with Herbert Eisenköck

Museum Leopold

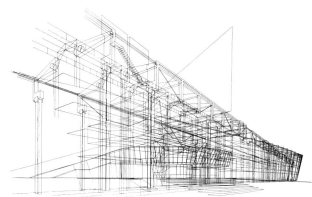

Museum Leopold in The Museum Quarter
Competition entry 1st prize, Vienna 1987, Laurids and Manfred Ortner

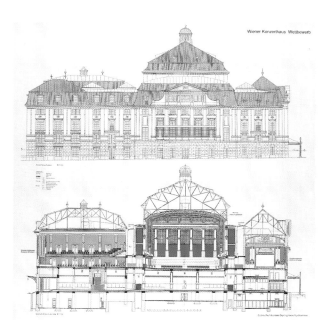

Concert House renewal
Competition 1st prize, Vienna 1994, Hans Puchhammer

University Institute Building III
Graz 1991, Adolph Kelz, Wolfgang Kapfhammer, Johannes Wegan, Gert Kossdorf

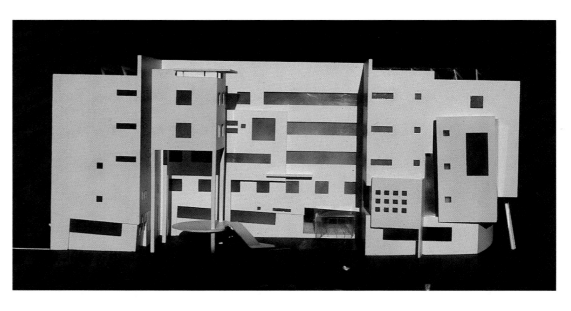

University Institute Building III
Graz 1991, Adolph Kelz, Wolfgang Kapfhammer, Johannes Wegan, Gert Kossdorf

House of Music
Prutz 1990, Anton Falkeis, Cornelia Falkeis-Senn

Polytechnic
Kaindorf 1993, Ernst Giselbrecht

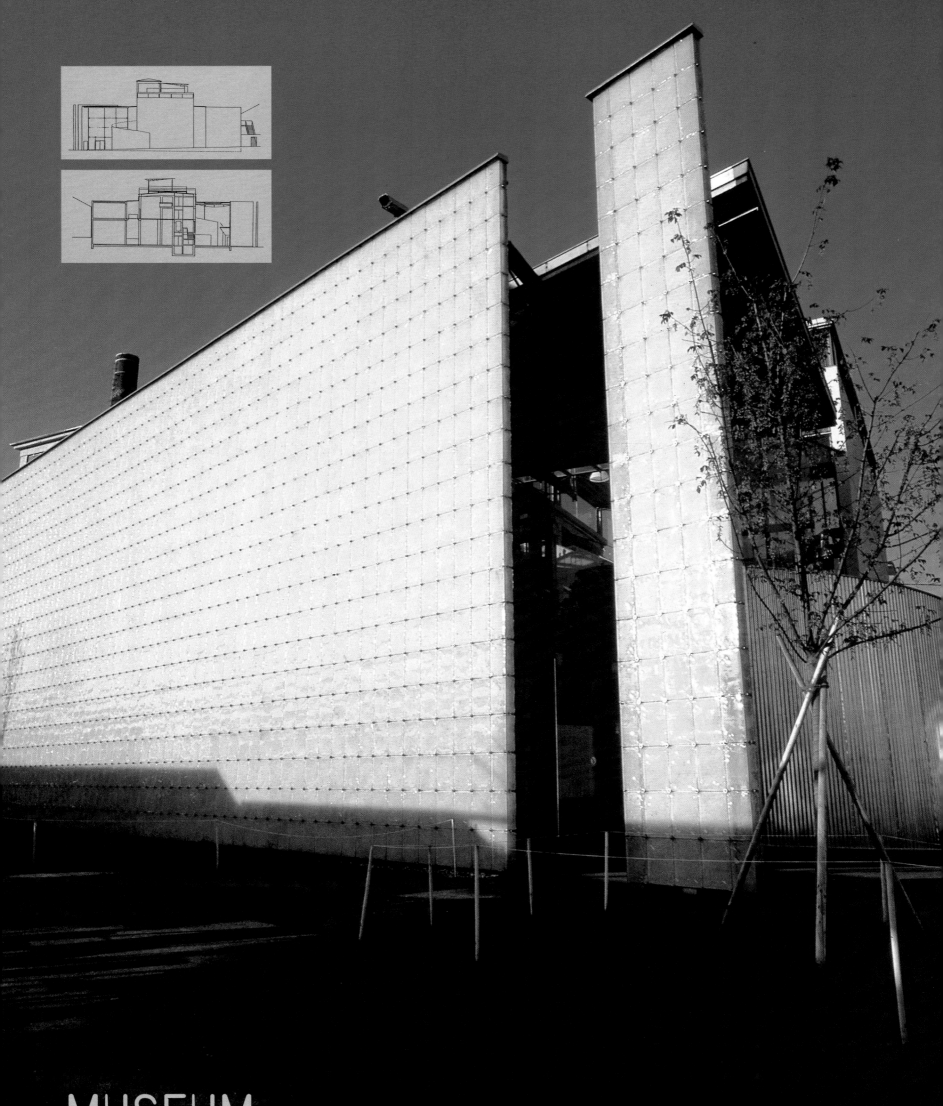

MUSEUM

GLASS MUSEUM
Bärnbach, Steiermark 1988
Architekt: Klaus Kada, b. 1940
Project team: D. Mitterberger, J. Reiterer,
J. Ebner, G. Gebhardt, E. Steiner, D. Feichtinger
Area: 1649 m2
Cost: 12.5 million ATS

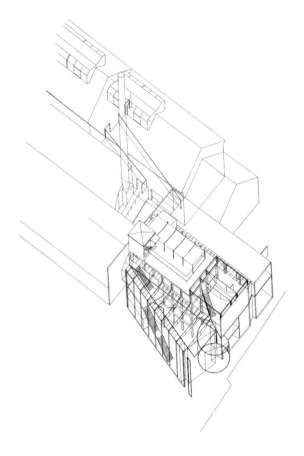

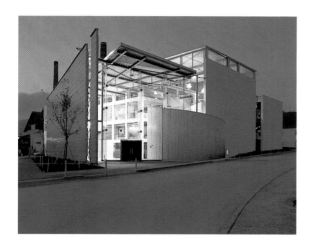

Due to the collapse of a hall in the Bärnbach glass factory which was to house a major exhibition on glass and coal, a competition was held for a new building as well as for the design of the exhibition to be shown in it. The winning project, which was transferred to another site with another concept at short notice was built within seven months with a relatively low budget. A central exhibit, a generator building of the 1950s, was enveloped as an 'objet troué' in handblown glass panes mounted on a filigrane steel structure that follows urban site lines and acts as a huge glass 'poster' for the exhibition. A second self-supporting facade consisting solely of glass plates dissolves the borders of the building to the city - the interior flows into the surroundings and vice versa. The contrast of these transparent screens with other, massive, opaque concrete walls (the connections being made with yet another industrial material - zinc sheeting) draw one's attention and directs it to the complex spatial experiences in the horizontal and vertical planes. The building shatters traditional concepts of built envelopes and spaces. Movement in the building occupies space and its absorption in unexpected ways. The constant insecurity caused by the visual separation of the construction elements and planes from each other by narrow glass strips that defy conventional logic of how materials come together bombards the visitor with the impression of anti-gravitational space travel without any specific science fiction-type elements. The glass building itself became part of the exhibition on glassware - in effect its largest exhibit.

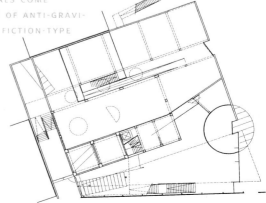

THE WINNING PRIZE IN A COMPETITION FOR A CENTRE FOR THE ARTS IN THE PICTUR-
ESQUE AND CULTURALLY AMBITIOUS TOWN OF KREMS ON THE DANUBE OFFERS A
STRAIGHTFORWARD SOLUTION TO A COMPLICATED PROBLEM. A DISUSED 19TH CEN-
TURY TOBACCO FACTORY WAS TO BE CONVERTED FOR USE AS A GALLERY, RESTAU-
RANT AND SERVICE SPACES. LARGE NEW EXHIBITION GALLERIES AND AN AUDITORIUM
WERE INSERTED BETWEEN THIS OLD TRACT AND THE COUNTRY'S MAJOR PRISON
BEHIND IT. AS NO OPENINGS WERE ALLOWED TOWARDS THE PRISON, ALL SPACES HAD TO BE TOPLIT. THE
COURTYARD BETWEEN THE OLD AND THE NEW TRACTS WAS COVERED WITH A SKYLIGHTED ROOF TO FORM A
HUGE SPACE FOR EXHIBITIONS AND OTHER EVENTS. THE CONNECTION BETWEEN THE DIFFERENT PARTS OF THE
BUILDING IS A GLAZED RAMP. PEOPLE USING THE RAMP AND THE VARYING VIEWS OFFERED FROM IT LIVEN THE
BUILDING. THE DOMINANT QUALITY OF THE MAIN SPACES LIE IN THEIR EXCELLENT PROPORTIONS. THEY HAVE
BEEN CARRIED OUT FRUGALLY IN EXPOSED CONCRETE AND GLASS TO PROVIDE A NEUTRAL AND MINIMAL BACK-
GROUND TO THE EXHIBITIONS.

KUNSTHALLE EXHIBITION SPACE
Krems, Niederösterreich 1995
Architect: Adolf Krischanitz b.1946
Engineers: M. Gmeiner and M. Haferl
Project Team: G. Schlager, M. Kerbler
Area: 5300 m²

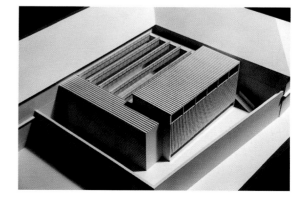

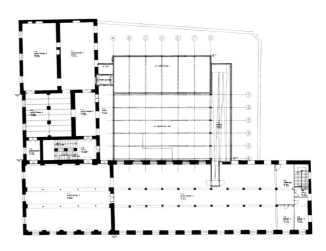

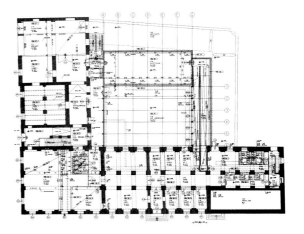

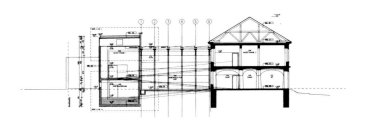

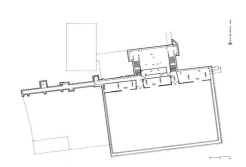
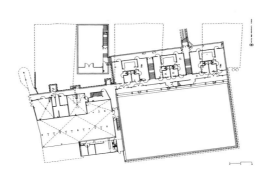
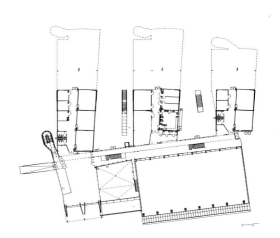

THE TRANSFORMATION OF ENERGIZED AMORPHOUS FLOWING ELEMENTS OF NATURE - WATER, SILICATE, LAVA, IRON - INTO MATERIALS WITH A SHAPE AND SIZE LIKE GLASS, CONCRETE AND STEEL IS ANALOGOUS TO THE REVERSE TRANSFORMATION FOUND IN GOOD ARCHITECTURE OF MATERIAL (GLASS) INTO THE IMMATERIAL (LIGHT AND SPACE). THIS BUILDING IS AN ALCHEMIC TRANSFORMATION OF INDUSTRIAL TECHNOLOGY INTO SPACES IN WHICH HUMAN BEINGS DELIGHT. IN THE FACE OF INITIAL OPPOSITION, A SCHOOL HAS BEEN BUILT WHICH WILL FORCE GENERATIONS OF CHILDREN TO LIVE, TOUCH AND ACT ARCHITECTURE. IT ACCORDS THEM WITH A FREE SPACE IN CONSTANT SIGHT OF THE SKY AND THE SUN, THE TREES AND THE CITY AROUND THEM. THIS IS DONE BY CREATING A FEELING OF IDENTITY AND TOGETHERNESS UNDER THE VAST ROOF, EVEN IF IT IS TRANSPARENT. CRITICS POINT OUT THAT THE SOCIAL ASPECTS OF SCHOOL DESIGN HAVE BEEN SOMEWHAT NEGLECTED IN FAVOUR OF A STRONG TECHNO-FORMALISM, WHICH, HOWEVER, HAS BEEN CARRIED OUT TO NEAR PERFECTION. THE IMPOSSIBLY BUOYANT USE OF GLASS, COMPARABLE ONLY TO A HANDFUL OF BUILDINGS IN BRITAIN, FRANCE AND JAPAN, IS VISIBLE PROOF OF THE CONSTRUCTIVE USE OF TECHNOLOGY: AN EXHILARATING CRY OF DEFIANCE AND DARING, AN EXCITING MANIFESTO OF FREEDOM AND LIGHT.

SCHOOL WAIDHAUSENSTRASSE
Vienna XIV 1994
Architect: Helmut Richter b. 1941
Engineer: E. Panzhauser
Project team: J. Dunkl, G.Gerner, H.Mehring
Area:11.000 m²
Cost: 250 million ATS

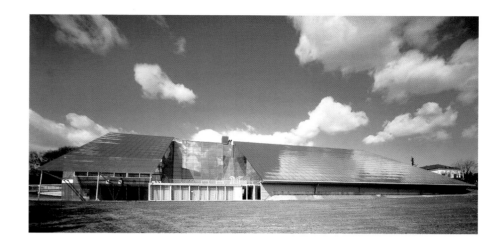

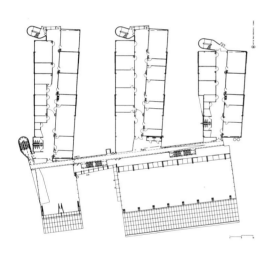
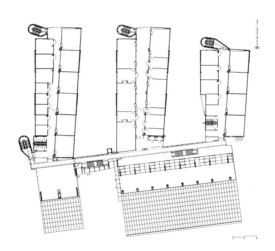
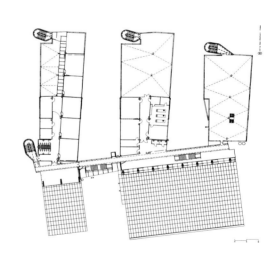

SCHOOL

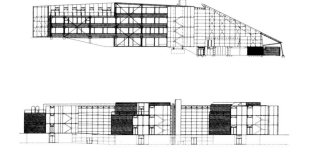

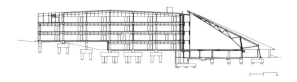

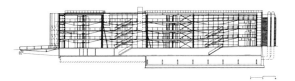

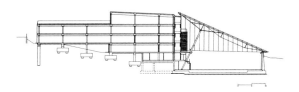

A SMALL VILLAGE IN THE ALPS 1500 M ABOVE SEA LEVEL, OFTEN SNOW-BOUND IN WINTER.
THE SNOW-BLOCKED ROADS FORCED PARENTS TO SEND THEIR CHILDREN TO AN ALL-YEAR BOARDING SCHOOL IN
THE VALLEY, AN INCONVENIENT SOLUTION WHICH BROKE UP FAMILIES. THE VILLAGE DECIDED TO DEVELOP A
NEW CONCEPT OF A SINGLE-CLASS SCHOOL FOR ALL THE TEN TO FOURTEEN YEAR OLDS IN THE VILLAGE, EVEN
THOUGH THERE WERE ONLY FIFTY OF THEM. THE BUILDING TO HOUSE THIS CLASSROOM WAS ALSO TO SOLVE
ANOTHER MAJOR PROBLEM IN THE VILLAGE - THE COMPLETE LACK OF COMMUNITY FACILITIES. EVEN THE TRADI-
TIONAL VILLAGE PUB WAS SEEN BY THE INHABITANTS ONLY FROM BEHIND THE COUNTER AS SERVING PERSONNEL,
A TYPICAL FATE OF TOURIST DESTINATIONS IN AUSTRIA. DUE TO THE STEEP SLOPE AND THE NECESSITY OF SEPA-
RATE ENTRANCES TO THE SCHOOL AND TO THE COMMUNITY SPACE, A TOWER-LIKE FIVE-STOREYED BUILDING
WAS PLANNED, WITH THE LOWER FLOORS FOR COMMUNAL USE AND THE SCHOOL ROOM ON THE TOP FLOOR. THE
LOWER STOREYS, PARTLY UNDERGROUND, HAVE A MASSIVE WALL CONSTRUCTION CLAD IN WOOD; THOSE ABOVE
GROUND ARE CONSTRUCTED SOLELY IN LARGE PREFABRICATED WOOD PANELS WHICH CARRY THE ROOF LOADS
AS WELL AS UP TO FIVE TONS OF SNOW WITHOUT INTERMEDIATE COLUMNS. THIS PRIMARY FORM HAS A CLARITY
THAT IS A RARE TRIUMPH OF MODERN ARCHITECTURE IN THE AUSTRIAN COUNTRYSIDE - A NEW BUILDING TYPE
THAT DOES NOT TRY TO DISGUISE ITSELF AS A COWSHED, BUT EXPRESSES ITS IDENTITY WHILE SUCCESSFULLY
INTEGRATING ITSELF INTO THE LANDSCAPE WITH THE USE OF A TRADITIONAL BUILDING MATERIAL - WOOD.

SCHOOL
Warth, Vorarlberg 1992
Architekt: Roland Gnaiger b. 1951
Engineer: Christian Gantner with Holzbauwerk Kaufmann
Project team: L. Danzer, G. Gruber, E. Zentner
Area: 1125 m2
Cost: 30 million ATS

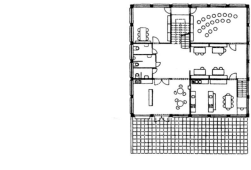

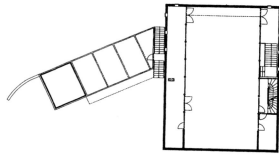

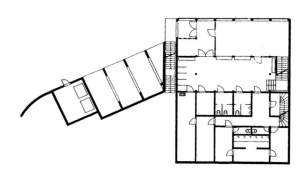

SCHOOL

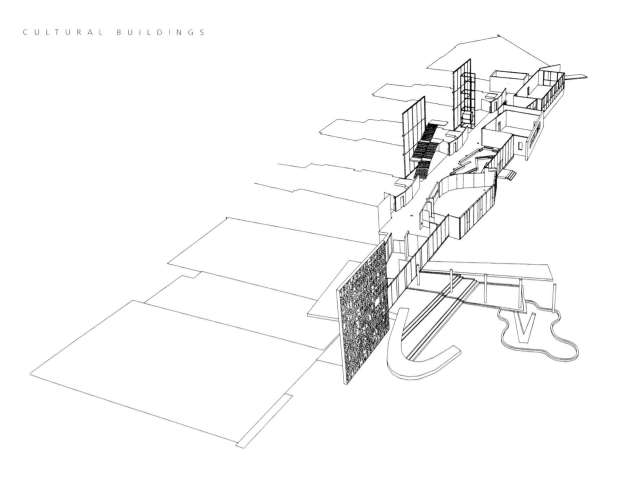

SCHOOL
Absbergasse, Vienna X 1994
Architect: Rüdiger Lainer b. 1949
Project team: H. Schild, B. Moos, K. Krummlauf, G. Auer,
Engineer: Helmuth Locher
Consultants: Anna Detzlhofer (Landscaping)
Oskar Putz (Colour), Erich Monitzer (Graphics)
Area: 8700 m2
Cost: 130 million ATS

The tenets of Modernism (less is more, form follows function) have often, in the last few decades, been dragged into disrepute by poor buildings based on them. Users and observers have frequently felt the lack of 'social space', the non-quantifiable patterns of behaviour that nevertheless need space to take place.If a design in the 1990s can be described as 'post-functionalist' without being post-modern, this school is a good example. The building has been placed sensitively in a rather uninviting site, with low-key visual barriers between itself and itssurroundings, allowing the landscape to flow through. The placement of building volumes and the bold use of colour signify entrances and other functions. A rational plan has been overlaid with specific spatial qualities that encourage diversity and unity, openness and privacy. Whereas the classrooms branch off in comb-fashion in fairly conventional rows from the main spine, they do look out on to varied courts, coloured and planted differently. The backbone of the design, as it were, is the main circulation spine itself, acting as an indoor street, a theatre, a river, a differentiated receptor for the movement and the noise that is the officially supressed part of school life. After all, what we remember most of our school days is what happened between classes, not in them. And if this extra-curricular activity has a pleasant landscape, a tangible stage set of its own, it is bound to informally enrich education and memories of early years, so much so that the classroom itself may fade into the background.

SCHOOL

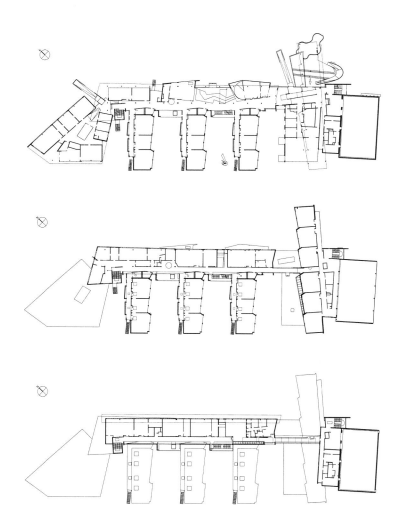

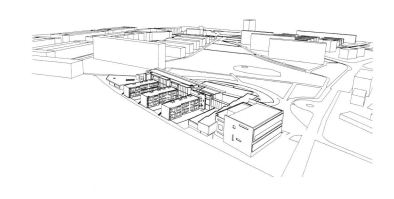

SCHOOL

KINDERGARTEN
Neue Welt Schule
Schwarzenstockallee, Prater, Vienna II 1994
Architect: Adolf Krischanitz b. 1946
Engineers: Manfred Gmeiner, Martin Haferl
Project team: M. Gilbert, E. Red
Consultant: Helmut Federle (colour)
Area: 900 m²
Cost: 14.6 million ATS

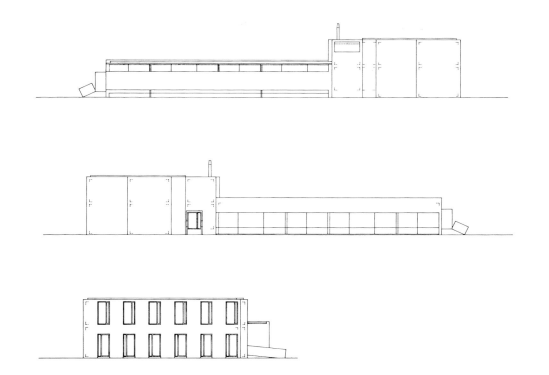

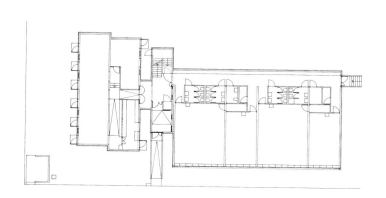

SCHOOL

And now for something completely different. Whereas grown-ups tend to terrorize their kids with their own concepts of fun, resulting in kindergartens that are colourful caricatures of childrens' drawings, this architect presents them with a black box that shocks. Paradoxically, it is the very simplicity and rawness of its surfaces that makes this kindergarten livelier than most. The architect himself says it is because the children enjoy an atmosphere as dissimilar as possible from home. The architectural critic Lilli Thurn und Taxis describes customary kindergartens as paint-by-numbers books, whereas this one is a book with white pages. The exposed concrete walls furnish a hardy surface that can take plenty of spirited action and any number of drawings scotch-taped on them without showing damage, thus offering the children a canvas for true creativity rather than just a chromatic impression of it. The children are obviously having fun in this building, a truly enjoyable sight. The building, in a beautiful part of a famous 200-year old park, seems to be almost immaterial in its use of solid and transparent surfaces and is marred only by the security wire fence around it that physically cuts it off from the landscape. The straightforward but refined volumes house a dining room on the ground floor with classrooms above it set against a one-storeyed tract of playrooms raised 90cm above the ground to protect the roots of a large black poplar. This tree also gives the building its colour - no dead black, though, but a living surface of coloured plaster that changes in tone and warmth with every day and season. One of the most unusual and striking buildings in recent years, its very minimalism evoking its richness.

THE REINTERPRETATION OF RELIGIOUS LIFE AND THE ROLE OF THE CLERICAL ESTABLISHMENT AFTER THE SECOND VATICAN COUNCIL IN THE 1960S LED TO A REDEFINITION OF CHURCH FORM ITSELF - NO LONGER HIERARCHICAL, AXIAL AND SYMMETRICAL, BUT COMMUNITARIAN, IN THE ROUND. THE SCULPTOR FRITZ WOTRUBA'S VISION WAS OF A SACRED PLACE, A CHURCH OPEN TO THE SKY, WHERE WORSHIPPERS WOULD STAND AND PRAY. THIS CONCEPT WAS COMPROMISED BY A PARISH THAT INSISTED ON A ROOF, GLAZED WINDOWS, PEWS AND CENTRAL HEATING, WHICH DECIDEDLY LESSENED THE CHURCH'S INCREDIBLE SCULPTURAL IMPACT. THE STRENGTH OF THE CONCRETE MASSES OUTSIDE IS ENHANCED ON THE INSIDE, WHERE THE RAYS OF LIGHT ENTERING THE SLITS, AND THE ACOUSTICS, WHICH WERE ACTUALLY IMPROVED BY THE ROOF AND THE GLAZING, UNITE TO CREATE A DIVINE ATMOSPHERE. ALTHOUGH THE ORIGINAL VISION WOULD HAVE RADIATED A MORE ARCHAIC STRENGTH, THE CHURCH REMAINS ONE OF THOSE UNCOMMON MONUMENTS TO A TIMELESS ARCHITECTURE, TO HUMAN ENDEAVOUR STRIVING BEYOND EVERYDAY NEEDS, AND TO SPIRITUAL QUEST.

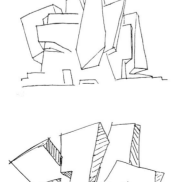

CHURCH OF THE HOLIEST TRINITY
Vienna XXIII, 1976
Design: Fritz Wotruba, b. 1907
Project architect: Fritz Gerhard Mayr
Project team: P. Clemens
Engineer: Psaffeneder
Area: 800 m2

CHURCH

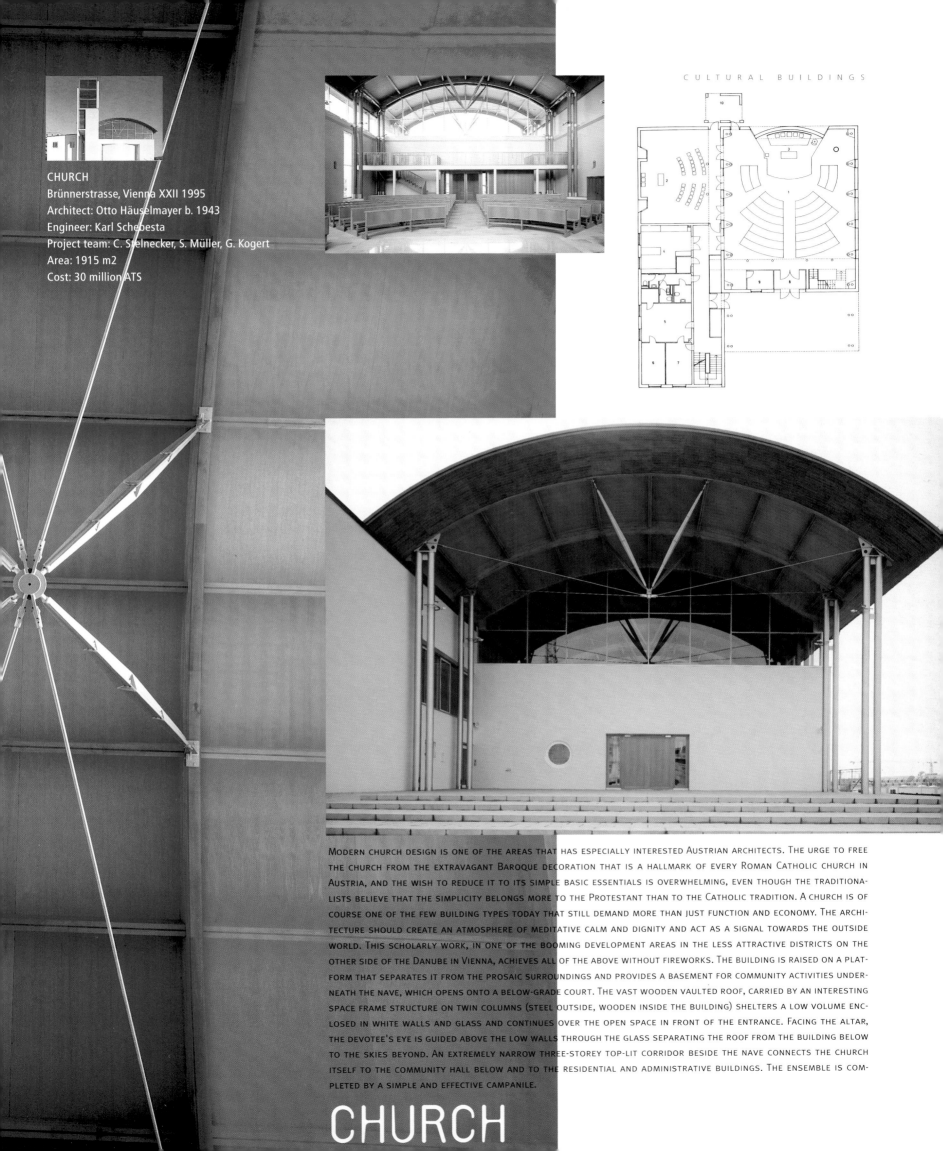

CHURCH
Brünnerstrasse, Vienna XXII 1995
Architect: Otto Häuselmayer b. 1943
Engineer: Karl Schebesta
Project team: C. Stelnecker, S. Müller, G. Kogert
Area: 1915 m2
Cost: 30 million ATS

MODERN CHURCH DESIGN IS ONE OF THE AREAS THAT HAS ESPECIALLY INTERESTED AUSTRIAN ARCHITECTS. THE URGE TO FREE THE CHURCH FROM THE EXTRAVAGANT BAROQUE DECORATION THAT IS A HALLMARK OF EVERY ROMAN CATHOLIC CHURCH IN AUSTRIA, AND THE WISH TO REDUCE IT TO ITS SIMPLE BASIC ESSENTIALS IS OVERWHELMING, EVEN THOUGH THE TRADITIONA-LISTS BELIEVE THAT THE SIMPLICITY BELONGS MORE TO THE PROTESTANT THAN TO THE CATHOLIC TRADITION. A CHURCH IS OF COURSE ONE OF THE FEW BUILDING TYPES TODAY THAT STILL DEMAND MORE THAN JUST FUNCTION AND ECONOMY. THE ARCHI-TECTURE SHOULD CREATE AN ATMOSPHERE OF MEDITATIVE CALM AND DIGNITY AND ACT AS A SIGNAL TOWARDS THE OUTSIDE WORLD. THIS SCHOLARLY WORK, IN ONE OF THE BOOMING DEVELOPMENT AREAS IN THE LESS ATTRACTIVE DISTRICTS ON THE OTHER SIDE OF THE DANUBE IN VIENNA, ACHIEVES ALL OF THE ABOVE WITHOUT FIREWORKS. THE BUILDING IS RAISED ON A PLAT-FORM THAT SEPARATES IT FROM THE PROSAIC SURROUNDINGS AND PROVIDES A BASEMENT FOR COMMUNITY ACTIVITIES UNDER-NEATH THE NAVE, WHICH OPENS ONTO A BELOW-GRADE COURT. THE VAST WOODEN VAULTED ROOF, CARRIED BY AN INTERESTING SPACE FRAME STRUCTURE ON TWIN COLUMNS (STEEL OUTSIDE, WOODEN INSIDE THE BUILDING) SHELTERS A LOW VOLUME ENC-LOSED IN WHITE WALLS AND GLASS AND CONTINUES OVER THE OPEN SPACE IN FRONT OF THE ENTRANCE. FACING THE ALTAR, THE DEVOTEE'S EYE IS GUIDED ABOVE THE LOW WALLS THROUGH THE GLASS SEPARATING THE ROOF FROM THE BUILDING BELOW TO THE SKIES BEYOND. AN EXTREMELY NARROW THREE-STOREY TOP-LIT CORRIDOR BESIDE THE NAVE CONNECTS THE CHURCH ITSELF TO THE COMMUNITY HALL BELOW AND TO THE RESIDENTIAL AND ADMINISTRATIVE BUILDINGS. THE ENSEMBLE IS COM-PLETED BY A SIMPLE AND EFFECTIVE CAMPANILE.

CHURCH

RESIDENTIAL BUILDINGS

CLINICS FOR HOUSING ADDICTS   122

HOUSING GRAZ   132

HOUSING VIENNA   134

HOUSING VIENNA   136

HOUSE STEINDORF   138

Detached house
Vienna 1995, Rudolf Prohazka

THE 19TH CENTURY WAS UNIQUE IN ITS ADDICTION TO RESIDENTIAL LIFE. IT SAW THE APARTMENT AS A LINED CASE FOR HUMANS WHO WERE EMBEDDED WITH ALL THEIR ACCESSORIES SO DEEPLY IN IT THAT ONE WAS REMINDED OF A BOX FOR A COMPASS, WHERE THE INSTRUMENT AND ALL ITS SPARE PARTS LAY IN DEEP VIOLET VELVET-LINED DEPRESSIONS... THE OLD WAY OF LIVING WAS ENDED BY THE 20TH CENTURY WITH ITS POROSITY, ITS TRANSPARENCE, ITS FREE RELATIONSHIP TO LIGHT AND AIR.

WALTER BENJAMIN[1]

WHEN HE WAS SETTING HIS HOUSE IN ORDER...HE HAD ALL THE PRINCIPLES AT HIS DISPOSAL, FROM THAT OF A STYLISTI-CALLY PURE RENOVATION TO THAT OF COMPLETE RECKLESSNESS; AND ALL STYLES, LIKEWISE, OFFERED THEMSELVES TO HIS MIND, FROM THE ASSYRIAN TO CUBISM. WHAT WAS HE TO CHOOSE?
MODERN MAN IS BORN IN A HOSPITAL AND DIES IN A HOSPITAL - HENCE HE SHOULD ALWAYS LIVE IN A PLACE LIKE A HOSPITAL. THIS MAXIM HAD JUST BEEN FORMULATED BY A LEADING ARCHITECT, AND ANOTHER, A REFORMER OF INTERI-ORS, DEMANDED MOVABLE PARTITION WALLS ON THE GROUNDS THAT IN LIVING TOGETHER MAN MUST LEARN TO TRUST MAN AND NOT SHUT HIMSELF OFF IN A SPIRIT OF SEPARATISM. A NEW TIME HAD THEN JUST BEGUN (FOR THAT IS, AFTER ALL, SOMETHING THAT TIME IS DOING ALL THE TIME), AND A NEW TIME NEEDS A NEW STYLE.

ROBERT MUSIL[2]

THE HOUSE IS THE SUBSTANTIATION OF THE EVERYDAY.

JOSE ORTEGA Y GASSET[3]

CLINICS FOR HOUSING ADDICTS

Walter M. Chramosta

Don't ever look directly at a magician's nimble fingers; the actual trick is being prepared on the side, only to be pulled on to centre stage at the decisive moment. The finesse lies hidden in the intricate movements preparatory and sub-sidiary to the main action. The art of building is no different. A view of the sluggish main flow of developments is not particularly exciting, though educational. It helps to understand the routes taken by the tributaries and side arms and makes one willing to surrender to the wild currents of really innovative ideas to be carried to new shores.

An overview of the imitative commonplace of most housing in Austria would perceive three styles: belated Post-Modernism, Alpine Style or Uninspired Indifference. Many planners seem resistant to spatial or functional innovation. The majority of the population and the politicians elected by them see dwellings primarily as eco-nomic goods that do not need to fulfill any require-ment other than that of an acceptable price. As in the fashion industry, several contradictory styles exist side by side. Fashions in building are similar in that they exploit familiar forms and ideas com-mercially until they collapse under the weight of this visual overexposure.

The aesthetic expectations of the public have largely been reduced to the extent that it is possible to build practically anything that can be sold on the property market by an advertising agency. The building by-laws and official standards tend to hinder the innovators and encourage the imitators. There is no doubt that a country with Austria's built heritage can afford to tolerate some fashionable banalities as a contrast to its avant-garde culture, at least in its cities and the more densely populated areas of its countryside. The everyday, the tasteless, the cheap and the personal obsession should also be given sufficient space to express themselves. The situation only becomes worrying when the majority of buildings at a given place and time are treated carelessly. Let us look briefly at some of these sins. One of the biggest burdens is to be found in the work of the painter Hundertwasser, who pretends to offer a better quality of living merely by apply-ing ornament. The mass media has latched onto his populist message and propagates it uncritically and mercilessly. Other artists have been commissioned to design apartment blocks which may be accepted as isolated curio-sities as long as they do not become prescriptions for residential building policy. Another burden, this time on the landscape, is the endless pro-duction of industrially prefabricated 'organic' timber and glass conservatory style that appeals to the current pro-environmental wave. To add

Gamerith house
Seewalchen/Attersee 1934, Ernst Plischke

to the misery some regional programmes for conservation and village-scape protection are being misinterpreted to such an extent that only reproductions of historic buildings are considered acceptable. The situation is afflicted by the culturally retrospective atmosphere, the social trend towards a retreat into the private sphere at the expense of community responsibilities, and financial restrictions caused by the reduction of state subsidies for housing.

The yearning for a better living environment in general and a more humane solution to the housing problem in particular is beginning to be taken seriously after several decades of purely economically determined functionalism. All housing in Austria - from the private single-family house in the village to the housing scheme in the city - is subsidized by legally regulated public money. This system potentially allows for great freedom within the parameters of maximum floor area and production costs per square metre. Houses or apartments exceeding this may be built, but they are not eligible for subsidy. Without this state support most housing in Austria could not be financed.

Housing is thus of national interest. More than in other places, housing does not merely have financial, but also political, cultural and psychological dimensions. Both government and business are heavily involved. Increased expenditure on housing is often a measure used to boost the economy and increase employment now that major investment in infrastructure, such as in motorways, railways and power stations, is no longer necessary. This means that housing policy is determined by party politics, ideological dogma and non-specialist influences. Cooperative housing societies are associated with one political party or the other and employ planners of the same leanings who are thus acceptable to them regardless of their abilities. Sometimes they even do the planning themselves to save the cost of an architect. Since building contractors and building societies are licensed to build, only a tenth of all building is actually designed by architects. The private client, the rule outside the cities, uses the taxes refunded to him for building to realize his own dreams; dreams that are often a nightmare for the planner or architect. For the reasons mentioned above, the non-profit cooperative housing societies use this money to produce largely unattractive housing. A few happy exceptions, which only prove the sobering rule, are widely published as representative of Austrian residential architecture, but those that achieve the levels of architecture discussed in this book are just part of a tiny section of residential building as a whole.

These distinctive signs of progress are scattered in a sea of commercial products of little artistic value. They are exceptions that stand in opposition to current regional practice, though not necessarily in opposition to regional building culture. Contemporary treatment of tradition is still generally considered a crime against history. One-dimensional reproductions of romantic buildings such as the farm house, the castle and the palace are in great demand. The repetition of the familiar is used to create the illusion of an intact settlement or landscape. In western Austria, it is the over extravagant use of wood that acts as a surrogate for country life, whereas, in the east of the country, it is the grand villa that acts as a model, though often grotesquely reduced to ridiculous proportions and questionable standards to suit the budget. The cities are dominated by a collection of worn-out quotations and copies of familiar styles, churned out by busy offices that do not have the time to develop a design thoroughly.

The source of innovative energy is ultimately the client: either the personal involvement of the private client or the rare example of the public body that expects high quality. There is no lack of architects, concepts for residential building, theories from the universities, statements from the architect's association, or Sunday sermons by politicians. What is lacking are good clients. The investor who risks his money in an architectural concept with the intention of raising the cultural value of a building commissioned by him cannot expect much public praise in Austria. The very best projects have always been attacked or viewed with suspicion by tabloids with a high circulation and great influence; the good works flourish in silence, and the mediocre are celebrated by the press.

Examples of progressive clients - regional building departments or mayors of specific towns or villages who free themselves of what they believe is the people's taste - in the public sector are found in the federal states of Steiermark, Vorarlberg and Vienna. Certain towns, Graz, Linz and

Salzburg for example, are also blessed with above average standards. They are places where there is an accumulation of buildings and projects worthy of discussion, where there is intensive debate on general questions concerning the culture of building, and where the schools of architecture, in Graz, Innsbruck, Linz and Vienna, work as catalysts of change.

The widespread built manifestations of historicism and the demonstrative use of money and fantasy do not run hand in hand with innovative spatial statements. In the early 90s, Austria experienced a boom in the total volume of housing built, but there was no broad debate at the same time on the future of living patterns. Public competitions that would have encouraged such a debate only took place in Vorarlberg and the Steiermark. In fact, there is as much cultural variety in building as there is in the country's landscape, and this variety is most clearly evident in its residential buildings. It is thus pointless to describe Austria's contemporary architectural scene as homogenous. What is on offer is a discursive division into sectors, into varying, independent developments. The discovery of surprising phenomena and of innovation in Austrian residential building should be considered in terms of region, function, typology and style. The regional pattern displays differences as well as interdependencies. The federal nature of the country, with its nine quasi-autonomous states, only partially reflects the variety of parameters within which architecture is created. Topography, climate, population structure, migration, socio-economic conditions, cultural and infrastructural networks determine the different character of the architecture in each state. Each state's specific political constellation results in regional preferences in residential policy. Whereas the detached single-family house, in the tradition of the farmhouse, is typical in the western states of Vorarlberg, Tirol and Salzburg, in the villages in the eastern states, Burgenland and Niederösterreich, the row house or terraced house is typical of the traditional concentrated village form along a street. These patterns correspond logically to the way of life and occupation: the mountain farmer in the Alps has been independent for centuries and is often a wealthy landowner, whereas the occupants of the plains in the east are descendents of bonded labourers. People's patterns of living subtly reflect their self-image and their subconscious, and building a house offers an opportunity to escape or influence the social system in which they are embedded. To achieve these aims, people are prepared to burden themselves with decades of debt and do-it-yourself labour.

Many urban dwellers now move into the country to take advantage of cheaper land prices in order to realise their dreams of autonomy in natural surroundings and simulate the life of a landowner. On the other hand, many rural dwellers dream of modernity, progress and comfort - ideals that they see embodied in the distant city. The house obviously compensates for any social or geographical disadvantages suffered, consciously or subconsciously, by the owner. These attempts often end in bewilderment. Neighbours' houses are copied and decorated with industrially produced decorated elements. Regional building styles, for example the Tirolean farmhouse with its wooden balcony and deep-eaved gabled roof, are the norm outside their home regions.

Buchroithner house
Zell am See 1930, Lois Welzenbacher

OT BUILD IN A PICTURESQUE WAY. LEAVE THIS EFFECT TO THE MOORS, THE MOUNTAINS AND THE
PERSON WHO DRESSES PICTURESQUELY IS NOT PICTURESQUE BUT A CLOWN. THE FARMER DOES NOT
IN A PICTURESQUE WAY. YET HE IS PICTURESQUE.

AS WELL AS YOU CAN. NOT BETTER. DO NOT BE PRESUMPTIOUS. AND NOT WORSE. DO NOT PUSH
ELF DOWN TO A LEVEL BELOW THE ONE YOU HAVE BEEN PLACED ON BY BIRTH AND EDUCATION. THIS
TRUE WHEN YOU GO TO THE MOUNTAINS. TALK TO THE FARMERS IN YOUR OWN LANGUAGE … PAY
ION TO THE SHAPES THE FARMERS USE IN THEIR BUILDINGS. FOR THEY ARE THE CRYSTALLIZED WIS-
F MANY GENERATIONS. SEARCH FOR THE REASON BEHIND THE SHAPE. IF TECHNOLOGICAL PROGRESS
ADE IT POSSIBLE TO IMPROVE UPON THIS SHAPE THEN THE IMPROVEMENT SHOULD BE USED. THE
HAS BEEN SUPERSEDED BY THE THRESHING MACHINE.

DING ON THE PLAINS REQUIRES VERTICAL ARTICULATION; THE MOUNTAINS DEMAND HORIZONTAL
JLATION. THE WORK OF MAN MUST NOT COMPETE WITH GOD'S WORK. DO NOT THINK OF THE ROOF,
RAIN AND SNOW. THIS IS HOW THE FARMER THINKS. IN THE MOUNTAINS HE THEREFORE BUILDS
ATTEST ROOF POOSIBLE. IN THE MOUNTAINS THE SNOW MUST NOT SLIDE DOWN WHEN IT WANTS
HEN THE FARMER WANTS IT TO. THE FARMER MUST THEREFORE BE ABLE TO CLIMB ON TO THE ROOF
IN ORDER TO REMOVE THE SNOW. WE, TOO, HAVE TO CREATE THE FLATTEST POSSIBLE ROOF
DING TO OUR ENGINEERING SKILLS.

JTHFUL! NATURE KEEPS THE TRUTH. IT GETS ALONG WELL WITH IRON TRELLIS BRIDGES BUT IT REJEC-
OTHIC ARCHES WITH BRIDGE TOWERS AND CRENELLATION. DO NOT BE AFRAID OF BEING
UNFASHIONABLE. CHANGES IN THE TRADITIONAL WAY OF BUILDING ARE ONLY PERMISSIBLE IF
ARE AN IMPROVEMENT. STAY OTHERWISE WITH WHAT IS TRADITIONAL. FOR THE TRUTH, EVEN IF IT
DREDS OF YEARS OLD, HAS A STRONGER BOND WITH US THAN THE LIE THAT WALKS WITH US.

ADOLF LOOS

Seeber hotel tower
Hall/Tirol 1931, Lois Welzenbacher

Tirol is an example of the difficulties and triumphs of modern housing in the countryside. Most building activity is occasioned by tourism, but even in regions less overrun by tourists, homage is paid - devoid of any feeling for the region's own past - to the 'International Style' of the 'Tirolean house', while attempts to achieve a more authentic architectural interpretation of today's requirements in Tirolean villages are scarce. There are, of course, a number of remarkable new buildings in Tirol, but the overall impression of the villages today is discouraging. The reason usually given is that tourists cannot be expected to accept modern architecture since they come from cities that have been spoiled and hence look for something different on vacation. Country life is, however, no longer based solely on agriculture. Recreation is replacing production in this mountain landscape. Attempts to ingratiate tourists tend to ignore the considerable capabilities of local architects, as the following examples illustrate.

Ernst Plischke's country home in Seewalchen achieves a direct spatial relationship to the charms of the Salzkammergut lake district, without using regional materials or elements of style to anchor the house in the region. Lois Welzenbacher achieved the relationship of his buildings to their context by a sharper perception of nature, not by formal similarities to typical local buildings. His work reflects the strength of nature more than that of culture. The relationship with the natural elements expressed in his hotel in Hall is rare. Unfortunately, contextual appropriateness is most commonly measured directly on the building itself, and not by its reciprocal interaction with its environment. Reductionist buildings like these need users sensitive to nature to understand their spatial logic, whereas the clichés of the bourgeoisie or the peasantry are self-explanatory. Rudolf Prohazka manages to escape the dictum of misunderstood regional tradition, to produce houses like solitaires in the landscape. His ascetic houses in the Vienna Woods confront their inhabitants with nature, but at the same time protect the private sphere through layers of filtration. Ernst Beneder emphasizes distance from trite normality and orientation towards natural beauty. His house hovering above a lake in Blindenmarkt is basically a rigid instrument to observe the untouched landscape, shielded off from the disturbing neighbourhood. Beneder's house becomes an independent cubic composition that ignores popular images of what a house should look like.

The conscious autonomy of the new directs Christian Lichtenwagner's addition to a badly planned and oriented existing single-family house in Bad Schallerbach. The perfectly executed steel-clad extension with an urban touch orients the new living and cooking spaces towards the garden. As living standards in urban and rural areas begin to approximate one another, farmhouses come under pressure to accommodate new standards of comfort. Wolfgang Feyferlik demolished one tract of a three-sided courtyard farmhouse in St. Anna am Aigen to replace it with a living and sleeping space. The removal of interior partitions, the introduction of large scale glazing and the replacement of many roof tiles with glass tiles was a fine tightrope walk between tradition and innovation. The roof becomes a translucent shield under which different volumes flow into each other, completely changing the interior within an unchanged external shape. The new is collaged with the old, with visible joints. Horst and Christine Lechner's timber atrium house in Kuchl is a minimalist but well planned open space solution to ecological and architectonic questions, proving that innovation does not necessarily always imply invention but can also mean optimal recombinations of the familiar. The Baukünstler, a group of young architects in Vorarlberg, have long been reinterpreting traditional timber houses. There are several convincing spatially and technically up-to-date solutions, like Hermann Kaufmann's house in Lech that combines rationalized prefabricated construction with a generous spatial concept. This is a house that satisfies the common wish for isolated single-family houses based on the historic precedent of simple wooden hut, as opposed to the free configuration of Arno Bereiter's house in Lustenau and Hugo Dworzak's house in Schwarzach. The common wish for a gable-roofed house is seen by the latter two as a restrictive corset to be perforated by conscious fragmentation and recombination of individual functional components, to create a useful whole organism of independent sub-elements. Bereiter separates semi-public and private spheres on the ground floors and upper floors respectively. Dworzak satisfies the clients' wish to enjoy the spectacular panoramic view in spite of an ugly construction in front of the site by splitting the parents' and children's wings into two tracts, each oriented towards its own view avoiding the barrier, and connected by a common space with an independent roof described by the architect as a cloud to manifest his dispensation of the traditional trinity of base, wall and roof. These two architects' gestures refer to zoological images or elements of uninhabited nature. This strategy of considering a construction as a mimesis of nature in order to escape from culturally determined forms leads to Günther Domenig's Steinhaus in Steindorf. As the function is not directly related to the form of this multifunctional house, its free composition can also be considered sculptural. Much more than a house, it is a subtle reaction to the natural potential of the site, of unique geological and morphological characteristics and of the family history of this lakeside site. Architecture as fine art that can be unequivocally ascribed to one person, the Steinhaus is an unrepeatable, radical and unaffordable work. The private residential space

Weekend house
Blindenmarkt 1994, Ernst Beneder

Feurer house
St. Anna/Aigen 1992, Wolfgang Feyferlik

Detached house
Lustenau 1995, Arno Bereiter

Raidel house
Schwarzach-Linzenberg 1995, Hugo Dworzak

Atrium house
Kuchl 1993, Christine & Horst Lechner

Detached house

Addition to house
Bad Schallerbach 1994, Christian Lichtenwagner

Detached house
Lech-Stubenbach 1995, Hermann Kaufmann

reaches a zenith of subjectivity in the Steinhaus that is an antipole to collective housing, that demands a high level of neutrality and flexibility. Max Rieder, Wolfgang Tschapeller and Hanspeter Wörndl apply Domenig's method of topological analysis to decode a fallow ground left by the destruction of a villa belonging to Wittgenstein's family on Vienna's periphery, as a basis for the design of many-layered housing, a social project with philosophical roots. An architectural healing is brought about here even though the formal vocabulary does not resemble that of the immediate environment. Norbert Fritz takes a diametrically opposite position in his terraced houses in Innsbruck to achieve a well-resolved interpretation of the south-facing slope. The spirit of rural building is reflected in the well thought-out details and the frugal character of the houses, without using a single romantic detail from traditional farmhouses. Fritz thus achieves a dignified transformation of the rural into the urban. This is a valuable and rare case of quiet innovation which integrates tradition harmoniously into today's needs. Mike Loudon's housing project in Bings relates to younger traditions and achieves a pragmatic aesthetic with economical construction, typical of new architecture in Vorarlberg. The clever combination of massive concrete and skeletal timber construction to create shells within which each resident can create his own home offers young couples affordable and identifiable housing.

In the cities, one comes across increasingly new variations within the strict financial limits laid down by subsidy rules. Adolph Kelz accomplishes a rigid functional layering of plans in Graz, which are nevertheless freed from the ground through the manipulation of material and planes. Also in Graz, neither Manfred Wolff-Plottegg nor Florian Riegler and Roger Riewe wish to disguise the harshness of building as an intervention in nature - on the contrary, they emphasize the serial geometry of the facades and their technical instrumentation. Their housing finds their manifesto-like expressions in the sober power of industrial mass-production parameters, not in the multiplication of private idylls. Helmut Richter as well as Dieter Henke and Marta Schreieck have redefined the skins of their recent housing projects in Vienna by retaining the urban edges but making them visually permeable with large translucent glazing - an innovative act in a city of plaster facades. This strategy also endeavours to assemble apartments out of evenly lit, generous and functionally neutral spaces. Klaus Kada's structural reform of a student hostel in Graz is reflected in its lively surface articulation. Temporally limited living is granted the quality of permanent residence through a variety of unit plans, with the added element of social communication enabled in the semi-public access galleries and prominent common spaces on the face of Kada's building. A hostel is, like a hotel, a place of gathering with retreat cells, a public event and an intimate refuge. The architectural expression of these two poles is a surprisingly rare theme in a tourist destination like Austria. Hanspeter Petri's extension of an old hotel in Steinberg and Much Untertriffaller's new hotel in Partenen are successful implantations of large volumes in the landscape, unifying the guest's demands for comfort, nature's right to respect and contemporary

Housing cluster
Pumpligahn, Innsbruck 1985, Norbert Fritz

Housing
Ziegelstrasse, Graz 1995, Adolph Kelz

architecture's values. Similarly, Erich Strolz's apartment house for hotel owners and staff calmly combines commercial necessity with aesthetic statements.

The debate on whether housing is part of architecture or urban design or just the fulfillment of a legal and financial programme is still going on, but housing remains the central task of architecture. The house, as the "substantiation of the everyday", is the scene of realization of everyday life — space must be created for the day's routine activities, but this space must contain conceptual options that go beyond the meeting of functional needs. Fifty years after the rigid work of post-war reconstruction began, the country is beginning to display greater humanization of public housing as well as a rectification of clichés in private residences, and has laid several milestones on its way towards more optimal "lined cases for people", towards a new state of private space.

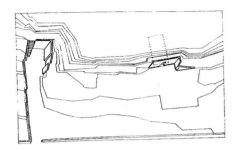

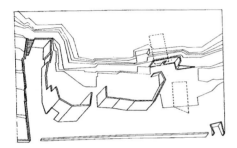

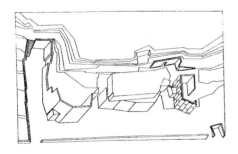

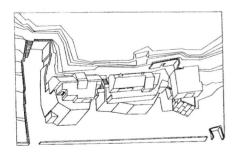

Housing
Wittgensteingründe Vienna 1990,
Manfred Maximilian Rieder-Wolfgang Tschapeller-Hans Peter Wörndl

Housing
Bings 1994, Mike Loudon

Housing
Vienna 1991, Rüdiger Lainer

Hochtannberg hotel staff housing
Hochkrumbach 1992, Erich Strolz

Hotel Windegg
Steinberg/Rofan 1989, Hans Peter Petri

Hotel Silvretta (lower 2)
Bielerhöhe/Partenen 1991,
Much Untertrifaller sen. & jun., Gerhard Hörburger

WIST Student housing (lower 2)
Graz 1991, Klaus Kada

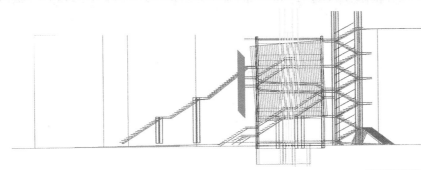

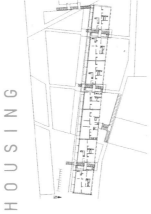

HOUSING

HOUSING
Seiersberg, Graz, Steiermark 1994 (second phase 1996)
Architect: Manfred Wolff-Plottegg b.1946
Engineer: Manfred Petschnigg
Project team: Mascher, C. Zechner
Area: 3123 m²
Cost: 28 million ATS

A statement against the dissipation and dispersal of low-rise suburban settlements, this housing scheme is at the beginning of the reurbanization of a low-density area on the periphery of Graz. An attempt has been made to deliberately break the suburban ideal of total privacy and isolation. The livening of the facade with architectonic means generated by random interactive computer-aided diagrammes and the interweaving of public access and private zones into communicative realms work to blur the definition of familiar elements of single-family houses such as borders, front or rear, symbolic or family use. Floor-to-ceiling glazing and trapezoidal rooms enlarge the rooms visually, as the eye measures and defines a space by its largest dimension. The transparent and generous nature of the flats within the usual tight economic constraints help to replace suburban living criteria with urban ones. Yet the individual needs and ways of life of the occupants have sufficient space and flexibility, as is obvious from the colourful way the building is used without compromising its architecture.

ÖBV HOUSING
Frauenfeldergasse, Vienna XVII 1994
Architects: Dieter Henke b. 1952, Marta Schreieck b. 1954
Engineer: Werner Lawugger
Project team: B. Eder
Area: 4400 m²
Cost: 82 milllion ATS

The treatment of the plot at the junction of two streets as an 'elbow joint', with each tract designed differently and accessible through a stairway acting as a social contact zone at the 'elbow', is the basis for this refined concept of urban housing. Maisonettes in one tract, fronted by two-storeyed loggias that act as mini-gardens, relate visually to the higher storeys of the older building it adjoins. This facade is characterized by two-storeyed adjustable louvered aluminium sliding panels that liven the building with patterns caused by the various positions and which 'immaterialize' the street front by lightening it in contrast to the heavy stone facades around it. The corridors on the rear of this tract are of a different type at every level, avoiding the 'sameness' that plagues multi-storeyed housing. The total of forty one-level flats in the other tract with the maisonettes offer a variety of ten types of flats as well as generous spaces and great flexibility within the flats achieved by sliding wall panels and floor-to-ceiling glazing. By dispensing with the habitual decorative and stylistic elements of Viennese housing and restricting their choice of materials and construction to a cool, almost industrial vocabulary, the architects have definitely provoked public taste. But by a sensible reallocation of resources they have offered the occupants of the apartments an unusually generous mode of urban living.

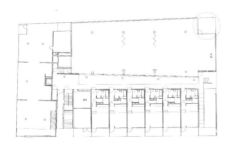

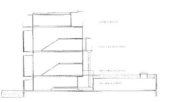

HOUSING
Brunnerstrasse 26, Vienna XXIII 1990
Architect: Helmut Richter b. 1941
Engineers: Wolfgang Vasko, Lothar Heinrich
Project team: A. Hengst, G. Kempinger, B. Dorfner, H. Rosner
Area: 5000 m²
Cost: 60 million ATS

The Viennese tradition of building council housing in the form of grand ensembles that resemble fortresses or castles for the proletariat often results in much money being spent on superficial decoration and status symbols at the cost of inadequate apartments behind them. The architect of this housing scheme has dispensed with symbolic elements such as a pretty facade and turned its back towards the noisy road. A structural glass facade protects the apartments, which are accessible from free standing corridor bridges, separated from the windows for privacy. The flats themselves are extremely flexible as the only fixed elements are one column, one load carrying wall and one sanitary point, thus allowing the residents to use or modify their flats as they wish. A pleasant living atmosphere is provided by the large transparent walls and the balconies, loggias and terraces oriented towards the rear garden. This building has also received international attention because of its remarkable construction: an extremely economical and imaginative application of prefabricated elements and industrial building components combined in original and precise details, some of which, however, suffer in everyday use. The materials and the elements all have a function and can be read as they are - there is no necessity for interpretation. Richter himself associates architecture with the spirit of invention, with a readiness to take risks, with perception. He quotes Prouvé, "To build is to create an osmosis between science, spirit and reality".

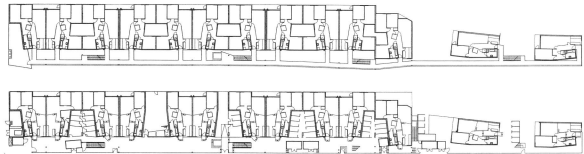

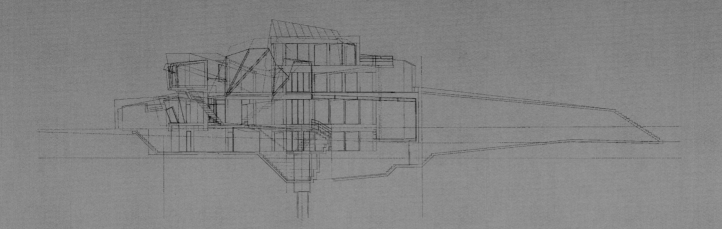

The title 'building' illustrates the difficulty of describing a project that is at once experiment, manifesto, idiosyncracy, sculpture and architecture. A

minent and prolific builder, Domenig began in 1986 to build for himself on this inherited lakeside site that he has known since his childhood. The first

ment in 1984 was a strange landing stage from which one could tumble into the water, a convoluted, aggressive concrete version of a dream follow

Slowly Domenig's story began to take shape, a metamorphosis of the mountaneous landscape and his own lifelong obsession with expressive and liv

form, the design developing as it was being built. Jagged edges cut through dark irregular volumes, vertical and sloping paths break through sunlit s

ces. As an autonomous life achievement, it is a unique, perso-

nal and uncompromising statement on the future of form and

space. An architect who has built many exciting buildings,

Domenig is constantly searching here, almost sleep-walking,

testing his own limits and the limits of architecture. The open-

ended project is to act as a centre for architectural discourse as well as a private retreat, a fusion of the conflict between the wish to share and the n

to retreat. A letter to the world at large and a private diary at the same time.

STEINHAUS, HOUSE AND MULTIFUNCTIONAL BUILDING
Steindorf, Kärnten (Work in progress)
Architect: Günther Domenig b. 1934
Engineer: Harald Egger
Project team: H. Dullnig, A. Gruber, G. Wallner, H. Liska, A. Lixl, W. Wimmer, P. Zinganel
Consultant: G. Schelling (Geometry)
Area: 1.000m²
Cost: unforseeable

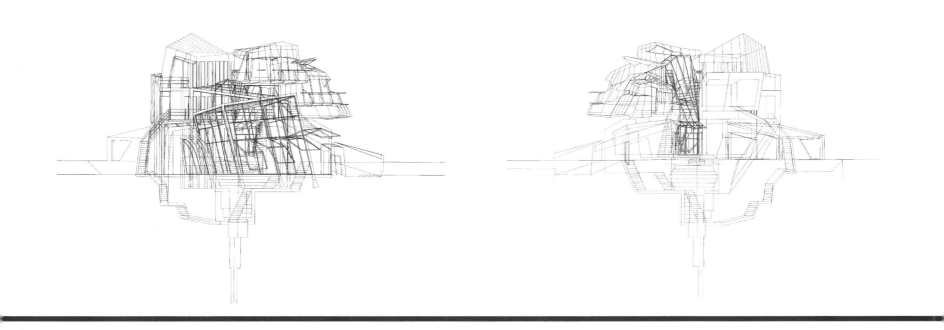

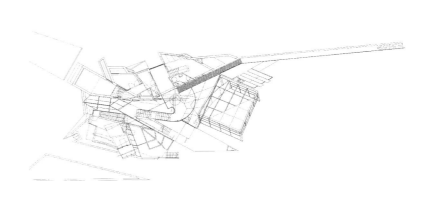

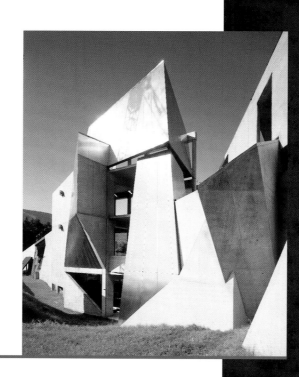

ECOLOGICAL BUILDINGS

INTERVIEW WITH EXPERTS   144

LOW-ENERGY HOUSE PROTOTYPE   150

ECOLOGICAL HOUSING GAENSERNDORF   152

DESIGN CENTRE LINZ   154

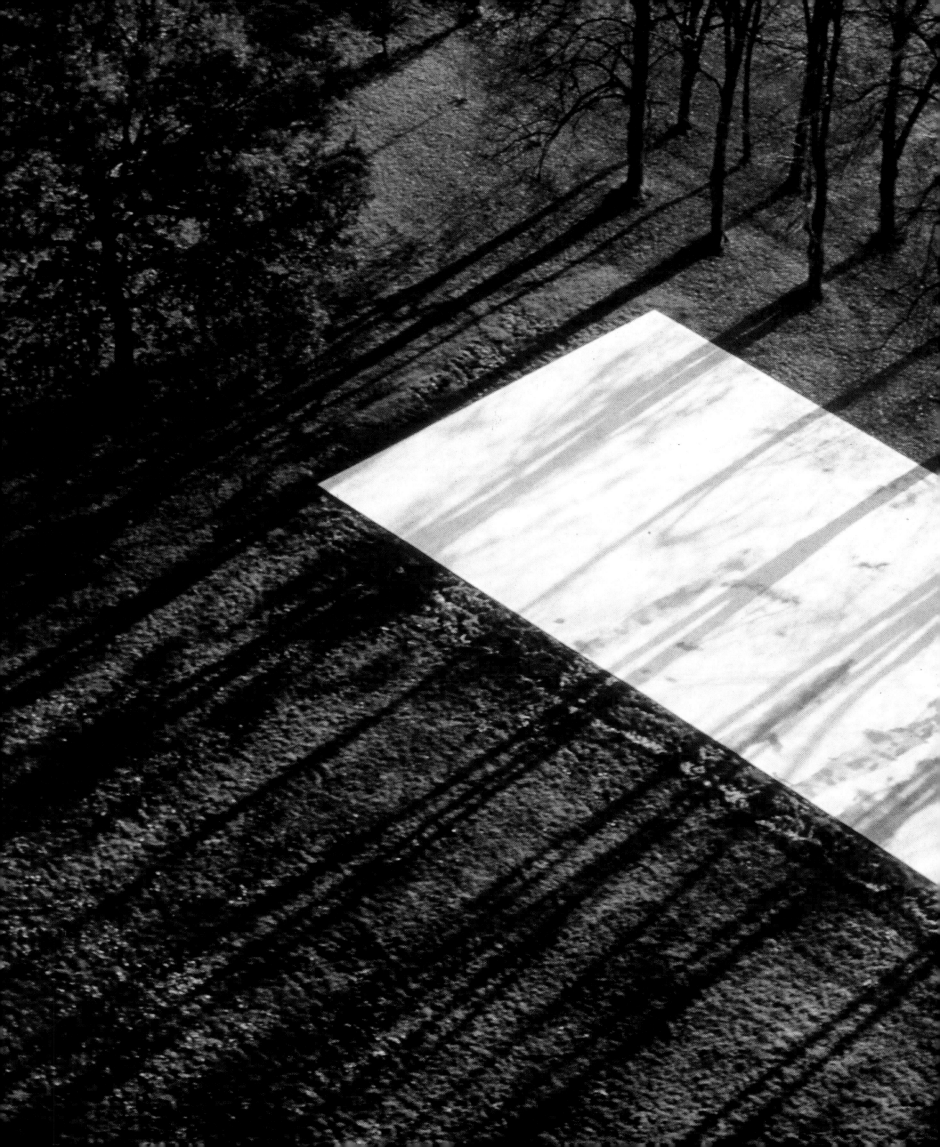

Untitled installation
Jöss 1990, Heimo Zobernig

GLOBAL ENVIRONMENTAL CONCERNS ARE NO LONGER MINORITY INTERESTS. RAPIDLY GROWING PUBLIC CONCERN OVER THE STATE OF THE NATURAL FOUNDATIONS OF LIFE HAS FORCED GOVERNMENTS AND EXPERTS ALIKE TO FACE THE MANIFOLD PROBLEMS OF THE ENVIRONMENT. SHELTER HAS BECOME ONE OF THE MAJOR BURDENS ON THE ECOSYSTEM. HOW IS THE PROFESSION IN AUSTRIA CONFRONTING THIS CRUCIAL ISSUE? **RAMESH KUMAR BISWAS** INTERVIEWED

THOMAS HERZOG, ARCHITECT, PROFESSOR AND WRITER IN MUNICH

THOMAS PROKSCH, LANDSCAPE DESIGNER IN VIENNA

ERICH RAITH, ARCHITECT OF ECOLOGICAL HOUSING PROJECTS IN VIENNA

BRUNO ERAT, PLANNER OF ECOLOGICAL PROJECTS IN HELSINKI, ULAN BATOR AND BHUTAN, AUTHOR OF SEVERAL BOOKS ON THE ECOLOGICAL HABITAT

RICHARD LEVINE, ARCHITECT AND PROFESSOR IN KENTUCKY

HEIDE DUMREICHER, EDITOR OF THE ECOLOGY JOURNAL 'OIKODROM' IN VIENNA

ROLAND RAINER, ARCHITECT AND FORMER CITY PLANNER FOR VIENNA

HANNES SWOBODA, EXECUTIVE CITY COUNCILLOR FOR PLANNING IN VIENNA

CHRISTOPH CHORHERR, PROPERTY DEVELOPER AND CITY COUNCILLOR IN VIENNA FOR THE GREENS

QUESTION: AN ARCHITECT DESIGNING ECOLOGICALLY ORIENTED BUILDINGS HAS TO CONSIDER SEVERAL ASPECTS: CONSERVATION OF ENERGY, MICROCLIMATE, WASTE MANAGEMENT, ENVIRONMENTALLY COMPATIBLE BUILDING MATERIALS (BAU-BIOLOGIE, TO USE AN ADOPTED GERMAN TERM FREQUENTLY USED IN ENGLISH), RECYCLING, LANDSCAPE AND GREENERY. DUE TO EXTERNAL FACTORS SUCH AS BY-LAWS AND FINANCIAL RESTRICTIONS, NOT ALL OF THESE ASPECTS ARE TAKEN INTO CONSIDERATION IN EACH PROJECT. WHICH OF THESE ASPECTS HAVE BEEN REALIZED SO FAR IN AUSTRIA? WHICH OF THEM HAVE BEEN NEGLECTED? WHICH OF THEM DO YOU CONSIDER DEMAND THE MOST ATTENTION IN THE IMMEDIATE FUTURE?

PROKSCH: The term ecology has become a consumer cliché directed at misleading buyers. There are three possible ways of looking at ecology: as a branch of the biological sciences, as a supra-scientific discipline in its own right, or as a Weltanschauung and political credo. When the latter view dominates, ecology is used by developers, bureaucrats and architects merely to legitimize current developments in the building industry. The solar collector on the roof has to make up for the poor orientation of the building, the pond in the courtyard for its unsuitable location in the landscape. Creepers and wood cladding on the facade suggest biologically compatible materials even if the construction is primarily of synthetic materials. The label becomes more important than the content. Out-of-date by-laws, standards and directives combined with exclusively financial criteria for building give the lie to Austria's self-definition as a model for environment-friendly policies. In my opinion, Scandinavian countries are far more advanced on this count. The danger of treating different aspects of environmentally appropriate building separately from each other is that a housing scheme that simply has better thermal insulation or passive solar energy storage (such as Harry Glück's 'ecohousing') appropriates the prefix 'eco' without deserving it. Helmut Deubner's housing in the Tannengasse in Gänserndorf, despite its positive aspects, suffers from its poor siting. It is so far outside the city that it generates individual motorized traffic, the single most polluting factor. These examples show that planning has to be done in a holistic way.

RAITH: The first generation of ecologically motivated buildings in Austria concentrated on 'alternative' energy use and building biology. Recently, high-density urban settlements that are admittedly energy-saving have been labelled as 'ecological' settlements, though I suspect that it is a disguise for the hard reality of high land prices and speculative development. The most obvious omissions are on the higher level of urban design and regional planning. Mistakes on these levels can rarely be compensated by well designed individual objects.

CHORHERR: Ecologically oriented building in this country has been limited so far to single-family houses focused on baubiologie and low-energy aspects. Even if such houses have a zero consumption of externally supplied energy, they require an expensive water supply and waste removal infrastructure. Worst of all, they waste land and energy on individual motorized traffic for access. An integrated approach is needed to solve all these problems together.

HERZOG: I would like to comment on two recent trends: the conversion of attic spaces into flats and the widespread use of glazed winter gardens or conservatories. The attic was traditionally an 'intermediate temperature space' that served as a thermal buffer zone. Converted roof storeys are selling like hot cakes, not just because of the widespread housing shortage. It is a mixture of a poor, bohemian poet romanticism and a smart penthouse image. I find it problematic and also morphologically wrong to use the attic in the same way as the floors below. However, if this space is indispensible, it must be designed differently. If the topmost level is not used, it can be turned into a green planted area - not with grass, but with other plants that only need a thin growing stratum. The green garden area lost on the ground is thus replaced at the top. This is nothing new: Le Corbusier advocated it a long time ago. With large-scale glass surfaces, which possibly lead to undesirable heat gain, one has to ensure that the heat can escape easily, or is kept out in the first place by means of reflective devices. In winter, problems arise if people want to use their conservatories as extensions of their living-rooms. One should withdraw into the house from a conservatory with single glazing (which I advocate for reasons of cost, function and aesthetic effect - constructional elegance being achieved with slimmer frames) as soon as temperatures sink. Under no circumstances should conservatories be heated. Nevertheless, these spaces are advantageous for the spatial climate of the core building as thermal buffer zones and as sun traps. I am aware that many experts on building performance and representatives of the glass industry do not share my views. The development of new possibilities in construction is an enormous area to be explored further. It has impressed itself on our awareness much more forcibly as a result of the re-evaluation of the energy balance of buildings. It is significant that we now speak of a building as a "skin" that affords more than just protection; it is one that "breathes", that regulates - in the broadest sense of the word - the climatic conditions and atmosphere between interior and exterior. It is a sign that one is beginning to regard this "skin" as analogous to that of a living creature. The need to recognize these analogies and to develop buildings with variable internal-external relationships and adaptable visual and

Traditional courtyard house in Peking
photographed by Roland Rainer

INTERVIEW

thermal qualities is something we suggested long ago.

LEVINE: Isolated measures are not the way to deal with the ecological crisis. Small steps, however realistic and well meant, often necessitate further and more difficult steps as a corrective. Ecological development demands a total view during design and realisation. It includes the use of passive solar energy, growing biological foodstuffs, freedom from cars, compact settlements, public participation and a host of other measures to be taken simultaneously. It is more a process than a fixed result.

QUESTION: IT IS OBVIOUS THAT THE PROBLEMS OF THE BUILT ENVIRONMENT CANNOT BE SOLVED ON THE SCALE OF THE INDIVIDUAL HOUSE BUT HAVE TO BE TACKLED ON THE SCALE OF THE CITY. WHAT CONCEPTS AND POLICIES ARE CRUCIAL FOR SUSTAINABLE URBAN DEVELOPMENT?

RAINER: The beautiful old cities in China and Iran I have visited so often have had a strong influence on my work and my teaching. They are the result of a culture less obsessed with progress than it is concerned with a stable relationship with the natural elements in a holistic world view. If the old centres of European cities like Vienna are really as wonderful to live in as they are reputed to be, why do their inhabitants escape from them every weekend to the green countryside, which they then proceed to destroy with their cars and weekend cottages? Most apartments in Vienna are located in the dense building blocks of the nineteenth century. They were built not to live in but to make money. That is, they were a result of high land prices, unprecedented urban immigration and speculative development. The streets that were built for horse carriages have to cater today to different kinds and speeds of traffic, which they fail to do satisfactorily. Present day urban development is still based on this 'sacred' form of building urban blocks. This is where I differ from the Krier school of thought. After all, this urban form is not much more than a hundred years old. Before that, in the pre-industrial age, urban culture existed in completely different forms - low rise houses with central courtyards, gardens and terraces in amenable surroundings. This type of housing, practically everyone's dream even today, can be achieved with the same average high densities that urban block development or high rise buildings have. I have often proved this in settlements I have built, and it is also the basis of the solar city I have planned near Linz, which is to contain housing designed by Richard Rogers, Renzo Piano and Thomas Herzog. Combined with high speed tramways and park-and-ride interchanges with public transport it is possible to offer urban dwellers a high environmental quality without being cut off from the city. The houses and gardens in my projects in Linz, Vienna and Kassel are all oriented towards the sun, which is impossible in block development. The extension of living spaces into walled gardens provides total privacy and makes it unnecessary for the inhabitants to flee their homes at the weekend, ensuring urban life seven days a week.

SWOBODA: One of the benefits of having a stable population in Vienna in the mid-90s is that we now have the chance to further improve urban design and the ecological aspects of city building. We are concentrating on basic planning premises as well as on actual building. A precondition for an ecological city is a dense and compact building pattern directly along the main public transport routes. Since two thirds of all flats are built in inner-city areas with high densities and good infrastructure, we are concentrating our efforts on environmental improvements in these areas. This improves the quality of life in the older districts, saves on investments in infrastructure and reduces the spread of the city into the surrounding countryside. Green belts around the city are protected from building activity by law, while at the same time small green areas within the city are intensified (the greening of roof surfaces, facades, courtyards and residential streets). Ecological concerns in city planning also embrace the microclimate, the topography, the orientation of individual buildings and city blocks. Above all, the City of Vienna believes in the importance of 'eco-mobility': the provision of extensive public transport and cycle paths, the reduction of car traffic through parking fees in the inner city, the financing of a car-sharing housing area, the establishment of teleworking stations and televillages in the periphery. My vision is that people living and working at home on the periphery would be connected by computer to their city centre offices, which they would only visit sporadically. This would mean a considerable reduction in commuter traffic. To limit the effects of isolation, we are proposing communal teleworking stations within walking distance of each housing settlement, where people could meet, work and still be in close contact with their families.
Besides the practical realization of projects, Vienna also provides space for ecological visions, such as the proposal to build a self-sufficient quarter, the 'city-as-a-hill', in the air space above the tracks of the western railway station.

CHORHERR: Compact high-density settlements are necessary although they are unpopular in Austria, where most people now wish to live in the suburbs or in detached houses in the countryside. The organization of everyday tasks should be based on easy access on foot or bicycle. Garages for cars should not be provided either by developers or by the city council. I, myself, move around in the city on bicycle - I have even got rid of my solar automobile because I found I did not use it. The re-mixing of separated functions and zones will contribute to a complex and compact city. A new symbiosis has to be established between working and living. I represent the Green Party but I am not a Luddite. I am in favour of using the latest technology to improve efficiency as well as the introduction of new models of energy consumption. The energy supplying companies should encourage the use of low energy household appliances instead of doing the opposite. They should also accept and pay a reasonable price for electricity fed into the net by individual users who produce it from the sun, water and wind. I think it is also possible to penetrate and change the present building industry. In my experience many industrialists and developers in the US and even here are far more willing to participate in energy-saving models than is generally believed.

LEVINE/DUMREICHER: What is the minimum activity, the smallest project, that holds the possibility of placing society on a sustainable path? In grappling with this query, we eventually came to reject all orthodox and prevailing environmental approaches and ecological strategies to social sustainability. Our social, historical and urban-architectural studies have always shown that the most appropriate level at which to negotiate sustainability is the scale of the city. Thus we concluded that the city of the future will again become the smallest entity for establishing a balance of all those present-day problems besetting the modern world, and the largest entity at which true ecological and social sustainability can be managed. Our early sustainability models were initially conceived as autonomous villages isolated from larger unsustainable processes. Soon we realized that sustainability for the few in such enclaves would soon be overwhelmed by the growing unsustainability of the larger society. Whereas various current environmental policies and programmes tend to be self-limiting in the sense that they undertake the easiest and least costly steps first while leaving the increasingly more difficult (and therefore more politically painful) steps until later, our strategy in advancing sustainable 'city implantations' is to ask the more important and potentially more productive question: what is the minimum ecological step necessary which would cause successive steps to become easier to accomplish and which would be subject to decreasing political resistance? Behind one of Vienna's main rail terminals lies a 1.5 km by 200 m train yard. The proposal to build a glazed vaulted roof over the terminal is in part in the tradition of many European railway stations except that here the hectares of glazing contain collectors and photovoltaic collectors to provide the 'city implantation's' energy requirements while modulating the climate and light. In our city-as-a-hill model the outer surface of the city contains all of the dwellings and neighbourhoods, the smaller scaled commercial and institutional activities and the network of public buildings and public spaces - that is, the streets, walkways, stairs and squares which give historic medieval towns their life affirming, pedestrian character. Inside the city-as-a-hill, daylit by courtyards and light wells, is a series of concourses and gallerias along which are located the large scale commercial, institutional, and industrial spaces as well as the infrastructure and other activities necessary to support a modern sustainable industrial economy. A network of greenhouses, ponds and a large terraced ecological park contain energy gnomons like a fountain, which is an indicator of the rate at which the 'city implantation' is exporting renewable energy to the larger city of Vienna.

ERAT: I believe that the transformation of existing buildings and cities to make them function better in environmental terms is much more important than the design of isolated new eco-settlements. Older buildings are wasteful of energy and need to be adapted in any case to meet today's needs and standards. The sheer quantity of older buildings in European cities makes it more sensible to concentrate one's efforts in this area rather than on new housing. Work in this area is also labour-intensive and would provide greater employment. People need not be displaced and can enjoy a higher standard where they already live. Urgent measures would include the application of additional insulation on external walls, better windows, the addition of a well-insulated attic which could provide communal spaces on top of housing blocks, the extension of small flats by the addition of a buffer zone of bedrooms on the north facade and of greenhouses on the south facade above streets and public spaces, the redensification of no-man's-land with parks and small community structures that improve the microclimate on the ground.

RAITH: The primary means of improving the environment in cities are the active protection of green areas in the city, the microclimatic improvement of inner-city areas, the encouragement of mixed uses on a small scale that offer a commercial infrastructure accessible on foot or bicycle in order to reduce journeys and traffic, solar considerations in layout planning and building design, the sensitive urbanization of the periphery, and the establishment of self-contained water and waste cycles.

PROKSCH: In order of importance: the reduction and minimization of compulsive mobility, the extension of the public transport system, the reintegration of urban life in all its facets, and the de-zoning of functions such as work and leisure, production and reproduction. It is true that official urban planning in Austria already follows these aims, but it is frustrated by the realities of the free market, builders' interests and other lobbys. Low density dormitory suburbs without any social infrastructure are still being built on green fields. Journeys between home, the work place, shops, schools, social and cultural amenities and leisure areas take longer than ever. This means people are more inclined to use their cars than public transport. One way to limit this in the future would be to make increased use of telecommunications for business and administration, but at the moment very few people live in Cyberspace. Other recent ideas, such as the biological approach to a new dialogue between city and countryside that tend to dissolve the boundaries of the inner city and the periphery, cannot be taken seriously. I do not consider projects naively based on urban ideas of the 20s and 30s, such as the 'city-as-a-hill' project over the western railway station, useful contributions to this debate.

QUESTION: MOST ECOLOGICAL ARCHITECTURE TODAY IS VERY VISIBLY ENVIRONMENT-FRIENDLY: THE POPULIST 'ECO LOOK' WITH WOODEN FRAMES AND AND WINTER GARDENS GALORE HAS AN OBVIOUS ICONOGRAPHY READILY UNDERSTOOD BY THE POPULAR PRESS AND THE PUBLIC. OTHER BUILDINGS, HOWEVER, USE STATE-OF-THE-ART HIGH-TECH SOLUTIONS BASED ON COMPLEX HEATING AND LIGHTING SYSTEMS. THESE BUILDINGS HAVE A SHINY INDUSTRIAL APPEARANCE THAT PEOPLE FIND HARD TO RELATE TO ECOLOGY. WHICH APPROACH APPEALS TO YOU PERSONALLY? DO AESTHETICS PLAY A ROLE IN ECOLOGICAL DESIGN? IS THE CONCEPT OF THE SCIENTIFICALLY AND VISUALLY 'ELEGANT SOLUTION' VALID IN THIS CONTEXT?

RAINER: Just as it is inappropriate for a Tyrolean mountain farmer to wear his alpine hat on the plains, it is inappropriate to build a wooden, sloping roofed, Tyrolean style house in the city, whatever its associations with nature may be. A sloping roof is often used to disguise a lack of design talent and tact. The built version of the Alpine hat has become a camouflage helmet, used to hide blind insensitivity to different landscapes and scales. This fatal misunderstanding has spread like a plague throughout the land.

PROKSCH: The aesthetic content of a building, a landscaped area or an urban space should be directly related to its functional form. If we could eliminate 'eco look' decoration and ornament, it would be possible to invest that money in houses that fulfilled ecological criteria more completely than at present.

CHORHERR: Ecology does not have its own official style or appropriate material. Concrete and glass elements can fulfill their functions just as well as wooden construction. What is important is basic principles of orientation. The rest is a matter of architectural creativity.

Atrium housing township
Puchenau I & II, Linz 1963-95, Roland Rainer

Atrium housing township
Puchenau I, Linz 1963-68, Roland Rainer

Sheltered public paths
Puchenau, Linz 1963-95, Roland Rainer

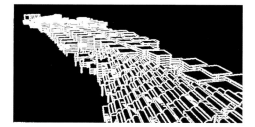

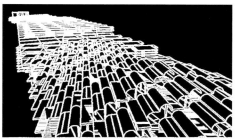

**City-as-a-hill, Project for an ecological urban district using
the air rights over the western railway station**
Vienna 1996, Heide Dumreicher, Richard S. Levine

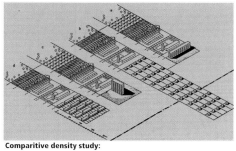

Comparitive density study:
land use by single-family houses, high rise housing and atrium houses
Vienna 1957 , Roland Rainer

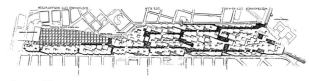

City-as-a-hill
project Vienna 1995, Richard Levine & Heide Dumreicher

Energy water and waste concept
Housing Gänserndorf 1993, Helmut Deubner

RAITH: Aesthetic judgements are related to several factors - only one of them being actual function. Designers of ecological buildings should define their work as a New Functionalism, use the entire repertoire of ideas as a matter of course, apply whatever highest-tech or lowest-tech means are most appropriate to their ends, be sceptical of all eco-symbolism, and leave the debate on style to those who have nothing more substantial to worry about.

HERZOG: New and unfamiliar things always provoke and annoy people. Conventional catagories of judgement are often no longer appropriate. I am not interested in being provocative, but in view of the state of the built environment and its wretched structures of the last few decades, I don't feel obliged to conform. You suggest that I am primarily interested in outward effects or, indeed, in architectural style - an aspect that is quite irrelevant to my work. I hope one can recognize a certain line in the things I do, but I am certainly not interested in a formal style, in the traditional sense of the term. Modernism - the Modern Movement - is not dead. It has become more complex, richer in its aims. The social, technical and artistic utopias of the first third of this century have been extended in the last third and have acquired an additional dimension - the interaction between the design of the material world and the conditions of nature, of the environment, in the broadest sense of the word. My projects and prototypes may appear to be new and often upsetting to many people, but I think that their apppearance has more to do with my basically conservative attitude. My aim is to keep sight of the ideals of the Modern Movement and to translate a brief into appropriate built forms or products, as far as possible with a free mind. Whether the end product then resembles something familiar or a completely new type is another matter. But it is logical that new thematic accents lead to new built forms. People often cannot stand tokens of independence, perhaps even elegance, especially in buildings of this kind that have a good ecological record. Most people prefer different images that represent a contrast to modernism - a semi-rural world of rough-squared timbers and grassed roofs. But I'm just not interested in that sort of thing.

QUESTION: THE BEST INTENTIONS LEAD TO NOTHING IF ENVIRONMENTALLY COMPATIBLE BUILDING IS NOT EASY TO REALIZE AND NOT ATTRACTIVE ENOUGH TO ALL SECTIONS OF BUILDERS, DESIGNERS, CONSUMERS AND BUYERS. HOW DO YOU PROPOSE TO INCREASE PUBLIC ACCEPTANCE AND THE ACTUAL REALIZATION OF SUFFICIENTLY LARGE NUMBERS OF PROJECTS TO MAKE AN IMPACT?

PROKSCH: The most important thing that we should concentrate on in Austria is an up-dating of the relevant by-laws to promote the efficient protection of resources (land, water and energy use). It is important to raise standards generally rather than to point to isolated exceptional projects. The concept of integrated environmental protection is more important than an 'ecological' image. As long as norms, by-laws and planning policies only demand very low standards in the protection of natural resources, ecological concerns will never be high on the list of priorities for profit oriented builders.

SWOBODA: In order to propagate the basic principles of ecological planning and to inform and motivate experts working in this field, the Vienna city council has commissioned a handbook on the subject for urban planners, architects and builders. We also intend to refuse building permission to projects that are not submitted with a detailed energy consumption balance sheet. The building by-laws in Vienna are to be modified by 1997 to encourage the increased use of natural ventilation, solar protection and thermally efficient spaces. In future, offices should receive as much attention as residential buildings do now.

RAITH: The mechanisms of the market should be activated to reward ecologically responsible activity. Laws along lines similar to consumer protection laws should be introduced to punish and fine builders of housing detrimental to the environment. An ecological balance sheet that includes indirect, hidden, and long-term costs should be made for each and every project. These mechanisms would probably only work for small scale projects. On the city scale the problem is more complex. Joint responsibility is a crucial ingredient for the success of ecologically oriented strategies. A pre-condition of this would be greater public involvement in decision-making. Only then would inhabitants feel motivated to participate actively in measures to ensure a better environment. Politicians and planners should also be willing to jettison their hierarchical, bureaucratic, linear and deterministic planning instruments in favour of more open strategies.

CHORHERR: All architectural competitions should have a strong environmental component besides aesthetic and urban design considerations. The administrative authorities need to be trained in the subject just as much as students of architecture and engineering. Building by-laws have to be reformed to include low-energy standards. Prices should be regulated to encourage the use of certain environmental technology. Non-renewable energy use should have its own progressive taxation. Building land should be concentrated on public transport routes and money reallocated from road building to improve real mobility. Publicity should be made for high-quality ecological housing projects - environmentalists should learn to live better, enjoy life and to show it.

ERAT: We should not forget that ecological building is more than a sum of technical and legal details. It requires the full involvement of every person in an effort to establish a sense of belonging, of being part of nature. It brings together the wisdom of many cultures that lived in harmony with the natural world long before the West 'discovered' the environment. We have to try to balance our needs with the demands of health, harmony and spirit - between our physical, biological and spiritual well-being.

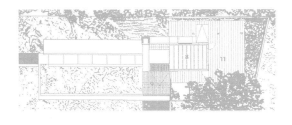

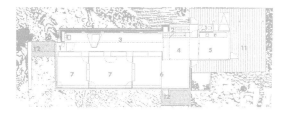

LOW-ENERGY HOUSE
Prototype 'Standard Solar'
Langenschönbichl, Niederösterreich 1990
Architects: Georg Driendl b.1956 Gerhard Steixner b.1953
Engineer: Ernst Illetschko
Technical installations: Franz Magerl
Area: 180 m2
Cost: 2.6 million ATS

THE REDUNDANT REPETITION OF ELECTRICAL AND HEATING PLANT, THE MANY EXPOSED SURFACES, THE EXTENSIVE INFRASTRUCTURE, THE ACCESS BY AUTOMOBILE AND THE INEFFICIENT USE OF LAND MAKES THE DETATCHED SUBURBAN HOUSE ONE OF THE MOST ENERGY-CONSUMING FORMS OF MODERN HABITAT. PREFABRICATED HOUSES INVOLVE AN EVEN GREATER CONSUMPTION OF ENERGY IN PRODUCTION AND TRANSPORT AND ARE RARELY DESIGNED ON ECOLOGICAL PRINCIPLES. GIVEN THE DEMAND, HOWEVER, ARCHITECTS SHOULD TRY TO ADDRESS THE PROBLEM AND MINIMIZE THE NEGATIVE ASPECTS. THIS PROTOTYPE FOR A LOW-ENERGY PREFABRICATED DETATCHED HOUSE IS BASED ON A MODULAR BUILDING SYSTEM WHICH OFFERS GREAT FLEXIBILITY DEPENDING ON SITE AND USERS NEEDS, AS TWO FURTHER BUILDINGS OF THIS TYPE CURRENTLY BEING BUILT SHOW. IT COMBINES THE ADVANTAGES OF MASSIVE CONCRETE AND BASALT STONE WALLS THAT STORE HEAT WITH THOSE OF A LIGHT SKELETAL STEEL OR WOOD STRUCTURE THAT OFFERS MAXIMUM BUILT VOLUME WITH A MINIMUM OF MATERIAL. JUST AS OUR CLOTHES PROVIDE US WITH A SECOND SKIN, A HOUSE SHOULD ACT AS A THIRD SKIN OFFERING SHELTER AND COMFORT. A LARGE DOUBLE-GLAZED SOUTH FACING SOLAR WINDOW COLLECTS PASSIVE SOLAR ENERGY. INSULATED SLIDING PANELS BEHIND THE GLASS CONSISTING OF TWO TRANSLUCENT POLYCARBONATE SHEETS OFFER PRIVACY AND PROTECTION FROM THE COLD AT NIGHT. SOLAR SHADING IS PROVIDED BY EXTERNAL BLINDS AND CANOPIES. THE HEAT IS STORED IN THE CONCRETE AND STONE WALLS INSULATED TOWARDS THE NORTH AND IN THE 70 LITRE WATER TANK UNDER THE FLOOR CONNECTED THROUGH HEAT EXCHANGERS TO THE LOW TEMPERATURE UNIT, MEETING ALMOST THE ENTIRE ENERGY NEEDS. IT WAS DECIDED NEVERTHELESS TO INSTALL AN UNDERFLOOR OIL OR GAS HEATING PLANT FOR EXTREMELY COLD DAYS, EVEN THOUGH THIS REPRESENTED AN INVESTMENT ADDITIONAL TO THE ENERGY-SAVING MEASURES, BECAUSE THE ARCHITECTS CONSIDERED EXISTING PROTOTYPES OF ZERO-ENERGY HOUSES TOO MUCH LIKE MACHINES THAT NEED CONSTANT ATTENTION AND OPERATION TO PERMIT THE FREEDOM AND FLEXIBILITY THAT IS A HALLMARK OF CONTEMPORARY LIVING. THE MATERIALS USED AND THE CLEAR ARTICULATION OF THE JUNCTIONS BETWEEN STEEL, GLASS, WOOD AND STONE COMBINED TO INTEGRATE THE HOUSE WELL INTO THE LANDSCAPE. NO WONDER THAT ARCHITECTS' JURIES HAVE HEAPED AWARDS ON THIS PROJECT, GIVEN THE ALMOST JAPANESE AESTHETICS, COMPLETELY LACKING THE KIND OF NEO-CLASSICAL OR NEO-VERNACULAR FRILLS TYPICAL OF PREFABRICATED HOUSES. IT REMAINS TO BE SEEN WHETHER THE CLICHÉ-RIDDEN TASTE OF THE BUYING PUBLIC WILL ACCEPT IT IN SUFFICIENT NUMBERS TO MAKE IT COMMERCIALLY VIABLE.

HOUSING

A COMPLETE FUNCTIONING SETTLEMENT BASED ON ECOLOGICAL PRINCIPLES IS STILL A RARE EVENT, ESPE-
CIALLY ONE THAT REALLY WORKS. THE AESTHETIC EXPRESSION UNFORTUNATELY PANDERS TO COMMON
CLICHÉS OF HOW ECOLOGICAL ARCHITECTURE SHOULD LOOK, AND THE LACK OF WORK IN THE AREA
MAKES IT A COMMUTER TOWNSHIP WITH LIMITED UTILITY AS A PLANNING MODEL. HOWEVER, THIS HOUSING
SCHEME IN A SMALL TOWN NEAR VIENNA IS A COMMENDABLE BUILT VERSION OF FRITJOF CAPRA'S CON-
CEPT OF HOLISTIC OR SYSTEMIC THINKING. THE MAIN PRINCIPLE THAT HAS BEEN REALIZED IS THE EFFICIENT
AND INTERACTIVE USE OF THE MAIN CIRCULATION SYSTEMS: ENERGY, MATERIALS, AIR, AND WATER. THE PAS-
SIVE USE OF SOLAR ENERGY HAS BEEN ACHIEVED BY SOUTH ORIENTED HOUSES AND CONSERVATORIES, THE
ACTIVE USE THROUGH SOLAR COLLECTORS. HIGH INITIAL INVESTMENT IN THERMAL INSULATION REDUCES
ENERGY COSTS DRASTICALLY. THE LOW-EMISSION GAS HEATING SYSTEM HAS WASTE HEAT-RECOVERY AND
HEAT-EXCHANGE SYSTEMS, JUST AS THE WARM WATER CYCLE DOES. THE USE OF NATURAL MATERIALS FREE
OF CHEMICAL TREATMENT CONTRIBUTES TO THE WELL-BEING OF THE INHABITANTS AND ELIMINATES DAN-
GEROUS WASTES WHEN THE BUILDINGS ARE EVENTUALLY DEMOLISHED. THE USE OF HIGH-TECH HUMUS TOILETS
AND RAIN WATER FOR SECONDARY DOMESTIC PURPOSES REDUCES THE USE OF DRINKING WATER BY 95
PER CENT. A WELL-LANDSCAPED NATURAL SEWAGE TREATMENT PLANT REPLACES EXPENSIVE SEWAGE
CANALS AND RECYCLES ORGANIC WASTE ON SITE WHICH IS THEN USED FOR THE COMMUNAL VEGETABLE
GARDENS. WIND ENERGY IS USED FOR VENTILATION. THE SEPARATION OF VARIOUS KINDS OF GARBAGE
REDUCES THE TOTAL QUANTITY OF NON-RECYCLABLE GARBAGE. THE PROJECT HAS BEEN A LEARNING PROCESS
IN ECOLOGY FOR THE INHABITANTS, ESPECIALLY FOR THE CHILDREN, AND HAS AN EXTREMELY UNUSUAL
ASPECT: THE ARCHITECT ACTUALLY LIVES AND WORKS THERE.

HOUSING

ECOLOGICAL HOUSING
Gänserndorf, Niederösterreich 1990
Architect: Helmut Deubner b. 1950
Engineer: W. Pistulka
Project team: O. Bischof, J. Dobler, E. Kunst, H. Schuller, M. Riegler
Consultants: W. Pokorny, Atelier Dreiseitl, I. Lambert
Area: 3900 m²
Cost: 47 milion ATS

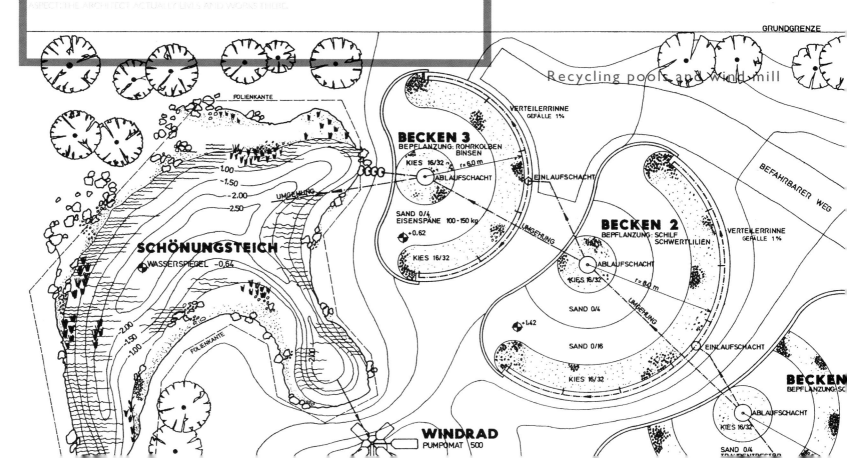

Recycling pools and windmill

DESIGN CENTRE
Linz, Oberösterreich 1993
Architects: Thomas Herzog b.1941, Hanns Jörg Schrade b.1951
Engineers: Sailer+Stepan, Kirsch-Muchitsh
Project team: R. Schneider, A. Schankula, K. Beslmüller, A. Heigl,
O. Mehl, V. Herzog-Loibl, A. Latz, H. Stögmüller
Area: 1600m2 (Hall)
Cost: 885 million ATS

MUNICH-BASED THOMAS HERZOG'S WINNING PROJECT IN AN INTERNATIONAL COMPETITION FOR A CONFERENCE AND EXHIBITION CENTRE IN THE UPPER AUSTRIAN STATE CAPITAL OF LINZ HAD TO ESTABLISH A STRONG SYMBOLIC PRESENCE WHILE SIMULTANEOUSLY KNITTING TOGETHER DISPARATE FUNCTIONS AND ELEMENTS IN ITS IMMEDIATE VICINITY. THE NEW HOTEL BLOCK ALONG THE MAIN ROAD, THE LARGE HARD-LANDSCAPED MULTI-PURPOSE SQUARE FACING THE CITY AND THE ACTUAL VAULTED HALL HOUSING THE CONFERENCE CENTRE, EXHIBITIONS AND TRADE FAIRS, CONCERTS, BANQUETS AND OTHER EVENTS MAKE UP AN ENSEMBLE THAT REDEFINE THE ENTIRE DISTRICT. THE HALL ITSELF WAS INSPIRED BY THE HUGE GLAZED EXHIBITION HALLS OF THE 19TH CENTURY THAT EXISTED IN LONDON (1851-1936), AND MUNICH (1854-1931) AND OTHERS STILL IN USE IN MADRID AND ELSEWHERE. AN IMPROVEMENT ON THE POOR THERMAL PERFORMANCE (OVERHEATING OR HEAT LOSS) OF THESE EARLY EXAMPLES WAS SOUGHT BY DRASTICALLY REDUCING THE HEIGHT OF THE DESIGN CENTRE TO THE MAXIMUM REQUIREMENT OF 12M IN SOME AREAS AND EVEN LESS IN OTHERS, GIVING RISE TO THE SWEEPING, LOW VAULT FORM OF THE ROOF BETWEEN STEEL ARCHES. THE EXPLOITATION OF BRILLIANT NATURAL LIGHT IN THE INTERIOR AND THE INNOVATIVE USE AND CONSERVATION OF ENERGY WAS ACHIEVED BY A SPECIALLY DEVELOPED 'SKIN' CONSISTING OF COATED INSULATING GLASS PANELS AND AN ALUMINIUM RETRO-REFLECTING SCREEN BETWEEN THE TWO GLASS PANES. THE CURVES AND ANGLES OF THE EXTRA FINE ALUMINIUM LOUVRES IN EVERY SINGLE ONE OF THESE SANDWICH PANELS DIFFERED ACCORDING TO ITS POSITION ON THE VAULT AND THE ANGLE OF THE SUN AT VARIOUS TIMES OF THE YEAR, AND WERE CALCULATED WITH A SUPERCOMPUTER. THE 'SKIN' TAKES ON THE FUNCTION OF REGULATING LIGHT AND TEMPERATURE IN ADDITION TO ITS TRADITIONAL PROTECTIVE ROLE, THUS ADDING NEW ASPECTS TO THE CONSTRUCTION, FUNCTION AND AESTHETICS OF BUILDINGS.

DESIGN CENTRE

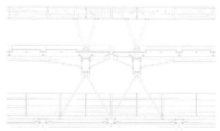

TECHNICAL STRUCTURES   **160**

INTERCHANGE, LANDSCAPE, LIMIT, NAVIGATION   **162**

BRIDGE FELDKIRCH   168

BRIDGE RENEWAL VIENNA   170

CAR SHOWROOM WAIDHOFEN   172

FACTORY LUSTENAU   174

STADIUM ROOFING VIENNA   176

AIRPORT GRAZ   180

Underground Railway U 4
Rossauer Lände, Vienna, Original by Otto Wagner 1894-1900,
Modernization by the Architektengruppe U-Bahn, 1978-1995
Wilhelm Holzbauer, Heinz Marschalek, Georg Ladstätter, Norbert Gantar

The transformation in the nature of technical buildings tends to be ignored even though it reflects important developments in industrial society. Decisions on planning and building are increasingly being rationalised and thus separated from the context of architecture as a whole. Criteria such as the mode of production, transport of materials, computer aided design, management and financial structure determine the way many contemporary industrial buildings are being constructed. The monotonous and unattractive results are being disguised by ludicrous colours and deceptive reflecting surfaces. This is all the more disgraceful when one considers that industrial building once inspired important architectural impulses and striking utopian visions. The most rational of buildings, the factory, with its vigorous mechanical technology, was a role model for the renewal of architecture in the first few decades of this century.

Machinery at the turn of the century had a very real and overwhelming physical presence that could not fail to influence architectural form. Current computerised technology has neither visible nor tangible dimensions, so that technical buildings today are rarely more than a romantic pandering to the market, an impervious abstraction. This no longer has anything to do with architecture, which is fundamentally a comprehensible discipline. The results are uncertain angles and fashionable curves decorated with

THE TECHNICAL IMAGE

Otto Kapfinger

TWO INNOVATIVE INDUSTRIAL BUILDINGS:
A BUILDING BOARD FACTORY AND A PAPER RESEARCH CENTRE

Funder Factory
St. Veit/Glan 1989, Coop Himmelblau (Wolf D. Prix, Helmut Swiczinsky)

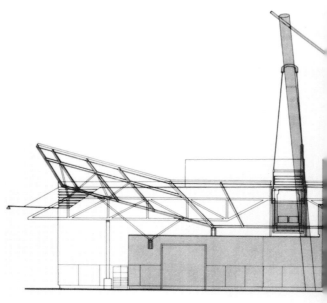

pseudo ornamentation. With a few high-tech exceptions, most construction is becoming coarser. In his time, Otto Wagner systematically and passionately attempted nothing less than a synthesis of building technology and the art of building, the transformation of traditional European culture into a technical civilization. His wafer-thin stairways have been succeeded by thicker and heavier slabs calculated by today's fail-safe engineers. The old wooden windows with slim and elegant profiles have been replaced by clumsy frames without any aesthetic profile. The reasons are manifold: double-leaf windows have been substituted by single frames with double or triple glazing to keep out the increased traffic noise; the larger the window panes the thicker they are; the unwieldy frames are less labour intensive as regards production and maintenance. On top of this, all the years of material surplus have made us wasteful. Aesthetics and common sense have little influence on the imperatives of technology, which has its own dynamics and its own rationale.

These are developments that have nothing to do with taste, either good or bad, but have a lot to do with the distortion of the relationship between man and his environment, between production and function. It is a perversion of the goals of technical thought, rendering them banal and materialistic. This state of affairs is obviously one part of the larger crisis of late industrial society.

KNP-Leykam Research and Development Centre
Gratkorn 1991, Klaus Kada

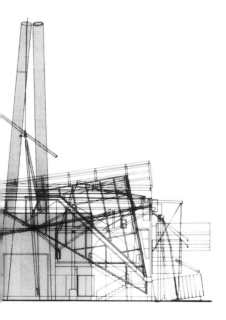

It is a fact that over the last decade the architectural project has often taken refuge in the heritage of the history of architecture, in the familiar urbanity of the city, and in the wretched everyday nature of the anonymous, in order to recover its lost certainties, to justify its failing vigour. And yet the work of some architects has succeded in undermining the conventional relationship between project and building. Work on the limits of the project, and that which often goes beyond them, seems to concern something that is not architecture but the architectural, in the sense that it transcends the constructed. It is no accident that the title of the forthcoming Biennale of Architecture in Venice in 1996, whose director is the Austrian architect Hans Hollein, is titled "Sconfinamenti e trasgressioni", manifesting a clear intention to investigate the overcoming of traditional borders. Of course this does not mean that architecture has suddenly ceased to offer roof and shelter. But sufficiency of construction is no longer an end in itself, and no longer constitutes the sole access to truth.

Kostas Axelos touches on the philosophical dimension of this condition when he asserts that "the experience of the poetry of the world can provide a response, from close up as well as from a distance, to the universal technicity. Of the two faces of Janus, one would find expression in the visible, while the other would attempt to penetrate the invisible. But what is the relationship between the poetic, whose element is metamorphosis, and the forms of daily life?"[1] Here is the crux. The visible and invisible aspects of which reality and of which interpretation of it? Phenomenological, structuralist, ontological, or deconstructivist? The ordinariness of the present day or that of age-old values? Accumulated tradition or the civilisation of the media? Tectonic insistence or technological challenge? Architects in Central Europe operate today on this basis through their work. Some demand the return of a lost paradise, others respond to the requirements of consumerism, while yet others seriously investigate these aspects. Ole Bouman and Roemer Van Toorn propose, in a similar way, a trifold taxonomy[2] —"three architectural strategies of resistence to mediocrity"— which bears a certain ressemblance to this: Archaism,

Facadism/Fascinism, Reflexivity: "they localise a view of reality that is shaped willy-nilly by the split, accelerated, artificial lifestyle of today", regardless of the 'heimliche' quality of a certain authenticity or the 'unheimiliche' quality as that evoked by technology and the virtualisation of society that the first two wish to pertain, or even the implicitly critical — politicised — aesthetic of the last one. It is more than interesting that among the architects included as exemplary references within these three strategies there is only one Austrian, namely Hans Hollein. In each case architecture conceptually redefines its relationship not only with technique and construction, but also with its physical and cultural context.

'POST-URBANISM'

For some time now the notion of the 'landscape' has retained a centrality, due to the ecological awareness and the restructuring processes of our post-industrial societies.[3] The 'periphery', 'zones of disturbance', 'intersticial spaces', the surrounding 'urban voids', the 'obsolete areas' — these are the sites on which the efforts of the municipalities and other responsible agencies are being increasingly concentred, and where some developers and construction companies are committed to innovative and bold design programmes. They stem from social needs for the improvement of the urban landscape and are based on concepts of feasibility and effectiveness. The existing city, according to the views of financial experts, is accumulating new urban activities in the sectors of commerce, the service industry and the tourism/leisure sector, which create a demand for new technical buildings and workplaces, together with certain types of housing in areas which have been classed as 'derelict' or 'abandoned'. These areas are usually located between the historic centre and the modern periphery. At the same time the diffusion of the city in its surrounding territory makes evident that it is no longer merely an image of culture but also a network of infrastructures. This would appear to be the main line of thought which has developed around coping with the crisis of the cities — a line of thinking which is founded on a re-assessment of the existing city, with a design strategy based on transformation and not on its constant

INTERCHANGE, LANDSCAPE, LIMIT, NAVIGATION

YORGOS SIMEOFORIDIS

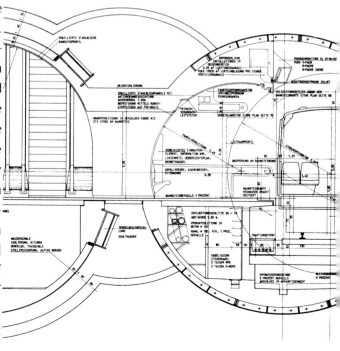

expansion. A typical case of this situation in Vienna has been the competition for the Vienna Museum Quarter, a collection of various museums to be built on the site of the 'Messepalast', converted court stables built in the Baroque period. The Vienna Architecture Seminar, an annual studio/ workshop with eminent tutors, has been focusing consistently on these areas during the last few years. At the same time, the EUROPAN competition sessions —through which a new generation of Austrian architects has had the chance to emerge— brought to our attention the existence of such sites and the transformations they undergo.

Describing 'post-urbanism', Anthony Vidler describes a culture "where suburb, strip, and urban center have merged indistinguishably into a series of states of mind". The human body moves "surprised but not shocked (this will be the difference with the modern metropolis) by the continuous repetition of the same, the continuous movement across already vanished thresholds that leave only traces of their former status as places".[4] Yet this is the critical turning point. One cannot deny — however much of a critical distance one may wish to maintain — that the concept of the urban periphery and the design of urban structures is subject to acceleration and displacement. For Arie Graafland, peripheral sites are perceived from rapid means of transport, while in connection with the centre the configurations of the intersection and the junction emerge as equally important. It is precisely in these places that a cinematographic effect appears in design which is governed by the relationships of observation and perception between reality and the observer (others, like Richard Ingersoll, describe this as 'jumpcut urbanism'). Related to this, following Paul Virilio and the gimmickry of virtual reality, is the phenomenon of the picnolepsy which is typical of our rapid displacements through the urban landscape, displacements in which the reality observed leaves no trace in the memory, thus causing a loss of perceptible points of reference and the disappearence of visual signs, despite the futile claims made by the advocates of 'Post-Modernism'. This seems to be a sina qua non condition of the contemporary environment, yet one that fully deserves fresh attention.

There can be no doubt that many contemporary projects seem to have liberated themselves from conservative perseverance and from the guarantee offered by the 'opening to history', and to be advancing in a more conceptual and expressive direction. Austrian architects appear to be more in search of the possible ways in which design gestures could manifest themselves in the amorphous structure of the modern city rather than in some metaphysical truth in the crystallised historical centres of those cities. The peripheral location, the special, open and natural character of these places — regardless of their scale — should not be neglected. "We shall have to find new methods in order to study the models that reflect the typical movements of these places in order to understand their properties, and finally we shall have to understand the innate abstraction of such places, the undifferentiated and non-symbolic styles towards which peripheral architecture tends, in which images disappear", suggests Marcel Meili.[5]

This is where the problem lies. The earlier generation of architects, politicians and managers is extremely reserved - not to say critical - towards these moves, which are often accompanied by impulsive spontaneity. In many respects they seem to be right, since tendencies in the second half of this century which waged war on the traditional concept of 'urban design' seemed to be motivated by aesthetic or pragmatic considerations and to lack a structural view of the problems. At this point Vidler is correct in arguing that "now a sceptical fin-de-siècle has invented the category of 'dirty realism' to domesticate what cannot be idealized: the margins, the wastelands, and the zones of ruined technotopias are celebrated in film, science fiction and now in deconstructivist architecture that emulates the rusting detritus it sees as its context".[6]

The processes of restructuring these areas relate to the new need for the definition of public/open spaces. For many, it is the empty space that gives form to the city, "the place where the city is seen and used". It is obvious to some that architecture has to assume the task of filling these 'voids', these 'empty spaces'. Nevertheless, this is not a task shared by many. The urge to do something, to fill these voids with architecture, and the need to do nothing — this is ultimately the paradox of our 'uncanny' metropolitan condition, a paradox displaced in the specificity of the

Underground mass transit railway U 1
Vienna 1973-78 , Architektengruppe U-Bahn
Wilhelm Holzbauer, Heinz Marschalek, Georg Ladstätter, Norbert Gantar

project, in the ideas which are implemented in it, each time.[7]

THE 'LOGIC OF THE LIMIT'

In those circumstances, the crucial question is how we are to approach the work of contemporary architects without resorting to useless stylistic categories or rhetorical constructs which reveal bewilderment rather than anything else. It is our undoubted duty to have an interpretative approach to contemporary architecture which involves a correlation to a shifting social and cultural setting.

The critic Ignasi de Solà Morales sets out from the absence of a clear system of values accorded collective acceptance as the foundation for practical activities such as artistic and architectural production. In a very interesting text on contemporary architecture that also applies to the Austrian situation, he distinguishes two types of architectural experience which are taken as personal answers to the crisis of values in contemporary architecture, an architecture that wavers in a 'state of weakness' between the architecture of identity and difference (the subjective refounding of architecture through references to its historical structures) and the architecture of the logic of the limit (a new system of foundations based on the elementary data of experience).[8]

The first of these two attitudes—which is in conscious opposition to the sentimental commercialism or reactionary historicism of post-modern architecture — is typical of the projects and work of those who have confined themselves to analysis of the place, personal memory and incidental allusions of an exclusively autobiographical nature: those who are in search of the simulacrum of a trace from which to start and to which they apply a process of differentiation so as to ultimately arrive at the rejection of the original over the remembrance of its image (architects such as Rossi, Graves, Moneo or Botta). The second approach is typical of the projects and work of those who —at some risk— approximate to a zero degree of architecture, those who insist upon the strict materiality of volumes and of building materials, incorporating into them a vibration, some slight gesture, an almost casual distortion, the fracture of some geometry, illustrated by the work of architects such as Krischanitz, Driendl & Steixner, Artec and Riegler & Riewe.

According to Morales, these two experiences correspond to the distinction between arte povera (which reworks an iconography already in existence, and especially that which stems from a knowledge of history and the accumulated experience of memory) and minimal art (which sets out from rudimentary kinaesthetic experiences such as geometry, colour and space). In effect, we could call the two experiences 'back to basics' and 'back to the limit', the central difference between them being the referential nature of the former and the self-referentiality of the latter.

Solà Morales clearly accepts the significant impact of contemporary art on architecture — natural in a period which has rightly been described as the age of the museum — in an allusion to the cultural diffusion of the artistic discourse into numerous other practices. Other critics such as Kenneth Frampton, have seen precisely the same phenomenon as the decline of contemporary architecture, which has been swept far away from its etymological roots (craftsmanship, tectonics, techne) and, consequently, from its inescapable incorporation into technical, economic and social evolution. Is it possible, then, to use this interpretative pattern to approach and describe the work of

Underground mass transit railway U 1
Stephansplatz, Vienna 1973-78 , Architektengruppe U-Bahn
Wilhelm Holzbauer, Heinz Marschalek, Georg Ladstätter, Norbert Gantar

contemporary Austrian architects? And if there is any such connection, can it be proved by specific projects, or do we need to look at the work of the architects in question as a whole? If I had to provide a quick answer, it would be that such patterns are extremely useful — even as provocative stimulus — in understanding contemporary architecture, especially in countries like Austria, where the impact of artistic discourse has always been determinant — though often disputed — for architectural practice. As a result, such an interpretative pattern could serve as one of the tools for an initial excavation of the landscape in which the younger generation of Austrian architects specifically has made its appearance: a landscape of isolated movements, not one of collective endeavours. Needless to say, the same pattern might be used for analysing other situations.

Hans Hollein, then commissioner of the 5th Venice Biennale in 1991, claimed that the panorama of Austrian architecture is marked by a complexity of positions, manifested not in groups, movements and schools but in personal, individual statements which have an impact on international developments in a situation of fertile fantasy. That is how one should see the work of Abraham, Coop Himmelbau, Czech, Domenig, Holzbauer, Krier, Krischanitz, Peichl, Prohazka, or Richter. Perhaps this hypothesis still holds good, However, I have the impression that continuing to the younger generation, there seems to be a shift towards an 'architecture of the limit', always conditioned from the particular tradition of the Austrian 'edge', seen in the work of Kada, Riegler & Riewe, Zechner & Zechner, PAUHOF, and others ...

What I am trying to suggest can be found in two statements, fragments from two interviews given by Riegler+Riewe and PAUHOF respectively, where a productive — undoubtely paradoxical — tension exists: "We don't design 'built images'. We arrange structures, open and yet precise, frames for the complex flow of the images of use..."[9]

"Le Corbusier speaks of the play of masses brought together in light: we dare to add to this the play of voids and in-between spaces, with a stratification that alienates, and an abstraction that leaves a great deal open..."[10]

The specific cultural tradition of Vienna still reproduces the basic pattern — integrated, synthetic and universalistic — which feeds on contradiction, permanent opposition, on a scepticism about integrated and unified systems, according to Friedrich Achleitner.[11] Nevertheless, two points should be stressed here: firstly, that "although the architectural culture of Austria may seem compact from afar..., a closer look..., however, reveals that the architectural 'continent Austria' is divided into several characteristic landscapes",[12] and secondly, that in the previous statements by the architects, we should be able to perceive an implicit critique of the discourses referring to specific cultural frameworks. Confronting each other like two boxers we had, in the mid-Eighties, the "decorative Expressionism" of the "Grazer Schule", and the "formalistic, elitist and historically charged" architectural discourse of the Vienna climate. A critique which tries to redefine a new — or a different — approach to reality.

Hydroelectric plant
Salzburg 1989, Max Rieder

In this setting, in fact, the discourse on architecture (and criticism in particular) presents itself as a strategic exploration of traces and signs, as navigation through a context that seems to be continually receding from view. It drifts among the terrae incognitae of contemporary architecture. So it is no accident that the new generations of architects of the nineties, who have not been obliged to liberate themselves from the so-called "prohibitions of modernism", have tackled the problem of technique in a different way, that they have shown more interest in the peripheries of the contemporary city than in historical centres, that they have devoted their attention to abandoned areas, or that they have displayed a 'familiarity' with the architecture of the thirties, the fifties and sixties, with positions such as 'rationalism', 'high-tech', 'brutalism' or the famous 'new minimalism'. So can we speak of a new situation, of new conditions for the architectural project? Can we carry on with the nostalgic visions of a past that is now totally lost, or should we be dealing with the surrounding artificial and cultural landscape as it is being formed? What will be the use and the role of architecture within current urban transformations, within the undergoing turmoil and competition among cities? To what extent can the architectural project be made to embrace the changes that are already under way in what are now such decisive sectors and concepts as those of tourism, time, speed and so forth? Are we seeing a return to the constituent materials of architecture, and a validation of its tradition of construction (from which it is in any case difficult to escape), as well as a redefinition of more 'subterranean' traditions, such as that of facing, or an attitude of laissez-faire towards the new synthetic materials? Are we capable of understanding differently,

Motorcycle Showroom Project
Vienna 1993, Helmut Richter

Mass transit railway U 1
Alte Donau, Vienna 1978-82 , Architektengruppe U-Bahn
Wilhelm Holzbauer, Heinz Marschalek, Georg Ladstätter, Norbert Gantar

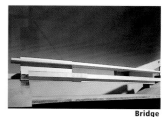

Bridge
Murau 1995, Marcel Meili / Jürgen Consett

Bank, wall sculpture
Vienna 1993, Günther Domenig

Supermarket
Deutsch Wagram 1994 , The Office

Austrian Railways
Station renewal scheme, Competition entry
1st prize, being realized.
Corporate Design Group Zechner+Zechner

at least touching on in extremis, or foreseeing 'domesticity', 'urbanity' in the new programmes that are already emerging around us?

However this may be, a revision of the traditional role of the architect is a prerequisite for all this. Perhaps we are now once and for all locked in the embrace of 'weak thought' despite the belligerent manifestations of the 'new order' or the the religious anxiety for the 'safe past', yet the conventions of rhetoric, persuasion and negotiation define a new statutory form for the architectural and urban project in terms of the cultural traditions of the communities to which they refer. In the end, those conventions set the boundaries for the assessments of the juries in large-scale architectural and urban competitions and determine relations with the client. Such conventions are evident now more than at any other time in history, precisely because they function as bonds for a shared culture for the development and management of a city which will, nevertheless, be absent.

Undoubtedly, negotiation, consent, and a new social contract are prerequisites and binding conditions for each new intervention. The differences are suggested in the formulation of the future image, in the collective visions which the cities themselves produce separately, based on their own distinctive features, an issue which does not concern individuals but social structures, within the framework of which the concepts of mediation and of engagement (of the agencies involved, of the political parties, of intellectuals) play a decisive role. The ultimate question is if and how far such a commitment of a moral and political order is feasible in this transitional age (for many, a period of crisis for established social and other structures), with direct implications for the co-existence of a collective vision as well as for trivial practice.

Ice rink
Vienna 1995, Sepp Müller/ Alfred Berger/ Werner Krismer

Earth relay station
Aflenz 1978 , Gustav Peichl

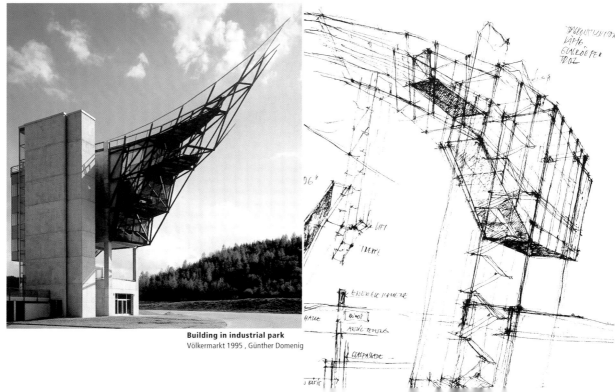

Building in industrial park
Völkermarkt 1995 , Günther Domenig

BRIDGE

BRIDGE ON THE RIVER ILL
Feldkirch, Vorarlberg 1989
Architect: Martin Häusle, b. 1953
Engineers: Klaus Bollinger, Manfred Grohmann
Project Team: J. Assmuss, R. Diem, M. Maier
Cost: 3 Million ATS

INNOVATIVE BRIDGE BUILDING HAS BEEN A TRADITIONAL STRENGTH OF ENGINEERS IN SWITZERLAND AND THE NEIGHBOURING WESTERN REGIONS OF AUSTRIA. THIS 36M LONG AND 3.5M WIDE STEEL BRIDGE FOR PEDESTRIANS AND CYCLISTS HAS AN ELEGANCE THAT HARKS BACK TO EARLY ENGINEERING WORKS, LONG BEFORE BYE-LAWS AND UNIMAGINATIVE ENGINEERS BEGAN TO PRODUCE OVERDIMENSIONED, 'SAFE' OBJECTS. THE UNIQUE CONSTRUCTION IS THE RESULT OF TEAM WORK — BOTH THE ARCHITECT AND THE ENGINEER SAY THEY COULD NOT HAVE DESIGNED THE BRIDGE WITHOUT THE OTHER. THE INCREDIBLE VISUAL LIGHTNESS IS DUE THE WALKING SURFACE BEING DESIGNED TO WORK SIMULTANEOUSLY AS THE UPPER MEMBER OF A TRUSS, THE FLOOR BEING A SINGLE 10MM THICK STEEL PLATE STIFFENED WITH A 100MM DEEP GRID OF STEEL STRIPS WELDED TO THE UPPER PLATE. DIAGONAL WELDED STEEL TUBES WITH A DIAMETER OF 60MM CONNECT THE UPPER PLATE TO THE SINGLE 140MM SOLID STEEL ROD THAT SPANS THE ENTIRE LENGTH. THE DOUBLE FUNCTION OF EACH OF THE ELEMENTS IS REFLECTED IN THE NON-SLIP SURFACE OF THE FOOTPLATE, WHICH ALSO ACTS AS A NON-CORROSIVE COATING. LIGHTING IS INTEGRATED IN THE SLIM HAND RAIL, CONVERTING THE BRIDGE INTO A BEAUTIFUL ILLUMINATED OBJECT IN THE DARK.

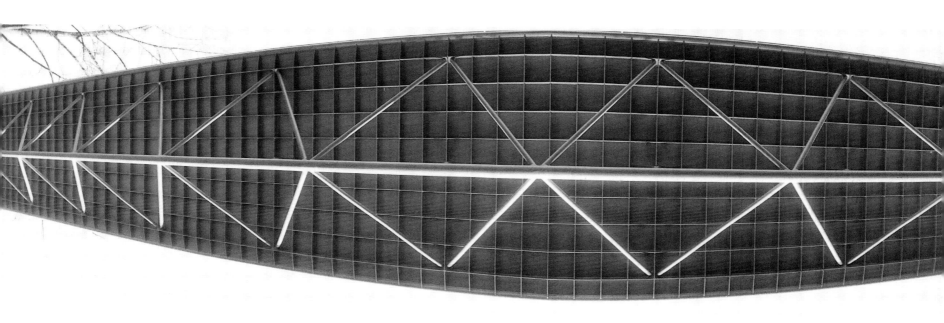

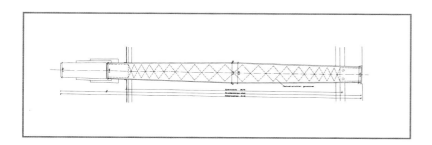

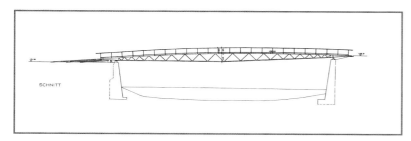

BRIDGE RENEWAL
Hackinger Steg, Vienna XIII 1994
Engineer: Wolfdietrich Ziesel b. 1934
Architects: Dieter Henke b. 1952
Marta Schreieck b. 1954
Project team: I.Brottrager, M.Koller
Area: 741 m^2
Cost: 28 million ATS

BRIDGE RENEWAL

The prominent place that this pedestrian bridge occupies
on the western entrance to the city, connecting one of
Otto Wagner's railway stations to residential areas
across the river Wien, demanded not merely a technically
adequate construction but also a prime quality urban
design solution. An existing monolithic bridge built in
the 60s, with poor functional and visual relationships
to its surroundings, was improved by the superimposition
of a structurally independent glass wall and roof.
Pedestrians are thus protected from the weather and the
noise of the autobahn that passes below it, which even
encourages them to pause and chat when they meet in this
unlikely place. Access was improved by better stairs,
ramps and a lift which form a filigree vertical counter-
part to the prismatic forms over the horizontal bridge.
The buoyant construction of maintenance-free, welded,
shining stainless-steel tubes and the unequal rhythm of
the glass elements raise the quality of the structure
above that of the utilitarian building it is.

CAR SHOWROOM
Waidhofen/Ybbs, Niederösterreich, 1992
Architect: Boris Podrecca b.1940
Engineers: Gerhard Wagner, Helmuth Locher
Area: 2723 m²
Cost: 35 million ATS

CAR SHOWROOM

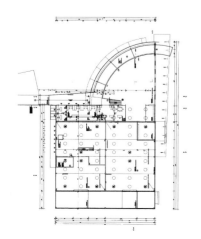 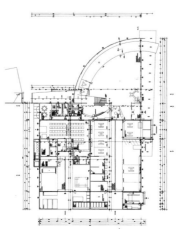 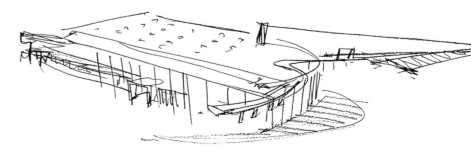

The car showroom is not a building type that receives the attention of architects, in spite of its ubiquity. Due to its relationship to the archetypal product of mass production, the automobile, it is usually a mass-produced industrial shed, although it rarely is the type of assembly-line product that Le Corbusier hoped for. This particular exception on the highway close to Vienna, although technical in nature, is asymmetrical, made to order and tailored to site, expressing the difference between a car that posses only mobility without physical context, and a building that is the opposite, between the car as an endlessly repeated article and the building as singular act. The association of images is, however, of utmost importance to both. In this light, it was interesting that Philippe Starck's recent exhibition was held in this space, in the midst of cars. The central wall acts as a kind of backbone which passes through the showroom and defines the open to sky space where the latest model is displayed. Whereas the workshops lurk unassumingly in the background, the rounded glass showroom faces the highway junction, and an open loggia-like form faces the city. The showroom is also used as a light and airy bar for technology fans; not cosy, but dominated by steel and glass. This buildings members are layered like scales, not unlike a Mikado game, and create a fragile envelope around the icon of our age - the car.

FACTORY

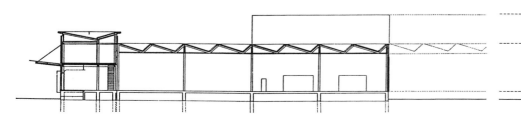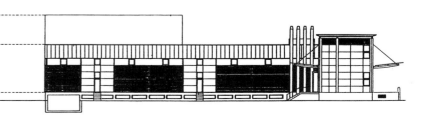

The clash between the breathtaking Austrian landscape and inevitable industrial buildings has been unsuccessfully disguised by populist pseudo-vernacular masks on factories, that are meant to make them fit in'. That an honest attempt to clearly define and differentiate between the specific complexities of the natural and the industrial world is more rewarding is proved by this project, a factory for heating systems. Inappropriate Mannerism, the use of unthinking off-the-rail systems or of the wrong scale in industrial buildings make other factories more out-of-place than this precise, polished, beautifully detailed, transparent structure that encourages a dialogue with nature. This is strengthened by the intelligent use of the site with 'green bridges' between the buildings that permit flora and fauna to coexist in a continuum. The skill with which young architects in Vorarlberg have worked with wood has been translated, seemingly effortlessly, into steel and glass. Working in the factory or its offices, one is in constant contact with the greenery and light of the outside world through the graded transparence of its exterior panels. The industrial materials glow in their natural colours and sheen and are joined in a refined manner, illustrating once again the very specifically Austrian use of high-tech as almost hand-made object art.

FACTORY, Lustenau, Vorarlberg 1990 (1st phase), Architect: Erich Steinmayer b. 1946, Engineer: Paul Frick, Project team: R. Dünser, N. Schobel, Area: 6200 m2, Cost: 109 million ATS

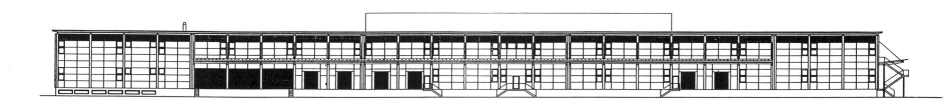

STADIUM ROOFING

Prater, Vienna 1986

Designers / Planners: Erich Frantl b. 1941,

Peter Hofstätter b. 1940

Engineers: Willibald Zemler b.1937,

Albert Raunicher b. 1944

Project team: R. Sturmberger (architect), H.Pircher,

W.Ploberger, P.Klement, K.Kratzer (specialist consultants)

Area: 32000 m² roof area

Cost: 140 million ATS

STADIUM

Of two proposals made to roof this 1920s stadium for 63000 spectators (the first being a complete roofing) the second, a partial roofing proposal, was chosen due to its innovative and economical construction which did not necessitate the strengthening of the existing stadium. The ingenious structure designed especially for this purpose did not have any supporting columns to interrupt the spectators view, thus seeming to float above the stands. The 48m wide suspended braced roof over the 270 x 215m oval stadium makes it one of the largest free span roofs in the world. The lambda-shaped steel columns on the axes of the existing columns carry the entire, purely vertical loads of the elliptical space frame consisting of a bowl-shaped network of steel rods and a unique multi-stabilized suspension frame. A free-floating, 460m long oval tensile inner steel ring at a height of 23m and a 760m long outer compressive steel ring at a height of 40m are connected by tubes tight-fitted into patented multifaceted steel nodes that were then injected with quick-setting concrete to make them resistant to tensile, compressive and bending forces as well as to protect the end of the rods from corrosion, permitting the entire erection of the roof from four mobile cranes without any scaffolding. The roofing plates are mounted on this network between the two rings and drained mechanically. The entire prefabricated production of steel members up to 34m in length and the assembly on site was carried out in a record period of 9 months, in spite of the development of several completely new solutions and inventions.

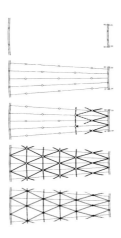

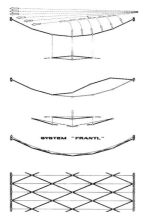

SYSTEM "FRANTL"

construction stages

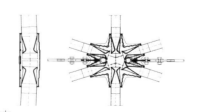

node

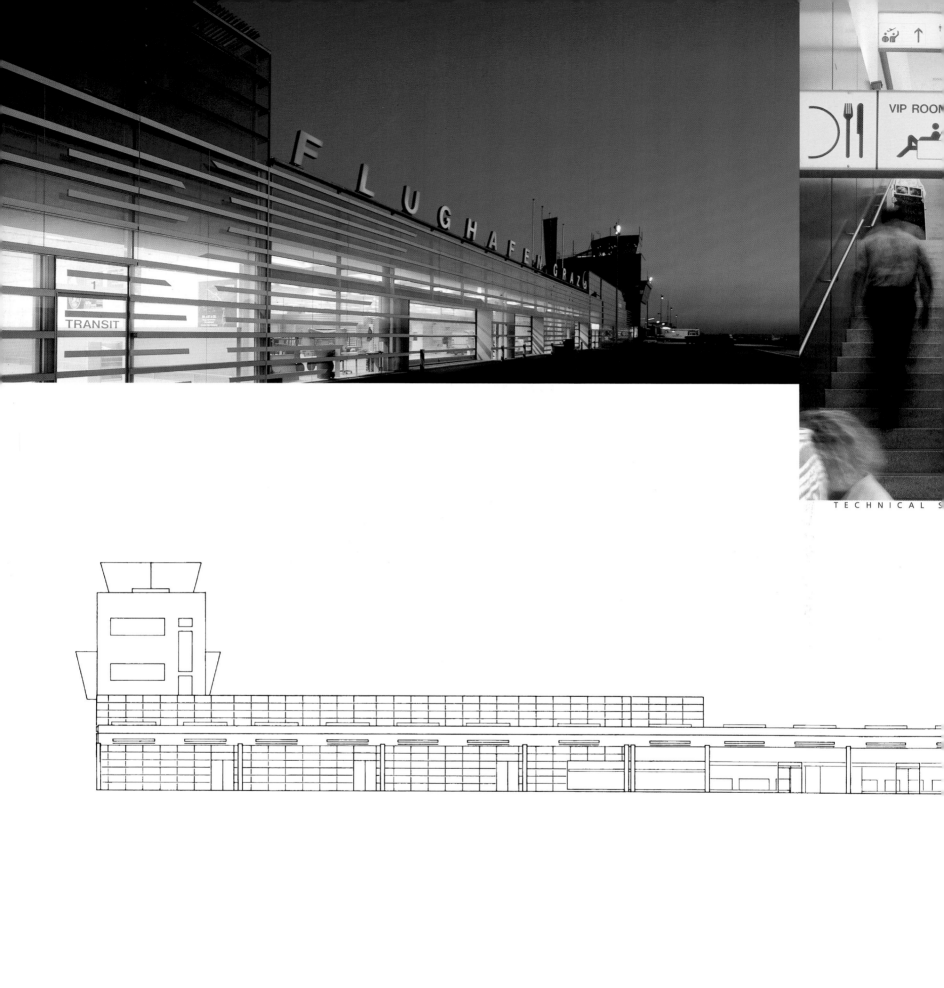

TRANSIT

FLUGHAFEN GRAZ

VIP ROOM

TECHNICAL S

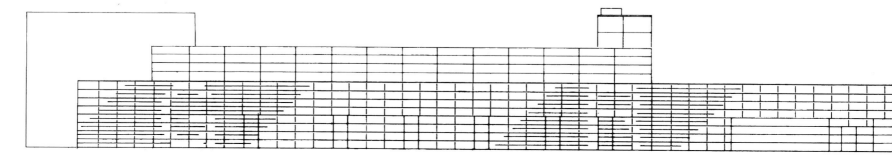

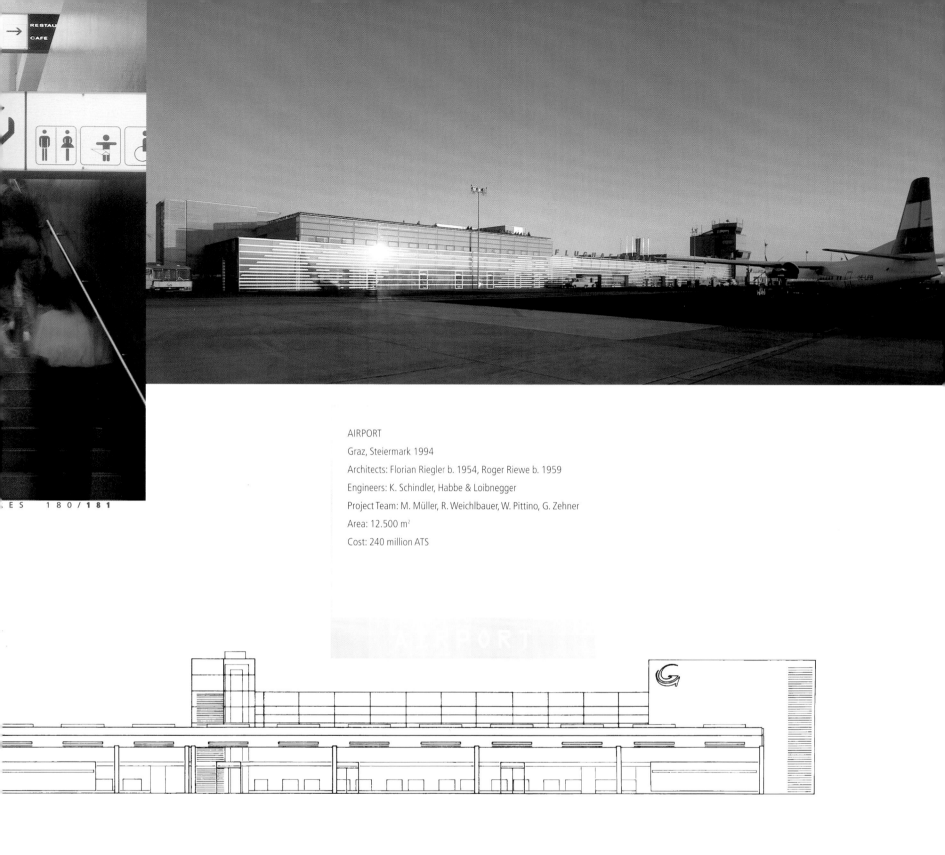

AIRPORT

Graz, Steiermark 1994

Architects: Florian Riegler b. 1954, Roger Riewe b. 1959

Engineers: K. Schindler, Habbe & Loibnegger

Project Team: M. Müller, R. Weichlbauer, W. Pittino, G. Zehner

Area: 12.500 m²

Cost: 240 million ATS

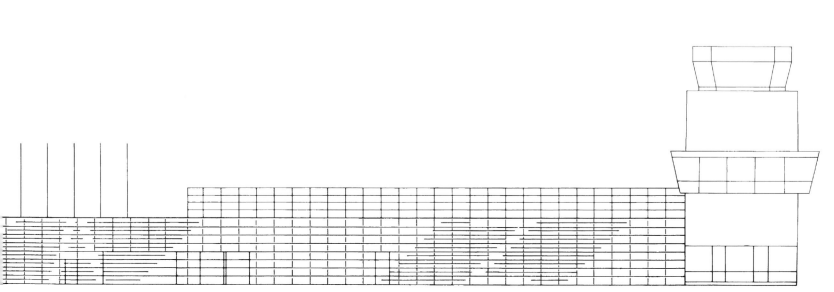

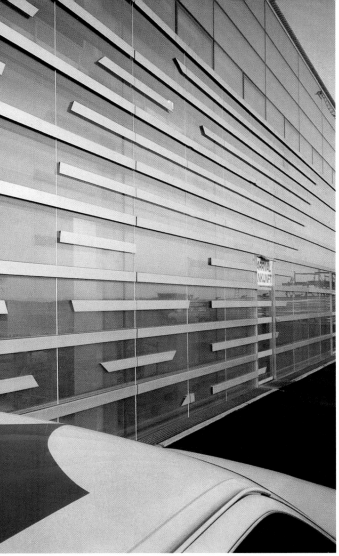

The metaphor of flight is seductive - airports which symbolize wings or flight are common, some of them breathtaking. This design for a small provincial airport with very few daily flights, on the contrary, surprises and refreshes with its restrained refinement - especially as the city it serves is so full of Expressionist members of the so-called 'Graz School' of architecture. A 30 percent expansion together with a reorganization of the existing airport has increased its capacity by a hundred percent. Visually it connects the speed of land travel to that of air travel through its transparency and clarity, thus harking back to early days when the passenger directly experienced the transition to and the excitement of travelling by air. Today complex security and other requirements have made travel all over a channelling of herds from one tube to another. The materials used here (steel, glass and aluminium) are common enough but achieve their high quality in the perfect minimalism of detail and atmosphere. The spartan simplicity of the airy glazed volumes that may be described as a kind of raw technical brutalism is wholly appropriate and yet not without its tactile pleasures. The architects have been able to house all the diverse functions (with the unfortunate exception of the shops and the cafe) without giving in to a visual or organisational chaos. The only thing that this airport obviously lacks is aeroplanes.

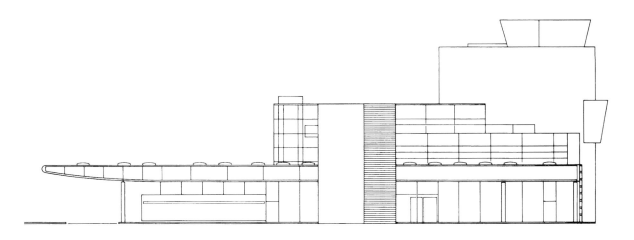

WORKPLACES

WORK, EAT, BUY   188

OFFICE BUILDING SALZBURG   190

Building department office
Competition project, 1st prize, Graz 1989
ARTEC – Bettina Götz, Richard Manahl

In an economy heavily dependent on work performance and consumption, it is striking how little attention is paid to the design of congenial workspaces. This may be true of most systems based on profit maximization and old-fashioned management styles. Innovation is surprisingly rare in the planning of office buildings, banks, laboratories, workshops, factories, hospitals and other places where people spend half their waking life. The strict labour regulations on workplaces are followed, but seldom is any more thought given to the subject. Where there is a noticeable design input it is mostly restricted to how the building fits into the urban context, and, of course, to visual details both in the interior and on the exterior. These few commercial buildings or offices are briefly documented here. Aspects such as natural lighting, heating or cooling, direct access to green areas, novel furnishings, facilities for social interaction between office workers and visitors or passers-by, individually adaptable workplaces, supporting infrastructure and recreational facilities are sparse, emphasising the unfortunate artificial division between private life and work life. However, the realization is slowly seeping into the minds of the bosses that high-quality flexible workplaces improve employee satisfaction and, consequently, productivity. It is to be hoped that this, together with the intel-

WORK, EAT AND BUY

Ramesh Kumar Biswas

**Architects' own office
in renovated former utilities building**
Vienna1990, Heinz Neumann

Commercial mixed-use building
(middle&below)
Graz 1990, Adolf Krischanitz

Kaufmann timber factory
Reutte 1994, Hermann Kaufmann

ligent use of changes in the patterns of work being brought about by information technology, will result in more interesting workplaces.

Commercial buildings in Austria are also not very exciting compared to the grand atrium shopping centres in Asia. This has not prevented some shopping malls from making their appearance on the periphery. But they are curious, faceless buildings that seem to present illusions of another world, and which apparently have a clientele sufficient to keep them profitable.

The fact that there are no grandiose shopping centres in Austria has its positive side - after all, many of those traffic-free enclaves in big Asian cities are a reflection of the lack of useable public space that is not walled-in or overrun by traffic. Vienna still has streets that are habitable, offering a dense infrastructure of small shops, markets and services. This is doubtless one of the most pleasant qualities of the city, one that the population obviously appreciates and wishes to retain. Another reason for this dearth of shopping malls is that Vienna's lively cultural life and restaurant scene ensures that consumption is not restricted to buying. This also explains the fact that the importance to Vienna of theatres and museums is relatively greater than that of shopping centres.

Bank
Favoriten, Vienna 1979, Günther Domenig

Bank interior
Favoriten, Vienna 1979, Günther Domenig

Architects own office 'Hobbyraum'
Vienna VI 1995, Steixner • Driendl

Kaufmann timber factory
Wolfurt 1994, Hermann Kaufmann

OFFICE BUILDING

Large office buildings do not often contribute benignly to the urban ensemble, especially when located on the periphery. Even less often do they offer their occupants better and more interesting working conditions than older offices do. This building for a large com-

WÜSTENROT OFFICE BUILDING
Salzburg, Salzburg 1992
Architect: Josef Lackner b. 1931
Engineer: H-D. Reichl
Project team: T. Fliri, H. Friesacher
Area: 9000 m²
Cost: 200 million ATS

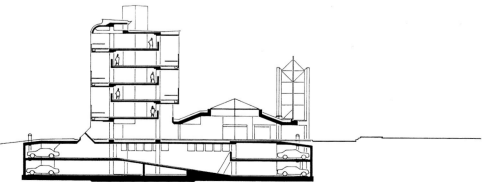

pany has a decidedly urban dimension and greater quality of workspace than many other flashy offices. An 80m long and 12m high glass wall held in place by a steel spider web-like structure protects the crescent-shaped office block from the highway in front of it, allowing the occupants to open their windows. The three different variable open plan, small group and individual offices are accessible from sunlit galleries. In section, service areas are housed in low-ceilinged rooms, whereas the workspaces have a generous ceiling height of 4.5m permitting the glazing for general illumination to be placed higher than usual, eliminating direct glare on computer screens. Small individual windows lower down can be operated manually by the occupants.

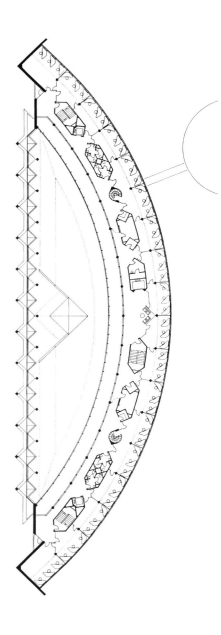

URBAN DESIGN

THE STREETS OF VIENNA   196

A UNIQUE EFFUSION   200

OF SONG-LINES AND SCORES   206

The Walking Maschine, urban performance art
Vienna 1972, Missing Link, Otto Kapfinger, Adolf Krischanitz, Angela Hareiter

Ernst Mach, the Viennese physicist who gave his name to the units that measure the speed of sound, used to illustrate the development of human consciousness by describing elementary physical processes. On his way to Vienna University on foot in the 19th century, passing various grand imperial edifices in the centre of the city, he was almost run over by a speeding cyclist on the Ringstrasse, the grand old boulevard that encircles the inner city. This small episode jolted him out of his train of thought and fantasies of the future. The cyclist, the "speed fanatic" who disrupted his walk, exposed the main factor that was to influence the future in general and urban life in particular - speed. In the European urban network Vienna lies between global cities like Frankfurt or Paris on one end of the scale and museal attractions such as Venice on the other. Vienna has not really been able to decide on either modernization or mummification of its structure. Perhaps this is what makes Vienna attractive to the long-term visitor. One finds, on a journey outward from the centre, quarters with a varied social and functional mix as well as skilled services that have long disappeared from the rest of the continent. A resident has a highly developed communal infrastructure at his disposal, from an excellent public transport system to hundreds of subsidised cultural events every day. One moves as a matter of routine between different time zones: aristocratic Baroque, bourgeois historicism and proletarian neoclassicism, but one has, nevertheless, a lively contemporary cultural scene - music, theatre and cinema of the highest quality. There is no doubt that the city possesses, to all appearances, all the characteristics that Richard Sennett described as the ideal political management of cultural differences, in "The Conscience of the Eye", his hymn to the metropolis.

Inside Vienna, however, there is little of this urban tolerance. Since the end of the communist system, the disappearance of the Iron Curtain and bizarre prophecies of mass migration from Eastern Europe, the city has closed its doors. The first sign was the result of a referendum on the planned Expo 1995, which was to be the first international exposition to be held by two cities in (at that time) two different political systems - Vienna and Budapest. Sixty four per cent of the Viennese population voted against the project, which would have made Vienna a focal point in Central Europe and given it badly-needed dynamism. The second sign was the inroads made into social democratic vote banks by a right wing populist opposition party with xenophobic slogans. In an effort to contain the losses, the central government introduced harsh (and heavily criticized) new laws, further strengthening already restrictive laws on immigration and the job market. There has always been resentment against foreigners here. A special "Jewish Police Unit" controlled the urban terrain until 1848, after which the so called "parallel society" of the silver-spoon upper class created an invisible wall against emancipated Jewish society. Sigmund Freud writes in his "Interpretation of Dreams" in 1900 of how his father was attacked by an anti-semitic hooligan and forced to step down from the pavement onto the street. Freud expressed bitter anger at the fact that his father did not defend himself. This scene was interpreted by Carl Schorske in his "Fin de siècle Vienna - Politics and Culture" as one of the experiences in which Jews of Freud's generation came up against the limits of political assimilation and as a consequence diverted their radicalism towards their literary and scientific work. But it also demonstrates something else: the audacity in forcing someone off the pavement exposes the symbolism of the street in Vienna.

The primary example is the Ringstrasse, built on the site of the old city walls after 1857. In "The City as a Work of Art", the social historian Donald J. Olsen has described this historicist ensemble as a framework for the self-representation of the liberal bourgeoisie and as an ideal forum for a "moral architecture". One may question to what extent architecture can force a moral position. But the stage-set image of the Ringstrasse has strayed into all other public space over time. Public space in Vienna is not a place where different social and political codes overlap. In a strange way, it is a place that establishes differences in meaning. This differentiation is a reflection of the history of the city, its revolts and revolutions, its festivals and ceremonies. Look at the workers' celebration on the 1st of May - an internationally unique demonstration from its beginnings in 1890 right

THE STREETS OF VIENNA - A VIRTUAL REALITY

Siegfried Mattl

up to the present day. A hundred thousand people march along the Ringstrasse to the square in front of the neo-gothic City Hall (when the weather is amenable) and occupy it not just physically but politically - no other party but the ruling social democrats would ever think of holding an event there. A recent plan by the Defence Ministry to hold its first post-war military parade on the Ringstrasse has met with widespread opposition. And in 1994 and 1995 young people twice turned the Ringstrasse into a large, noisy freewheeling rave, a techno party to demonstrate their presence in a city with one of the largest numbers of very old people (who turned up in large numbers to grumble about the event and who strangely enough made no mention of the noise of the tens of thousands of cars that use the Ringstrasse every other day of the year).

Or look at the Heldenplatz: the Heroes' Square - a vast empty space in front of the unfinished Imperial Palace. It is an indelible part of the international bank of historic images as the place where the Viennese jubilantly greeted Hitler's triumphal march into the city in March 1938. This image occupies in one's imagination the second, unfinished half of the square, a strikingly neurotic occupation of a public space, even though we know today that the image was manipulated by Hitler's photographer to give the impression of an overcrowded square and mass hysteria. Recently this loaded image was weakened and replaced to some degree by the impressive impact of hundreds of thousands of lit candles carried in a late-night demonstration against racism. That moving event is referred to as the "Ocean of Lights" and is still discussed with some emotion.

The 15th of July 1927. The Ringstrasse once again. Flames devour the Palace of Justice, set on fire by a spontaneous mass demonstration to protest against the freeing of a right-wing murderer. The police fire into the crowd causing a bloodbath without managing to disperse the crowd. The Nobel Prize-winning author Elias Canetti witnessed the scene and wrote of it in his autobiography, "The bullets whipped them together, not apart. The impression of fleeing masses on the street was an illusion, because even while they were running they could see that some of them fell, never to rise again. This inflamed the fury of the masses just as much as the fire itself, causing them to gather again. On this terrible, brightly-lit day I realized for the first time the role of the crowd in our century." What was the tragedy of that black July? Canetti analyses the anthropological motivation in "Crowds and Power". But there is a specific Viennese colour to the story. It was the misjudgement of power and its places of representation. The roots lie deep in history. No less than five groups divided the pre-1848 city into zones - the imperial court, the merchants, the university, the catholic church and the landowners. Difficult indeed to develop an urban consciousness or citizen's identity under such conditions. The democratic reforms of the 19th century paradoxically strengthened the Emperor's hand. He used the expansion of the city in 1857 and 1892 to reshape the city in imperial pomp and splendour. The crux was formed by the incomplete Emperor's Forum with the new Imperial Chancellery (now the National Library), the Castle Gate and the Museums of Art History and National History. Government was a version of Bonapartism, the Emperor putting pressure on Parliament and City Hall by allowing nationalist, socialist as well as antisemetic demonstrations on the Ringstrasse. It gave the impression that the periodic fall of the government was caused by mass demonstrations, whereas their destiny had in fact already been sealed by the Emperor. He himself enjoyed the increased loyalty of his subjects to whom he conceded this illusory feeling of power. The longer this went on, the more did various social groups and classes labour under the fatal impression that it was they who were shaping politics on the street. Public space is not considered by the Viennese as a metaphor to define the liberal democratic political system, but literally as political topography, which one can use like a board game. The political view was an image of the city as a mechanism, long before Le Corbusier's machine concept. This led to misunderstandings with serious consequences. In February 1934, the Vienna City Council was removed in a putsch, the mayor arrested and the extensive council housing, the pride of Red Vienna, besieged, fired at and damaged by government troops. The internationally famous Gemeindebauten (the council housing of the 1920s with over 60.000 units including the great kilometre-long "Karl Marx Hof", radical in their conception of community living) were nevertheless based on a slightly antiquated urban typology. They were inward-looking as castles once used to be

The Justice Palace on fire
Vienna 1927

The form of the internal court unconsciously signalled the social utopia of a Charles Fourier rather than that of a modern urban pragmatism. The defeat of the working classes and their political party was total because they had prepared for street battles of the type common in the 19th century. Their right-wing opponents, on the other hand, had, in spite of their own mobilization of the masses on the street, concentrated their force elsewhere - in the takeover of the radio transmitter in the city centre. The power over the city had been transferred from the street to the air waves - the age of the mass media had begun. To this day governments keep an eye open for the opinion of the gutter press - many a politician has experienced a premature end to his career if he did not come to an arrangement with a certain tabloid (where the most successful mayor in recent times began and ended his career).

The social democrats, who had ruled the city from 1920 till 1938 seemed to want to somehow wreak revenge on the city after 1945 for their own illusions of public space by planning its active destruction. Every decade after the war saw new plans, which, had they been implemented, would have turned the city into a network of motorways. One is relieved today that Vienna did not "modernize" itself in such a brutal way.

The reasons for this, however, are problematic: until a few years ago the city did not conform to the usual laws of market economy which would have forced this modernization. An uncommon fate caused by many factors, above all the steady decrease in population till a few years ago from a city with two million inhabitants at the end of World War I to one and a half million now, as well as the loss of its function as the trade, banking and communication centre of Eastern Central Europe. The generous infrastructure it inherited forms the backbone of the city to this day. To add to that, the strong rent control law of 1917 with its extremely low rents have made private investment in housing unattractive, until its recent reform. All this prevented major structural changes except on the periphery. In spite of extensive war damage, Vienna has remained a city with an unusually intact and functioning historical centre, with a traditional mix of uses and all the conservatism that a lack of competition entails. A symptom of this is the social, political and architectural obsoletism of the central districts. It is only recently that the city has begun to show movement.

But not all this movement is positive. Things have not changed fundamentally since Ernst Mach's days. The straightforward bicycles of the day have given way to 21-speed city bikes that terrorize pedestrians just as the cyclists themselves are terrorized by car drivers. The biggest shopping centre in Europe, just outside Vienna, opened in 1972 and has been growing ever since. It causes constant, long, creeping traffic jams - a robber recently escaped on cycle while the police were helplessly immobile in their cars. Driving to shop there isn't quicker or more convenient than shopping in the city centre. It's just that the shopping centre is forcing the city shops to close down, leaving

Imperial procession on the Ringstrasse
Vienna 1908

Demostration against National Socialism
Ringstrasse, Vienna 1933

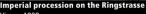

no alternative. To take an example, the modern version of the plague befell Vienna in 1977 when McDonald's opened its first eatery. There are 30 of them now with seven million customers annually. Modernization of this kind is frightening - especially if it involves the decline of the traditional Viennese restaurants. So the city comes up with measures to protect both the small shops and the traditional eating houses - subsidies, easy loans.

To attempt to counter the threatening big shopping centre in the countryside around Vienna, pedestrian shopping streets have invaded the city, furnished with pine trees in tubs flowers and meadow-like strips of grass in an embarrassing attempt to bring nature into the city, whereas the rows of twee shops in the fully airconditioned indoor mall outside Vienna perversely imitate the old inner-city streets and lanes.

Forces of change tend to come from outside rather than from inside. Several large urban projects such as the Museum Quarter or the new Danube City across the river which would have given a new impetus to the use of public space in these districts, are delayed and castrated beyond recognition. Much of the conscious change in the city is directed towards small-scale operations which enhance the admittedly high quality of traditional urban life in Vienna. In many ways this has parallels to the architectural scene, where the most interesting projects until recently were small renovations and shop interiors. The risks taken in Vienna are those characteristically small risks of the 19th century, whether they concern cyclists, pedestrians, the historicist mentality or the fate of modern architecture.

Due to the 500 km long network of cycle paths, Vienna has recently become a Mecca for cyclists from all over Europe, a fact which leads the city to proudly describe itself as an environmentalist city. However, the creation of the cycle path has followed the path of least resistance. The conquest of public space by the bicycle, a hundred years after it was invented, is one of the cheapest or easiest planning measures that one could take. After all, it is extremely cheap to paint two parallel yellow lines on the pavement. And presto! One has an efficient, noiseless, and pollution-free transportation system. But the cycle paths have been built at the expense of the pavement the pedestrians use, and not at the expense of that major part of the street that is used today by the automobile. As a result, there are constant collisions between speeding cyclists on 'their' cycle path, where they feel safe from the dreaded automobile, and the promenading pedestrians on the Ringstrasse who have developed a false sense of security over the centuries. The problem is solved at the wrong level, which gives rise to new problems, typical for the attitude to many things in this city. This is where Vienna begins to become dangerous, as Ernst Mach rightly pointed out, all those years ago.

The Free Party on the Ringstrasse
Vienna 1995

Clearing up after the Free Party, a Techno rave on the Ringstrasse
Vienna 1995

1st of May demonstration
Workers with the Imperial Theatre on the Ringstrasse
in the background, Vienna 1932

Parade of the
Parade of the authoritarian guilds, Vienna City Hall 1934

Perhaps the most persistently controversial building in Vienna is the Hundertwasser Haus. Located far from the tourist maelstrom of the First District, it attracts busloads to gawk at its lavishly ornamented facades and quirky details, shoot rolls of film or dine in its two cafes. While its fundamental tectonics are conventional, the project - with its roof gardens, arcades, undulating sidewalks, and psychedelic coloration - has managed to both engage and delight the public as no other modern architectural work in the city.

Nevertheless, this is the building which (along with a similar project down the street) Viennese architects and intellectuals love to hate. The vehemence always comes as something of a shock. After all, whatever it may represent, the Hundertwasser Haus is simply a sweet, slightly kitschy, modestly-scaled public apartment building in a relatively obscure part of town. Clearly, the disproportion of this reaction suggests anxieties far exceeding any immediate architectural particulars. To account for it, one must do no less than account for Vienna: no reading of the Viennese architectural avant-garde can ignore the unfathomable weight of the town itself.

Vienna, with its historic culture of irony and self-pity, sentimentality and rigor, is a condition, an emotional substrate, that hangs over the lives of its citizens like a cloud of perfumed smoke. No city exceeds its constant inspiration for exile and repatriation, psychical and physical. No city rivals it in its weighty configuration of irrationality and self-congratulation, a dynamic that produces, by turns, astonishing wit, limpid form, and utter despair. No city can match the simultaneous allegiance and animosity it seems to inspire in its community of architects. Yet no city has a richer, more battered, history of architectural experiment.

The tendency comes and goes. The most recent return - after a half century of eclipse - coalesced in the the sixties and seventies - bringing Vienna once more (with London its only serious rival) to the center of the world architectural avant-garde. A generation schooled in the demonstrative, insubordinate, imaginative styles of 1968 became absorbed in an effort to fuse the studio and the street, to produce an architecture of action, passion, rebellion, and clarity. The result was an unprecedented outpouring, much of it on paper as polemics and proposals, more as temporary structures and events, more still as a crust of small-scale building: shops, bars, renovations. The aggregation still astonishes.

That this unique effusion should have happened in Austria was overdetermined. Of course, the global rising of youth culture was nowhere uniform nor monochromatic, despite the shared anthems and habits. But the Austrian scene was still singular, product of a special set of precedents and traumas. It had, to begin, a superior darkness, an oedipal hum. The children of that criminal generation which had been the death of the predecessor avant-garde were obliged to deal with a rage and an official amnesia that the children of France, Britain, or America could scarcely know. And, the traditional educational style - the Masterclass system (to this day taught by an exclusively male professoriat) - was a clear incitement to patricide, succinct microcosm of all that was both oppressive and irrelevant about the hollow imperium of a culture that had lost its agenda. Although architecture was uniquely freighted with all of this, it was, paradoxically, during this period of rebellion that architecture - the discipline most intrinsically connected to structures of power - established itself firmly as Austria's dominant - and most consistently successful - art form. This vitality, of course, was not exactly ex nihilo. Austria is one of modern architecture's wellsprings and the site of many of its monuments. Architecture enjoys a quotidian prestige (as well as levels of patronage) within Austrian culture that is both strong and enviable. Indeed, in this tension between sanction and rebellion lies the core Austrian modernism's meanings.

Two streams of this modernity emerged clearly in the latter nineteenth century, emblemmatized by Austria's two great protagonists of urban form: Otto Wagner and Camillo Sitte. Although both embodied expressions of common cultural feelings, from each might be said to descend one of the poles of a dialectic that continues virtually unabated to this day. The great debate over the Ringstrasse, the founding of the

A UNIQUE EFFUSION

Michael Sorkin

Viennese Secession, the stinging critiques of Adolf Loos, the social transformations of Red Vienna, and the rebellious innovations of the sixties and seventies, all participate in this fundamental - yet complex - rift.

Otto Wagner was the apostle of a post-Cartesian rationalism, of a somewhat scientistic, technical, therapeutic view of the city, of a metropolis of grids, arithmetic hierarchies, and unlimited growth. His urban fantasies were of order and enormity, the high modernist dream that has so dominated the twentieth century urban sensibilty. Wagner was a great visionary of infrastructure, one of the first to seize upon the engineering programs of waterworks and mass transportation as suitable sites for architectural invention. In his case, the potential oppressions of such a position were leavened by the genius of his practice, by an amazing sense of detail, and by a subordinate yet juicy sense of decoration. In his simultaneous deployments of gigantism and subtlety, Wagner became an archetypal practitioner (and an architectural Father) whose unrivallable achievement has - for both better and worse - framed desires for over a century.

Sitte, on the other hand, was an up-front avatar of urban joy, arguing for a frankly artistic approach to the question of designing the city, condemning traffic-based and "systems" approaches and calling for styles of informality and intimacy rather than the gridded regularities advocated by Wagner. Sitte's work also embraced a distinctly historical (even historicist) vector, expressed via analyses of numerous medieval, 'organic' towns which he felt held the graceful qualities of the urbanity he sought. Like that of Pugin or Morris, Sitte's advocacy of the pre-modern city anticipates a critique that was to re-emerge a century later (reinforced in part by a rediscovery of Sitte's work) amidst the wreckage of modernist hegemony: the Wagner/Sitte split does not simply presage a characteristically Viennese schism, it summarizes a global urbanistic debate that burns hotter than ever.

Both Wagner and Sitte represent the high side of tendencies which have frequently and easily lapsed into low modes. If for Wagner, the degenerating path is the mechanistic road to alienating scale, formal uniformity, and social minima, for Sitte, the risk is sentimentality and kitsch, the post-modern failings of forms wrested from their originating contexts of meaning. Vienna has a taste for both degeneracies. The Ringstrasse - that grandest of achievements of Viennese civic architectural culture - manifests these twin pulls in both its form and in the alternatingly adulatory and damning reception it has received in the city. Today, it can be seen both as the sure expression of a class at a moment of confidence and as a kind of lateral Disneyland, a parade of civic buildings in apt ersatz: classical parliament, gothic town hall and palazzi for the haute bourgeoisie.

But the Ringstrasse carries a message about Viennese architectural life that exceeds either its grandiosity or style. Under its new liberal government, nineteenth century Vienna developed an administrative culture that transformed the city's infrastructure, its sewers and roadways, its public transportation and municipal services. This civic impulse was undimmed by the collapse of the Hapsburgs and was taken up again in the great days of Red Vienna when the public obligation to construct housing was set in the city's consciousness via a vast number of remarkable projects. Today, this sense of municipal responsibility is unabated. Services continue to be modernized and housing construction (at a scale comparable to the Red halcyon) is almost completely dominated by the public sector. Indeed, this construction - and the wide availability of commissions to collaborate in it offered even to younger architects - forms the special context of Viennese architecture and urbanism.

The on-going vehemence of the reception of the Hundertwasser Haus becomes far more explicable as a restoration to visibility of this convergence of historic anxieties. As an instance of urban public housing, it presents a gaiety at odds not simply with local proprieties but also with the facades of rationality that have long accompanied the social project of subsidized housing. More, that Hundertwasser is an artist seems galling to the proprietary sensibilities of a 'mastery' that fetishizes titles. And, of course, Hundertwasser's hippie-kitsch 'decorative' manner is, for most intellectuals, the most fearsome aspect of the local repressed, of the bathetic picturesque

Haus Rucker which glowed bright at the time but lapsed into more ordinary routines), Himmelblau turned to the apparently destabilized, anti-gravitational tectonics, skittish lines and surrealist technologies which have made their reputation. If their forms were largely sui generis, the assault on pat Wagnerite symmetries - the obsessive alterity (not to mention the hippiesque spirit of performance) - was shared with the organic bravura of Hundertwasser or (most notably), the fabulous Gunther Domenig from Graz.

Coop Himmelblau also well embodies the anxious, filial, relation of the Viennese avant-garde to the town. However much their work is forged in a reaction against both a parentage of the Nazi generation and the received certainties of a modern architecture that had failed to save the day, much of their form-making addresses a more current sense of exclusion; historical, psychical, and practical. This is nowhere better symbolized than in their relation to the Innere Stadt, the area hemmed by the Ring, the fortress of the Viennese establishment. As with so many others, Himmelblau's reaction holds elements of both subversion and longing. Many early projects (including several executed ones) contain cutting and piercing elements which seem to simultaneously rend existing tissue and embed within it. Others - like many experimental projects of the time - propose structures floated above the city, whether (like some early collages of Hollein), as huge megastructures or (as with projects of Haus Rucker, among others) simply sitting atop or grafted to historic structures.

This polemic of forced entry continues to shape their practice, a dream of another city muscling its way into the old center, a glowering, reprimanding cohabitation. Although Himmelblau have largely shed the overheated rhetoric of prowling panthers lurking like Fantomas above the roofs of Vienna, their work carries on the notion of this second city, superimposed on the body of the first, the insistence that their difference be recognized within the context of the old city. The dialogue is crucial, skirting cooptation. In the frustrated project for the Ronacher Theater and the brilliant roof-top offices built for a Viennese law firm there's an abiding sense of both otherness and renewal; a vulture-like pose over a landscape of rot with a simultaneously generous collaboration in the extravagant play of profiles of the gothic and baroque roofscape, anger and desire synthesized. Whether in Hollein's self-conscious good taste, Hundertwasser's treacly phantasmagoria, or Himmelblau's jagged superpositions, all of this work locates a kind of limit of decorousness and points up one of the two key problematics of Austrian urbanism: the question of insertions within the texture of historic cities. This sensibility of appearances - of both their narrow range and of keeping them up - is at the center of the national style, historic focus of both solidarity and rebellion. Hardly surprising in a country where - even in the jaded, sophisticated, capital - citizens dressed in the dour black of cafe intellectuals jostle equal numbers clad in various modifications of folkloric garb. Both fitting and myopic, architectural debate in the media is disproportionately concerned with the propriety of additions to historic urban cores (something Vienna does well), slighting the second and greater problematic, the increasingly ill-disciplined development of the urban periphery.

The search for models is both local and further afield. Like Schindler and Neutra, those great Viennese exiles of half a century ago, Coop Himmelblau are fascinated with Los Angeles, maintain an office there, find its antithetical urban pattern pure refreshment after the tight strictures of the Innere Stadt. This fascination seems to be shared more generally (if less explicitly, less intensely) with the local collective unconscious, in an ironic return of the American repressed. If the great project of Red Vienna was to build a home in the city for the enfranchised proletariat, the rush of construction today is for a burgeoning suburbariat. Vienna's huge program of housing construction (the municipality subsidizes between eight and ten thousand units a year!) is increasingly a phenomon of the edge.

There's a certain inevitability here: the compact (and intact) center of town is largely full and the periphery is where the land is. But it's also clearly where the sensibility - both home-grown and global - is. As a result, contemporary Viennese architecture's main typological research (the glitzier manifestations more familiar abroad notwithstanding) is into low density, automobile-dependent, attached, suburban housing typologies. The yuppies newly ensconced in their Transdanubian Arden, the strand-dandies of the Copakagrana, the newly arrived looking for space, all describe the fresh subjectivity of the leisure age. Situated somewhere between American-style suburban and European center-city densities, these developments seem decidedly, perhaps irresistably, the future.

At the time of the construction of the Ring, a proposal was put forward that its new residential construction be not in the palazzo style that ultimately prevailed but in the form of the English semi-detached town house. As Vienna builds its milennial ring at the town's periphery, the old debate about rational versus romantic construction is rejoined, if less than explicitly. The great problem of Vienna is now its suburbs, another sort of second (or perhaps third) city, inscribed not over the top but at the sides of the historic one. As in the nineteenth century, the question is how to approach a voided or green perimeter, now not the glacis or the Wienerwald but a jagged fringe at once sloppy and energized, the battle ground of Wagner's expansiveness and Sitte's compaction. If the Austrian avant-garde can said to have a blind spot, it is in its lack of interest in questions of the real growth of the city, in inventing a compellingly new urbanism for the urban edge. Caught between the dreamy subversions of superposed megastructural fantasies and the architectural assault on the sacred center, no clear vision of the new city - or much sympathy with the project of its research - emerged from the raucous nose-thumbings of the seventies. While there have been some recent exceptions - notably Rudiger Lainer's competition-winning scheme for the abandoned Aspern airfield - the conversation about the growth of the Austrian city has been not-ably quiet among the most innovative architects of the cohort, still too wedded to invasive or collagist strategies.

Absent compelling new models, the pattern for these new sites has largely remained the social-democratic beau-ideal of the 1920's: the garden siedlung. There's a certain irony here. Vienna's great contribution to the history of public housing (unlike that of Germany or Great Britain, for example) has been its dense, center-city, infilling projects and, in that sense, the new profusion of low-rise peripheral schemes represents a typology without substantial local precedent. As a result, while the architecture of these places is of generally high quality, their urbanism is subur-banism. Lacking a relationship to an existing texture, the projects tend to float. Monofunctional and car dependent, dependent on a road and transit-reinforced, radial relationship to the city, they seem neither sufficiently autonomous nor sufficiently linked to find a satisfying coherence. This isolated quality reflects a more general condition in contemporary architecture, part of the political crisis of post-modernity and its critique of the masterplan.To its credit, Austria has largely managed to escape the banal ravages of the historicist urbanism that has become an almost uni-versal default mode. A Green sensibility - an inevitable pillar of any appropriate urban future — has begun to pervade the conversation, although too few of its advocates seem to be architects. Transportation planning is unusually advanced. Strides are being made for the inclusion of far more public participation. The physical debate, however, remains framed by planning documents tied, however notionally, to a traditional modernist sensibility.

The Ur-text is the beautifully produced 1962 plan executed under the direction of Roland Rainer (who,at 85, remains the grand old man of Austrian architecture). Graphically marvellous, it's a

Vienna's centre:
The inner city with St. Stephan's Cathedral
grew up on the site of a Roman camp

Vienna's centre:
The Imperial Forum and the Heroes' square
at the edge of the inner city

modernist classic, a vivid relic. While offering acute analysis, strong and protective propositions about green and open space and sensitive propositions for the historic core, its proposals for new development are firmly rooted in the forms of the 1920's and 30's, the light-filled and spacious, but ultimately one-dimensional architecture of the modernist siedlung. It's vision of growth is firmly radial, a sensibility of carpeting and equivalence. As diagram, it's seductive, as urban design banal.

The best features of the Rainer plan are carried forward in Vienna's current official planning document, the Stadtentwicklungsplan (STEP), promulgated in 1984 and revised ten years later. A sophisticated document, the STEP is filled with numerous constructive propositions but - like so many liberal plans of the period - it is reticent both about specifying form and about operating at large-scale, save in general zoning prescriptions. This is understandable, given the miserable performance of most modernist urban schemes in post-war European (and American) experience. Still, in its still too piecemeal vision of the city's fringes, the STEP leaves open a set of questions which are only beginning to find satisfactory answers. To its credit the revised document recognizes many of the shortcomings of its predecessor and a current flurry of energetic activity harbingers the possibility of solutions that are as physically progressive as the social impulses behind the plan.

Fortunately, there seems to be a rapidly growing sense among the public authorities that the dormitory suburb is deficient as a general model for the city's expansion. What remains is to develop a truly coherent vision of the edge: for Vienna, this is the most crucial physical question for the future. Still relatively bounded and compact, the city retains the possibility to end itself at once gently and crisply, to find a definitive border. Comprised of a structured mosaic of coherences, such an edge might allow Vienna it to pioneer a kind of third urban typology, one which combines the openness and greenery of the suburb or seidlung with the sociability and mixture of the town. In this fertile territory of urban invention, the historic Viennese architectural dialectic might find many satisfying syntheses.

Vienna's periphery:
The Danube dividing the Prater park with its stadiums on the right bank, from the United Nations Centre and the new urban expansion areas on the left bank.

Vienna's periphery:
The city and its edge. New housing areas on the periphery meet green fields and canals.

Modernism's programme for the city was a social programme, a manifesto for the new city. Those were the days of iron-clad certainties and unshakeable beliefs. Architects today, however, seem helpless and perplexed when faced with the uncontrolled growth of cities. Urban design has been reduced to isolated pockets, to the connection of growth areas to old sub-centres with traffic routes like umbilical cords. Plans that are merely form without social content alternate with academic concepts lacking appropriately developed forms. What one does observe today is an attempt to translate the theories of the early part of the century, as well as the ideas developed during the economic recession in the West in the 70s and 80s, into actual schemes. A closer look at the motivation for and the mode of translation of these concepts reveals differing degrees of success. It is, after all, success that matters in the global rivalry of major cities; success in their efforts to survive as commercially viable entities while offering a high quality of life. The Austrian contribution to the debate began in 1909 with Camillo Sitte's sensitive proposals, in his book "City Planning According to Artistic Principles", to repair cities damaged by megalomaniac Baroque monumentality. His interventions were based on the lessons learnt from the Italian towns to which architects make pilgrimages. Sitte's book was translated into English only in 1965, thereafter having an enormous impact on academic circles in the English-speaking world. As a consequence, it received renewed attention within Austria and seemed to be applicable to the amelioration of the ravages of building in the 60s and 70s. Luxembourg-born Rob Krier, who teaches in Vienna, was one of the main proponents of this school of thought in the 1980s. He proposed the basic, time-tested elements of the European city - the street and the square - as the foundation for the renewal of cities destroyed by planning and speculation. This was doubtless a necessary corrective to certain abstract and destructive ideologies of urban development. His built projects, such as a large housing scheme in Vienna, where his master plan was partly filled out with his own buildings and those by other architects, were pleasant enough and popular amongst the residents. They avoid that enormous

weakness of post-war housing: SLOAP (space left over after planning), offering peripheral settlements a familiar urban ambience reminiscent of city-centre living. Beyond a certain point, however, they were considered insufficient in several areas – definitely no panacea to the new problems and demands that cities face today. Nevertheless, this approach was salutory in that it reminded architects to integrate elements of what they personally enjoyed, such as beautiful Italian towns built on a human scale, in their own projects. An enormous number of small scale projects to repair or transform parts of the city came out of architecture schools in the 80s and 90s. Some of these interventions have actually been carried out: a park here, a square there, an arcade, an urban space. Though probably not sufficiently grandiose to satisfy the ego of the profession, they have definitely improved the quality of life of residents and users.

Although almost all the attention of urban designers is concentrated on Vienna (which we will come to later) and a couple of other cities, it is the rural areas which seriously need consideration. The distinction between settlement and surrounding countryside maintained for hundreds of years is now being dissolved due to changes in the economic and social profile of the population. Most people in rural areas no longer work in agricultural occupations. This and the atomisation of the family into its component parts has led to an indiscriminate carpet development of inappropriate single family dwellings over the mountains and valleys. This could be described as a kind of built diarrhoea spilt over the spectacularly beautiful Austrian countryside. Villages themselves are fast losing their centres to vehicular traffic and their borders to the encroachments from the next village. One of the few examples of an attempt to rectify this trend and save a village from falling apart is the intervention by a young couple, Anton and Cornelia Falkeis, in a small 'one-street' village in mountainous Tirol. The commission, which started out with a small music pavilion, expanded successively to include several communal, cultural, administrative and banking facilities, which were used to reestablish a village structure. They rightly recognized that a kind of 'reurbanization' of the village was the only way to recover its identity and to redefine its boundaries by

OF SONG LINES AND SCORES

Ramesh Kumar Biswas
Research by Gottfried Pirhofer,
Peter Klopf, Manfred Schenekl
and Ariane Müller

concentrating forces and forms. The simple buildings and a geometrical central public square have a calming effect on the stylistic and functional chaos. Modest as the results may appear, anyone who knows the atmosphere in small towns - hostile to anything overtly modern while sensitive to criticism of false developments - will appreciate the achievements of this intervention and hope for further constructive proposals from architects in other small towns and villages, which still house the majority of the country's population.

Of course, it is Vienna which houses most of the architects and attracts most of the urban design effort. An amazing rash of building activity has spread over Vienna recently, reminiscent of the great expansion of the city in the so-called Gründerzeit (the Founders' Era in the second half of the 19th century). The sheer numbers, the heterogeneity and the volume of the projects is impressive. Yet the performance is less striking under closer scrutiny. In the Gründerzeit building and city building were complementary processes; architecture was equivalent to urbanism, creating the urbanity for which Vienna is famous. The projects being built today, however, can be easily classified into specific functions - housing, commercial, educational, multifunctional centres - but, in spite of conscious efforts by the city planning department to encourage comprehensive planning, ordering principles like those of the Gründerzeit are difficult to trace.

When the Iron Curtain fell in 1989 and a new Gründerzeit was announced with great enthusiasm, a heated debate broke out about the future development of the city. Earlier, Budapest and Vienna had begun planning a common World Exposition for 1995. The interesting thing about Expo 1995 would have been its location in two cities, one in the capitalist West, the other in communist Eastern Europe. The bridge between two cultures collapsed prematurely with Hungary shedding its communist government and the population of Vienna voting in a referendum against an event that they feared would raise rents and increase immigration. By that time, an international architectural competition had been held. Sepp Frank's winning project which was visually based on a wave referring to the riverside site on the Danube, was expected to include adaptation for future use after the Expo. Preparatory construction had already begun on the site. After the Expo was jettisoned, the site was declared the future second business district for Vienna and renamed 'Danube City'. Two other architects, Adolf Krischanitz and Heinz Neumann, rejected Frank's monolithic and commercially unviable design and based their new urban layout on a modernized version of the Gründerzeit grid. The size of the individual sites to be bought by single developers and the building volume were fixed, but no setbacks or access roads were determined. The aim is to encourage building on the edges of the plots and to ensure sufficient natural light, leaving investors to build at any future point in time under the same conditions as those who built first. The monolithic platform base over the motorway on which the development was to take place was punctured to allow light to penetrate and trees to grow through the recesses in the platform. Public access via bridges, green areas and streets are to be woven in between the private properties, transferring some of the responsibility for public use from the res publica to the private realm.

On the city side of the river, an urban development area has been demarcated on the site of the former Northern Railway Station, the largest reserve of building land in the city. It is adjacent to the underground line and the road that lies on the major axis connecting the cathedral in the city centre to the Danube City on the other side of the river and beyond to the new urban expansion. Heinz Tesar's and Boris Podrecca's pragmatic high density layout, also based on the Gründerzeit grid, is organized around a central park with all the infrastructure. A mix of uses is planned with flats above and commercial use of the lower floors, unfortunately likely to be vacant for the first few years, making the area unattractive in the beginning. The plan to realize the scheme in phases is pragmatic but will mean that the initial residents will be living in an unpleasant building site for many years. This scheme, which started off with various grand titles such as The City of the Future, A City for Cyclists, The Waterfront City, or The Ecological City, demonstrates how quickly utopian ideas dissolve into a safe and commendable but finally uninteresting effort, with the main concern being the avoidance of any big mistakes. The situation is similar to that in Berlin now,

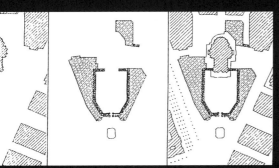

Reurbanization of the Votivkirche square
Vienna 1909, Camillo Sitte

where all the experimental urban design concepts have been discarded in favour of traditional city block forms.

Utopian projects of great magnetic power have emerged since the 1960s. Hans Hollein's super-imposed, floating and underground cities, the Haus-Rucker-Co group's gigantic non-functional stairways, Carl Pruscha's infrastructure for a continuous global city, Missing Link's critical commentaries on the dehumanization of urban life, Raimund Abraham's metropolitan core and other such utopias have been fundamentally questioning the nature of urban settlement in the twentieth and the twenty-first centuries. These visions force the formation of new viewpoints and new syntheses.

A high-risk visionary project is Pauhof's project for both the above sites. The two young architects Wolfgang Pautzenberger and Michael Hofstätter made a radical break with the traditional street/block system. They proposed the freeing of the terrain at ground level for public use by transferring all private functions into a megastructural development raised high above ground level. It was one of the few projects that enthusiastically embraced the developments which followed the fall of the Iron Curtain: the immigration, the black markets, the new cultural constellations. Pauhof's work is based on the Concept Art term of Non-relationism that does not relate directly to a given environment but embodies abstract philosophical principles. On the one hand, it projects an uncompromising strangeness which provokes negative reactions in this city, on the other it is integrated in its context in a precise and highly complex manner. The architects express their conceptual plans in a bold and intensive language which also accepts the temporary destabilization or even destruction of well-known elitist formal models.

The theoretical discourse has given way, inevitably, to practical development. Utopian schemes, though apparently not en vogue at the moment, obviously survive in the form of remnants in the minds of the advertising branch. Catchwords are used to connect the fragments of sagas and fairy-tales that float somewhere in the collective memory. Ideas from other areas of technology, ecology and the consumer industry are used as key-notes for new developments. This is hardly surprising, considering that the merciless competition for primacy between European cities is all about attracting ever larger business concerns and even more tourists. Vienna's neighbours are also operating with slogans: Prague presenting itself as fresh, audacious and dynamic, Berlin as the booming capital of Europe. The debate about the end of narrative architecture and the abdication of models of legitimation exposes the displacement of story-telling on to other planes. Architecture is no longer a text that reflects society. Society uses architecture as a symbol or medium. What is transmitted is not a whole, but isolated themes.

Architecture and city-planning are also confronted with the general trend towards individualization. Classes in society have internal contradictions, and these do not stop at their blurred edges. The logic of the international economic system and the forces which structure economic dynamism are both beyond social control. Personal experience, on the other hand, is organized within specific locations in a system. Manuel Castells says that this split - between locally determined processes under social control and placeless processes - reduces social movements to defensive reactions and limits their ability to organize social projects that protect specific local interests.

Valley in Tirol with Prutz
in foreground

Village reorganisation
Prutz 1989, Anton Falkeis, Cornelia Falkeis-Senn

Vienna's major vegetable mar

scientists. The apartments were unfortunately too expensive for the original target group of musicians, artists, teachers and social workers. Though the intentions are honorable, it may have been more important to concentrate on the integration of the many immigrant workers in other districts of the city.

The urban expansion planned on the former Aspern airfield in the north-east of the city is an exception. Four thousand residential units and six thousand jobs are to be created on a 130 acre site. It is one of the few active attempts at improving the quality of life on the periphery, as well as to give a befitting physical form to it. A diagram of predetermined lines, areas, heights, parks and traffic systems defines different points on the site. Some of these points or foci are detailed, especially those where public facilities and reference points are to be built. The rest of the plan is considered a free field that can be occupied, built upon and constantly rebuilt as long as certain heights or borders are respected. These restrictions are not in place throughout the site, but are based on lines of sight to dominant elements of the surrounding environment or on existing geographical features. This diagram, described as a score (like a musical score which defines a structure but allows interpretion) appears to be radically utopian. At the same time it uses the familiar tools of existing building regulations, urban structures and building types - a pragmatic approach that improves the chances of fulfilling the plan.

This new concept has a glittering vocabulary: 'urban score', 'corridor', 'field', 'communicative space'. House owners are apparently encouraged to feel that talking about urbanism is not the exclusive privilege of academics in intra-university discourse. Almost anyone can become a scholar overnight. Who cares if all these concepts do not make much sense, as long as they are packaged in attractive language, and the design is surrounded by an aura which demands worship. It is difficult for consumers to react in any way other than emotionally to terms like 'Urban Score', 'Viennese Loft' and 'Women's City', when they do not actually signify very much more than phrases mentioned in quotation marks.

However, these examples are the better ones - they correspond to the menu of a posh restaurant. The rest of the expanding city is being served by a fast-food chain. What is truly alarming are the 'themeless cities', housing schemes that may look prettier but are no better than the faceless mass housing of earlier decades, with a repetition of their high long-term social costs. Almost eleven thousand flats are being built in 1995 by various private developers and housing cooperatives,

Aircraft carrier - City in the landscape
Vienna 1964, Proposal, Hans Hollein

with no aesthetic pretentions or sophisticated urban concepts involved whatsoever. The quantity of flats and other statistics are more important here than anything else, something which arouses the scepticism of the educated classes who are the potential buyers or tenants. This is why some of these settlements have been given labels or a themes. They aestheticize the banal products on offer on the market. These flats have to be sold, and the buyer has to be able to identify with a specific situation, with something that gives him the illusion of living in an exceptional environment, and which consoles him for the lack of urbanity in the periphery. Other buyers are looking for the opposite of urbanity, and the builders of these theme schemes cater to this need for pseudo-rural village-like clusters.

In certain ways these projects express the need for small socio-cultural groups to organize them-selves within the anonymity of the metropolis. The city, which used to be a medium that brought different groups together and concentrated their interaction, is now losing its ability to create a consensus. The demands of all these groups are now being satisfied by a shopping mall type of solution: a variety of products are being offered next to each other but they still do not make a whole. Furthermore, some of these 'theme cities' are laboratories, a useful glimpse into the future. They are in fact going to change the familiar structure of Vienna to a greater degree than the more spectacular projects like the 'Danube City', the 'High-Rise City', 'Vienna on the Danube' and the other high-visibility projects that are oriented towards the global horizon of Los Angeles, the terrible future of all cities.

It is true that many other cities are developing much more radically in this fragmentary and dis-integrative manner than Vienna, where it is only happening on the periphery. Vienna is still a cen-tralized city, readily accessible on foot or by public transport, homogenous in its urban typology. In its neutrality of function it is the antithesis of Los Angeles. There is practically no area or building in Vienna that is not accessible to any and everyone. Many Viennese institutions, such as the café, the wine-garden, the tables on the pavement in summer, the sausage kiosk, the small local family restaurants, the vegetable markets, indeed entire districts, base their existence and their charm on the heterogenous mix of people who use them. The commercial infrastructure of a city also determines to a great extent the way it functions. This has been recognized by the city council, which now offers financial support for its retention. The dense small-scale network of shops and facilities, becoming rarer by the day in other European cities, owes its existence to an imperial

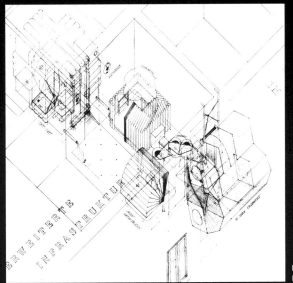

Experimental extension of residential cells in the city
Proposal 1970, Missing Link - Otto Kapfinger, Adolf Krischanitz, Angela Hareiter

law that allowed a shop only to sell one kind of product or offer only one kind of service - an iron-monger could not sell furniture, a hatmaker was not permitted to tailor coats. It was only towards the end of the last century that this tradition began to be abandoned and multi-product shops and, later, supermarkets came into being. The splintering of groups within a city and their physical displacement began in the second half of this century. Certain classes of people fled the inner city, which they considered to be premodern and unsuitable for the car, and moved to large housing projects on green fields. They expected happy families, air, light, sun, refrigerators, American-style kitchens, large windows, balconies and television. Of all these expectations, it was only the slight improvement in the consumer standard of the flat that was fulfilled. But the belief in progress is obviously still there, it has merely been transferred to other planes.

The theme settlements, also familiar as a motif of property developers in the US and in South-East Asia, offer their consumers a kind of consolation or moral justification for the disturbing fact that meadows, forests and corn fields have been destroyed to build their flats. At the same time their socio-pedagogic programmes initiate a process of identification for those who are leaving the city. While they offer these groups some kind of 'homeland', they enact a politically acceptable

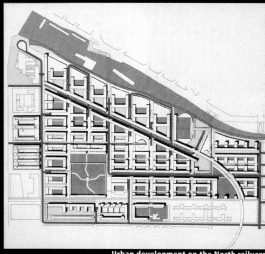

Urban development on the North railyard
(above and below)
Vienna 1995, Boris Podrecca and Heinz Tesar

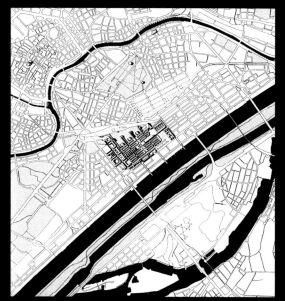

Urban development Aspern
Vienna 1995, Rüdiger Lainer

segregation of old people, yuppies, multicultural cosmopolites, women, or eco-freaks. Critics dislike this isolated manner of problem-solving. These 'homelands' do not satisfy the actual quantitative need for good housing schemes. Some of the targeted groups are people living at the social edge of society who cannot pay for the high costs of participating in the project. Others, such as teen-agers without buying power, are ignored completely. Ultimately, the consumers are the middle classes who are, curiously enough, expected to be sensitive to the social problems of marginal groups, and to enjoy living in housing designed for completely different life-styles. Some of the projects do reduce and divide urban growth into comprehensible units and portions, and they attempt to enrich quantity with quality. The paradox lies in the fact that until now quantity was multipliable whereas quality was considered holistic. The weakness of these projects is that they draw attention to certain problems and shortcomings in the city without being able to solve them. The next step would be to find solutions and syntheses which are truly useful, possible and desirable.

Urban development project for the North Railway Station area
Vienna 1994, PAUHOF (Pautzenberger & Hofstätter)

Housing development on the Wagramerstrasse
Vienna 1995, Raimund Abraham, Coop Himmelblau, Mark Mack,
Eric Owen Moss, Carl Pruscha, Michael Sorkin, Margaret Schwarz

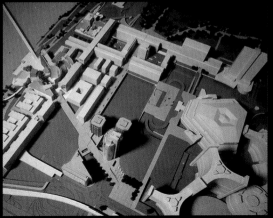

Extreme left and left: **Danube City Project**
Vienna 1995, Towers by Arata Isozaki and Gustav Peichl
School and Museum by Hans Hollein
Masterplan Adolf Krischanitz, Heinz Neumann

Katerina Ruedi

ONE: WAR AND PSYCHOANALYSIS

"THE CONTRADICTION BETWEEN THE PHILO-
SOPHY OF THE UNCONSCIOUS AND THE
RULING ECONOMIC ORDER BECOMES COMPLI-
MENTARY IN VALUE; THAT THEORY IS MEANT
TO MAKE UP FOR WHAT IS LACKING IN REALITY;
WITH OTHER WORDS, IT IS EXPLOITED AS
IDEOLOGY."

THEODOR ADORNO

The declaration of the Rights of Man following
the French Revolution of 1789 enshrined a
completely new relationship of social obligation
between citizen and state. The exchange of
freedom and security for taxation and con-
scription became the base of a new social contract
that insolubly linked warfare and welfare. The
majority of European states, including Austria
in 1848, adopted similar forms of the social
contract during the subsequent hundred
years. The capitalist system was greatly accelerated at this moment. Men became 'free' and
equivalent; simultaneously they were drawn
more tightly into a system of abstract social
relations that eventually led, in the twentieth
century, to the emergence of the welfare state.
The new 'universal' social contract introduced
in nascent form the concept of the identical
citizen. This concept was further strengthened
by the development of industrial capitalism
and the production of mass-produced cultural
artefacts, which further eroded the diversity
of traditional structures through which culture
and social relations were previously reproduced
and understood. This gave rise to a second
phenomenon that attempted to mask the
equivalence of the new universe of the mass-
citizen and the mass-product.

In The Fall of Public Man, Richard Sennett
links commodity fetishism to mass-production
and a new urban audience and in the process
touches on its connection to the appearance
of psychoanalysis. Commodity fetishism, in
Marx's words a projection of "metaphysical
subtleties and theological whimsies" onto a new
category of anonymous serial objects, occurred,
in Sennett's opinion, as a complementary

response to the meaninglessness of the new
universe of industrial objects. Such fetishism
attempted to invest objects with attributes
largely divorced from the nature of their production process. In a new fabrication of the
aura through decoration, exotic juxtaposition
and a shift to a minute reading of detail in
order to discover 'signs' of unique meaning,
previously insignificant detail suddenly acquired
enormous importance.

The secret life of objects was paralleled by that
of their human counterparts. The appearance
of psychoanalysis was crucial to the development of capitalism. Indeed, psychoanalysis as
a science of the unconscious was proposed by
Freud to have an 'economic point of view'.
Through this conceptual framework the
unconscious (as a source of desire necessary
to drive consumption) could be quantified as a
process of circulation and distribution of
instinctual energy. Desire could thus be harn-
essed as an instrument of excess and a source
of profit. Within architecture this production of
excess led to a new form of urban experience
and a new type of audience - the distracted,
'dreaming collective'. It inhabited the new
opulent 'dream-palaces' of commerce - the
arcades, cafes, department stores - and was
both reflected and constituted by their utopian-
images-made-into-architecture.

These new urban and architectural phenomena
served to map desire onto commodities. The
channelling of desire was necessary to divert
instinctual energy from its more politically
threatening aims - the demand, by the growing
numbers of the poor, for food and shelter. The
repression of political desires and their displacement into images of plenitude paralleled
the repression of sexual libido identified by
Freud. Physical deprivation was the counter-
part of visual excess. Like the repressed wish of
the unconscious, desire could not enter reality
undistorted - until the phenomenon of war
blew away its veil of concealment and reaffirmed
the relationship of obligation between citizen
and state. The cyclical return of the repressed
characterises the map of both the individual
and the political unconscious of the twentieth

century - where war acts as the collective trauma through which repressed desires can return to haunt their creators.

TWO: PRIVATION AND EXCESS

"I AM HUNGRY THE WHOLE DAY. WITH HALF A LOAF OF BREAD PER WEEK, WITH THE GREATEST AUSTERITY, I CAN SURVIVE FOR ABOUT FOUR DAYS, EATING ONLY ONE SLICE FOR BREAK-FAST...PROBABLY THE WAR WILL CONTINUE FOR SOME YEARS YET, AND THE INFLATION WILL GET WORSE. ONE GETS USED TO EVERYTHING."   ALFRED SILBERSTEIN

The story of the two world wars in Vienna was one of the extreme privation of individuals. In order to appease the hunger and homelessness of the working class and middle classes in period following WWI, the Viennese administration spearheaded a massive housing programme and sweeping legislation protecting the rights of tenants. This 'architecture of the social contract' relied on the concept of the identical citizen of the production process, not the dreaming individual consuming visual excess; it consciously ignored one half of the machinery of capital. Economically, the housing programme and the tenancy protection acts in effect 'froze' the value of Viennese property, preserving the city, as it were, in aspic. As a result, following the end of WW2 the city was not attractive to investors; like Berlin, it was partitioned, and, not merely in a geographical sense, peripheral to the future of Europe.

Yet, though devastated by the legacy of two global conflicts, desire returned to eventually disavow the legacy of war. Today, to remind Viennese citizens of the brutality of the hunger that was once a part of everyday experience is to awaken memories of an era that most wish forgotten. This cyclical 'forgetting' of trauma could be argued to have led to some of the most outstanding architecture of the post-war period; architecture that, for a time, influenced architects throughout Europe and beyond.

Following a period of slow post-war reconstruction, tiny but intense outbursts of architectural opulence characterised the seventies and eighties, particularly in Vienna. Hans Hollein's travel agencies and Schullin jewellery shops, Boris Podrecca's celestial conversions and Gunther Domenig's visionary bank in Favoriten and Humanic shops all profoundly rejected the sober inheritance of the past. Vivid points of brilliance on every architectural tourist's itinerary (and brought to international visibility through the most tourist-like of architectural consumables - Charles Jencks' coffee-table book Postmodern Architecture), these small projects were a celebration of excess in an economic and political climate without large scale development of architectural quality. In their footsteps, Coop Himmelblau, Friedrich Hundertwasser and the architects of the 'Graz School' all lay their buildings on the same sacrificial altar - symbolic offerings of plenitude to a seemingly 'frozen' city. With little inward economic and architectural immigration from the rest of Europe, these vignettes of desire instead travelled outwards to influence the drawing boards of Europe and North America. In the same period key figures also temporarily left to study, work and teach abroad: Hollein, Pruscha, Abraham and Ortner are a few names amongst many.

Today Austria is once again the physical and cultural heart of post-1989 central Europe; an influx of workers, refugees and tourists as well as membership of the EU has opened doors to new finance and industry. New building projects and new architects are emerging; structural change at a large scale - urban planning, housing, retail and office development - distinguishes this era from the previous one. Today, when desire surfaces, it is no longer focused on a doorway or a ceiling but on an entire city; nor is it any longer necessarily the work of Austrians. Raoul Bunschoten's fascinating and controversial urban proposals for the city of Linz celebrate the act of 'forgetting' by harnessing the city's future-filled desire for political fulfilment. In Bunschoten's project the embryonic form of the brass flame crowning Hollein's Schullin jewellery shop now reappears in the 1:50 000 urban plan and subsumes an entire district of the city. This is a phenomenal gesture of optimism — architect, client and citizen are all caught once again within the dreaming collective. Such architectures of desire characterise much of the avant-garde in Austria today.

THREE: RETURN OF THE REPRESSED

"A Klee painting named "Angelus Novus" shows an angel looking as though he is about to move away from something he is fixedly contemplating. His eyes are staring, his mouth is open, his wings are spread. This is how one pictures the angel of history. His face is turned to the past. Where we perceive a chain of events, he sees one single catastrophe which keeps piling wreckage upon wreckage and hurls it in front of his feet. The angel would like to stay, awaken the dead, and make whole what has been smashed. But a storm is blowing from paradise; it has got caught

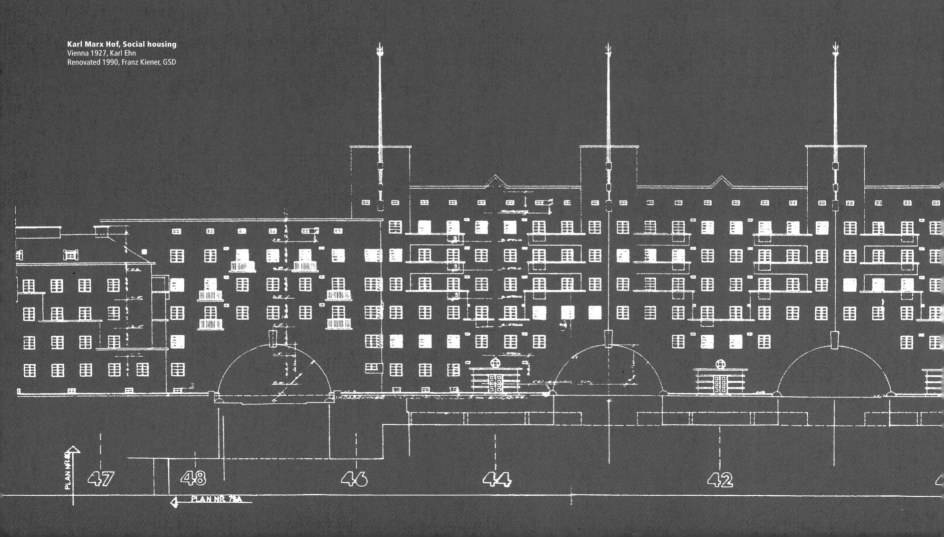

Karl Marx Hof, Social housing
Vienna 1927, Karl Ehn
Renovated 1990, Franz Kiener, GSD

in his wings with such violence that the angel can no longer close them. This storm irresistibly propels him into the future to which his back is turned, while the pile of debris before him grows skyward. This storm is what we call progress."   Walter Benjamin

Yet these utopian acts of excess, these act of forgetting, these rituals of disavowal, also point to the cyclical return of the repressed. European turmoil continues close to Austria's borders —the flame of war burnt in Bosnia, bringing a steady stream of humans that have lived with hunger and death, without shelter, within collective trauma. Racism and anti-Semitism is rising as the stream of refugees continues and the welfare state is stretched to accommodate them. As with the phantasmatic architecture, art, literature and theatre of the Fin-de-Siécle, which rose to a crescendo of physical excess just prior to the outbreak of the First World War, momentarily concealing profound political ruptures, today too it seems to me as if architecture heralds the cyclical return of the repressed. The storm that haunted the paradise of Mitteleuropa once, gathers strength on the horizon once again.

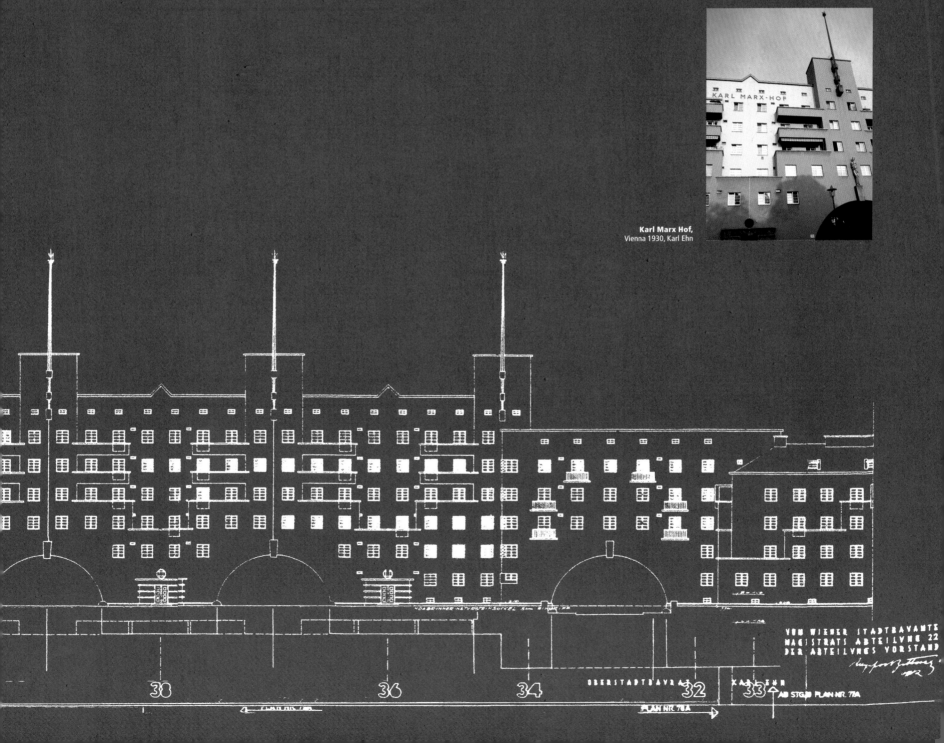

Karl Marx Hof,
Vienna 1930, Karl Ehn

AALTO, Alvar, 11, 39, 73
ABRAHAM, Raimund, 72-75, 165, 208,
   213-14
ACHLEITNER, Friedrich, 5, 20, 67, 165
ADORNO, Theodor, 214
AICHINGER, Hermann, 22
ALEXANDER, Christopher, 10, 68, 69, 71
ALSOP, Will, 73
ARENDT, Hannah, 13
ARTEC (GÖTZ-MANAHL) 37, 164, 186-87
ATELIER 4, 81
ATTATURK, Kemal, 67
AXELOS, Kostas, 162

BALZAREK, Mauriz, 21
BARTOS, Armand, 69, 70
BAUHAUS, 16
BAUKÜNSTLER, Vorarlberger, 126
BAUMANN, Franz, 23, 21, 24
BAUMANN, Ludwig, 20
BAUMGARTNER, Franz, 21
BAUMSCHLAGER, Carlo, 92
BEHRENS, Peter, 20, 22, 73
BENEDER, Ernst, 125-26
BENJAMIN, Walter, 122, 217
BENKO-MEDGYASZAY, 66
BEREITER, Arno, 126
BERGER, Alfred, 167
BEUYS, Joseph, 79
BISWAS, Ramesh Kumar, 1, 4-6, 8, 13, 34,
   40-41, 66, 146-49, 188-89, 206, 222
BOECKL, Matthias, 5, 20, 67
BÖHM & HEGEDÜS, 21
BOLLINGER Klaus & GROHMANN Manfred, 168
BOLTENSTERN, Erich, 25
BORROMINI, 17
BOTTA, Mario, 164
BOUMANN, Ole, 162
BRAMBERGER, Alfred, 33, 38
BRANZI, Andrea, 13
BREUER, Marcel, 67
BUNSCHOTEN, Raoul, 214
BUNUEL, Louis, 70
BUONAROTTI, Michelangelo, 17

CACCIARI, Massimo, 10
CALDER, Alexander, 70
CANETTI, Elias, 197
CASTELLS, Manuel, 8, 208
CHORHERR, Christoph, 146-49
CHRAMOSTA, Walter, 5, 122
CONDER, Josiah, 76
COOP HIMMELBLAU (PRIX & SWICZINSKI),
   16, 38, 52-55, 70-71, 73, 77, 82-83, 160-61,
   165, 202-03, 213-14
CORBUSIER, Le, 13, 76, 197
COSENZA, Luigi, 17, 67
CZECH, Hermann, 38, 165

DAHINDEN, Justus, 73
DALÍ, Salvador, 70
DELEUZE, 11
DE STIJL, 16-17
DEUBNER, Helmut, 149, 153
DOESBURG, Theo von, 70
DOLFUSS, Engelbert, 24

DOMENIG, Günther, 16, 26, 34, 41-45, 77, 93,
   95, 127, 138-41, 165-67, 189, 202, 214
DOSTOEVSKY, FYODOR, 34
DRIENDL, Georg & STEIXNER, Gerhard, 38-
   39, 150-51, 164, 189
DUMREICHER, Heide, 146-49
DWORZAK, Hugo, 126

EBERLE, Dietmar, 92
EGGER, Harald, 138
EHN, Karl, 22
EICHHOLZER, Herbert, 67
EICHINGER or KNECHTL, 32, 37-39
EISENKÖCK, Herman, 93, 95
ERAT, Bruno, 146-49

FALKEIS, Anton & Cornelia, 97, 206, 208
FELLERER, Max, 25, 27
FERSTEL, Bernd, 47
FERSTEL, 21
FEYFERLIK, Wolfgang, 37, 126
FISCHER v. ERLACH, Johann, 37, 93
FOURIER, Charles, 197
FRAMPTON, Kenneth, 9, 164
FRANK, Josef, 19-20, 22-24, 67
FRANK, Sepp, 207
FRANKL, Paul Theodor, 22
FRANTL, Erich, 176-79
FREUD, Sigmund, 20, 35-36, 39, 66, 196, 215
FREY, Konrad, 38, 48-49, 93-94
FRICK, Paul, 174-75
FRITZ, Norbert, 127
FUCHS, Rudi, 71
FUKSAS, Massimiliano, 73

GANTNER, Christian, 106
GAUDI, Antoni, 16-17
GEHRY, Frank Owen, 19
GESSNER, Franz Hubert, 22
GISELBRECHT, Ernst, 92, 97
GMEINER, M. & HAFERL, M., 99, 112
GNAIGER, Roland, 92, 106-107
GÖDEL, 35
GOFF, Bruce, 17
GOLDMANN & SALATSCH, 21
GRAAFLAND, Arie, 163
GRAF, Oskar, 54
GRAVES, Michael, 164
GROPIUS, Martin, 40
GROPIUS, Walter, 10, 26, 67
GRUEN, Victor, 17, 19, 67-69
GSTEU, J.G., 26
GUATTARI, 11

HADID, Zaha, 73, 78
HAECKEL, E., 35
HAERDTL, Oswald, 25
HAGMÜLLER, Roland, 69
HAREITER, Angela, 194-95, 211
HÄRING, Hugo, 73
HASENAUER, 21
HAUS RUCKER, 202, 208
HÄUSELMAYER, Otto, 117
HÄUSLE, Martin, 168-69
HENKE, Dieter & SCHREIECK, Marta, 120,
   128, 134-35, 170-71

HERZOG, Thomas, 146-49, 154-55
HETMANEK, Alfons, 22
HILBERSEIMER, Ludwig, 71
HITCHCOCK, Henry Russell, 67
HITLER, Adolf, 24-25, 67, 197
HOFFMANN, Josef, 17, 20-21, 25-26, 66
HOFMANNSTHAL, Hugo v., 36
HOFSTÄTTER, Peter, 176-79
HOLLEIN, Hans, 16, 27, 37-40, 67, 70, 72-74,
   79-81, 93, 162, 165, 202, 210, 214
HOLZBAUER, Wilhelm, 26-27, 67, 71-72, 75,
   158-59, 162-63, 165-66
HOLZER, Michael, 71
HOLZMEISTER, Clemens, 17, 20, 22-27, 67, 75
HÖRBURGER, Gerhard, 131
HUNDERTWASSER, Friedensreich, 16, 72, 77,
   123, 200-03, 214
HUTH, Eilfried, 26

INGERSOLL, Richard, 163
ILLETSCHKO, Ernst, 150

JANAK, Pavel, 66
JENCKS, Charles, 12, 78, 214
JOHNSON, Philip, 67
JUDD, Donald, 50

KADA, Klaus, 93, 98-99, 128, 131, 160-61,165
KAFKA, Franz, 11
KAPFHAMMER, Wolfgang, 93, 96
KAPFINGER, Otto, 5, 36, 92, 160, 194-95, 211
KAUFMANN, Hermann, 126-27, 188-89
KAUFMANN, Holzbauwerk, 106
KAYM, Franz, 22
KELZ, Adolph, 93, 96, 127
KIESLER, Friedrich, 17, 24, 69-70, 73
KISHIDA, Hideto, 76-77
KLEE, Paul, 216
KLIMT, Gustav, 21
KLOPF, Peter, 206
KOCH, Markus, 92
KOOLHAAS, Rem, 10
KOSSDORF, Gert, 93, 96
KOTERA, Jan, 21, 66
KRAUSS, 21
KRIER, Rob, 18, 73, 147, 165, 206, 209
KRISCHANITZ, Adolf, 37-38, 94, 100-01, 112-
   115, 164-65, 188, 194-95, 207, 211, 213
KRISMER, Werner, 167
KURRENT, Friedrich, 26

LACKNER, Josef, 26, 190-91
LADSTÄTTER, Georg, 158-59, 162-63, 166
LAINER, Rüdiger, 52-53, 93, 108-11, 130,
   204, 210, 212
LANG, Fritz, 39, 40
LAWUGGER, Werner, 134
LECHNER, Christine & Horst, 126-27
LECHNER, Ödon, 21
LEMOINE-LUCCIONI, Eugénie, 13
LEVINE, Richard, 146-49
LEVI-STRAUSS, Claude, 8
LICHTBLAU, Ernst, 22
LICHTENWAGNER, Christiane, 126-27
LISSITZKY, El, 70
LOCHER, Helmuth, 52, 109, 172

LOOS, Adolf, 8, 17, 20-23, 25, 27, 33, 36, 66-
   67, 122
LOOS, Walter, 70
LOUDON, Michael, 92, 127, 130
LOVELL, Philip, 17, 19, 22

MACH, Ernst, 1, 196, 198-99
MACINTOSH, Charles Rennie, 16
MACK, Mark, 73-74, 213
MAEKAWA, Kunio, 76
MARKUS, Helmuth, 85
MARSCHALEK, Heinz, 158-59, 162-63, 166
MARX, Karl, 214
MATTL, Siegfried, 5, 196
McLUHAN, Marshall, 8
MEILI, Marcel, 163, 166
MENDELSOHN, Erich, 16
MIES van der ROHE, Ludwig, 39
MISSING LINK, 92, 194-95, 209, 211
MOHOLY-NAGY, László, 70
MONEO, Rafael, 164
MONITZER, Erich, 5, 109
MONTAIGNE, Michel de, 8
MORALES, Ignasi de Solà, 164
MORPHOSIS, 74
MORRIS, William, 16, 201
MOSER, Koloman, 21
MOSER, Thomas, 92
MOSS, Eric, 74, 77, 213
MUCHA, Alfons, 21
MÜLLER, Ariane, 206
MÜLLER, Sepp, 36, 50-51, 167
MUSIL, Robert, 122
MUSSOLINI, Benito, 25

NEUMANN, Heinz, 188, 207, 213
NEUTRA, Richard, 8, 17, 19, 22, 24, 67-68,
   73, 203
NOEVER, Peter, 50
NORBERG-SCHULZ, Christian, 8
NOUVEL, Jean, 73-74, 77, 79, 209

OFFICE, The, 166
OHMANN, Friedrich, 20, 26
OLBRICH, Josef-Maria, 17, 21, 24, 37, 66
OLSEN, Donald, 196
ORTEGA Y GASSET, Jose, 122
ORTNER, Laurids & Manfred, 95, 214

PANZHAUSER, 103
PAUHOF (PAUZENBERGER & HOFSTÄTTER),
   38, 41, 165, 208, 213
PAXTON, Joseph, 39
PEICHL, Gustav, 27, 71, 74, 84-85, 165, 167
PELLI, Cesar, 68, 73
PERCO, Rudolf, 22
PERRET, Auguste, 20
PETRI, Hanspeter, 128, 131
PIRHOFER, Gottfried, 206
PISTULKA, W., 153
PIVA, Paolo, 33, 37-38, 73
PLATO, 13
PLECNIK, Josef, 21, 66
PLISCHKE, Ernst, 66, 70, 123, 125
PODRECCA, Boris, 37-39, 41, 71, 94, 172-73,
   212, 214

PROHAZKA, Rudolf, 121, 125, 165
PROKSCH, Thomas, 146-49
PRUSCHA, Carl, 34, 37, 69-71, 208, 213-14
PUCHHAMMER, Hans, 73, 95
PUGIN, 201
PUTZ, Oskar, 32, 38

RAINER, Roland, 25, 70, 146-49, 204-05
RAITH, Erich, 146-49
RAUNICHER, Albert, 176-79
REICHL, H-D., 190
RICHTER, Helmut, 93, 102-05, 128, 136-37,
 165-66
RIEDER, Manfred Max, 127, 129, 165
RIEGLER, Florian & RIEWE, Roger, 37, 127,
 164-65, 180-83
RIEPL, Peter, 92
RIETVELD, Gerrit, 73
ROSSI, Aldo, 18, 164
RUDOFSKY, Bernard, 17, 24, 67-69, 73
RUEDI, Katerina, 5, 214

SANT ' ELIA, Antonio, 66
SCHEBESTA, Karl, 116
SCHENEKL, Manfred, 206
SCHINDLER, K. & HABBE & LOIBNEGGER,
 180-83
SCHINDLER, Rudolph M., 17-19, 22, 25, 66-
 67, 73, 203
SCHMID, Heinrich, 22
SCHÖFFAUER, Friedrich, 90-91, 93
SCHÖNBERG, Arnold, 16
SCHORSKE, Carl, 196
SCHROM, Wolfgang, 90-91, 93
SCHUSCHNIGG, Kurt, 24
SCHUSTER, Franz, 25
SCHÜTTE-LIHOTZKY, Margarete, 66
SCHWAIGHOFER, Anton, 69
SCHWANZER, Karl, 25, 27
SCHWARZ, Margaret, 213
SCHWARZ, Rudolf, 26
SEIDLER, Harry, 73
SEMPER, Gottfried, 20
SENNETT, Richard, 196, 214
SERRES, Michel, 13
SILBERSTEIN, Alfred, 215
SILVESTRIN, Claudio, 39
SIMEOFORIDIS, Yorgos, 162
SIMMEL, Georg, 36
SITE, 50
SITTE, Camillo, 200-01, 206-07
SORKIN, Michael, 5, 74, 200, 209, 213
SPAGOLLA, Bruno, 92
SPALT, Johannes, 26
STEINMAYR, Erich, 174-75
STRAND, Oscar, 20
STRNAD, Oskar, 22, 23
STROLZ, Erich, 129, 131
STURMBERGER, R., 176-79
SUZUKI, Akira, 5
SUZUKI, Hiroyuki, 5, 75
SWOBODA, Hannes, 146-49

TAFURI, Manfredo, 12
TALIESIN, 17
TANGE, Kenzo, 76

TESAR, Heinz, 46-47, 212
TRIPOLT, Albert, 43
TESSENOV, Heinrich, 22
TSCHAPELLER, Wolfgang, 90-91, 93, 127, 129

UHL, Ottokar, 26, 73
UNTERTRIFFALLER, Much, 128-29, 131
URBAN, Joseph, 16-17, 20, 22, 25

VAN TOORN, ROEMER, 162
VASKO, Wolfgang & HEINRICH, Lothar, 136
VETTER, Hans, 26
VIDLER, Anthony, 163
VIRILIO, Paul, 163

WACHSMANN, Konrad, 26, 73
WAGNER, Gerhard, 52, 172
WAGNER, Otto, 8, 11, 14, 16-17, 20-22, 25,
66, 74, 76-77, 200-03
WALLACH, Franz, 27
WAWRIK, Gunther, 73
WEGAN, Johannes, 93, 96
WELZENBACHER, Lois, 24, 124-25
WLACH, Oskar, 23
WITTGENSTEIN, Ludwig, 127
WOLFF-PLOTTEGG, Manfred, 127, 132-33
WONDRA, Heinz, 92
WONDRACEK, Rudolf, 25
WÖRNDL, Hanspeter, 127, 129
WÖRLE, Eugen, 25, 27
WOTRUBA, Fritz, 116
WRIGHT, Frank Lloyd, 17, 19-20, 22, 24

ZECHNER, Christoph & Martin, 165-66
ZEMLER, Willibald, 176-79
ZEVI, Bruno, 16
ZIESLER, Wolf-Dietrich, 50, 170-71
ZOBERNIG, Heimo, 144-45
ZUMTHOR, Peter, 94

ACHLEITNER, Friedrich, 23, 26-29, 30
ALLISON, Peter, 60, 61, 64, 65, 66, 67
ARCHIVE ACHLEITNER/BOECKL, 18-21
ARTEC, 67, 186-187
BASSEWITZ, Gert von, 140-141

BISWAS, Ramesh Kumar, 36, 38, 39,
 41, 102-103, 112-113, 117, 132,
 155, 182, 189, 213, 217
BLAU, Anna, 50, 51, 167
BONNER, Tom, 74, 84
BRAMBERGER, ROEMER, 33
BOECKL, Mathias, 69, 70, 77

CHRAMOSTA, Walter M., 123-127, 131
DELTSIOS, Martha, 158-159, 164, 166
DEUBNER, Helmut, 152-153
DOGL-CHERKOORI, 32, 75, 102-103,
EICHINGER OR KNECHTL, 39

ELLERT, Lucia, 16
ERLACHER, Gisela, 78, 79, 80, 81
FALKEIS & FALKEIS-SENN, 208
FISCHER, Christian, 198, 199
GRUEN, Victor, 6, 71

HAEUSLE, Martin, 168
HISTORISCHES MUSEUM, Stadt Wien,
 209
HOLLEIN, Hans, 74, 76, 82, 83, 210
KADA, Klaus, 98-99
KAUNAT, Angelo, 48, 49, 97, 128, 188

KIENER, Franz, 216-217
LACKNER, Christof, 190-191
LANDESBILDSTELLE WIEN, MA 13,
 204, 205
LIEDL & GRONEMANN, 90-91
MAURACHER, Michael, 46, 47

MISSING LINK, 194-195
NEVIDAL, Hans, 71
OTT, Paul, 126, 180 - 183
ÖSTERR. INSTITUT F. ZEITGESCHICHTE,
196, 197
PILLHOFER, Markus, 75

PRUSCHA, Carl, 72, 73
RAINER, Roland, 146, 148
RAU, Uwe, 86, 87
RICHTER, Helmut, 102-105, 136-137
RIHA, Georg, 40

SCHILD, Hannes, 53, 111
SCHMID, Alfred, 100
SCHULMAN, Julius, 20, 21
SCHUSTER, Michael, 144-145
SIGMUND FREUD MUSEUM, 35

SPILUTTINI, Margarita, 32, 52, 53,
 84, 85, 86, 100-101, 106 -107, 108-
 111, 114-115, 116, 120, 127, 130,
 134-135, 150-151
STEINER, Rupert, 166
STIFTUNG DEUTSCHEN KINEMATEK,
 40
SCHWINGENSCHLÖGEL, 67
TRAUTTMANNSDORFF, Octavian, 63

UTIMPERGHER, Paolo, 33
VEIGL, Mathias, 41
WILLIG, Hajo, 121
ZOBERNIG, Heimo, 66
ZUGMANN, Gerald, 42-45, 54-57, 94,
 129, 160, 161, 172-173

Techno-Waltz Innovative Austrian Architecture
Biswas

1   Michel de Montaigne, On the Education of Children, Essays, Penguin, London 1958
2   Manuel Castells, Informatisierte Stadt und soziale Bewegungen, in: Stadt-Räume, hg. v. Martin Wentz, Frankfurt/Main 1991
3   Claude Levi-Strauss, Mythologica (transl. Suhrkamp, Frankfurt/Main 1971-75)
4   Christian Norberg-Schulz, Genius Loci - paesaggio, ambiente, architettura, Gruppo Editoriale Electa, Milano 1979
5   Kenneth Frampton, Tyrolean Regionalism. A Critical Postscript, in: Kuz/Chramosta/Frampton, Autochthonous Architecture in Tyrol, Hall in Tirol 1992
6   Massimo Cacciari, Architecture and Nihilism: On the Philosophy of Modern Architecture, Yale University Press, New Haven 1993
7   Rem Koolhaas, The Paranoid-Critical Method, Architectural Design 2/3, London 1978
8   Mark Hillegas, Introduction to H.G. Well's A Modern Utopia, University of Nebraska Press 1967
9   Walter Gropius, proclamation for the exhibit Arbeitsrat für Kunst, Berlin, April 1917
10 Deleuze/Guattari, Kafka: Towards A Minor Literature (transl. Für eine kleine Literatur, Suhrkamp, Frankfurt/Main 1976)
11 Charles Jencks, The Architecture of the Jumping Universe, Academy Editions, London 1995
12 Manfredo Tafuri, History of Italian Architecture 1944-1985, MIT Press, Cambridge, Mass. 1989
13 Daniel Odier, The Job, Interviews with William S. Burroughs, Penguin, New York 1974
14 Eugénie Lemoine-Luccioni, Partage des Femmes, Paris1976
15 Michel Serres, Hermes I: La communication, Minuit, Paris 1969
16 Andrea Branzi, Learning from Milan: Design and the Second Modernity, MIT Press, Cambridge, Mass. 1988
17 Hannah Arendt, The Human Condition, The University of Chicago Press, Chicago 1958
18 Wolf Prix, in conversation with the editor

Innocents abroad
Biswas

1   Friedrich Achleitner, Die geköpfte Architektur. Anmerkungen zu einem ungeschriebenen Kapitel der österreichischen Architekturgeschichte, in: Gabriele Koller (Ed.), Die Vertreibung des Geistigen. Zur Kulturpolitik des Nationalsozialismus, Vienna 1985
2   Josef Frank, Annual Program of the New York School for Social Research, New York 1942
3   Matthias Boeckl/Otto Kapfinger (Ed.), Visionäre & Vertriebene. Österreichische Spuren in der modernen amerikanischen Architektur, Ernst & Sohn, Vienna 1995
4   Bernard Rudofsky, Architecture without Architects, Museum of Modern Art, New York 1964
5   Christopher Alexander, The Timeless Way of Building and A Pattern Language, Oxford University Press, New York 1979
6   Refer to work by Eduard Sekler, Carpenter Center for the Arts, Cambridge, Mass.
7   Ernst Bliem (Ed.), Austrian Cultural Institute New York. An Architectural Competition, Haymon, Innsbruck 1993
8   Friedensreich Hundertwasser, Verschimmelungsmanifest, Vienna 1958

A certain lack of respect - the re-interpretation of time
Biswas

1   Fyodor Dostoevsky, Notes from Unterground (1864), Penguin Books, Harmondsworth, 1981
2   Leopold Kohr, The Breakdown of Nations, (Das Ende der Grössen, Vienna 1986)
3   Douglas R. Hofstadter, Gödel, Escher, Bach: an Eternal Golden Braid, New York 1979
4   Herbert Marcuse, Kultur und Gesellschaft, Frankfurt/Main 1965
5   Sigmund Freud, The interpretation of Dreams, transl. by the editor, Traumdeutung, Vienna 1900
6   Otto Kapfinger, Grundsätzliche Anmerkungen, in Victor Hufnagl (ed.), Reflexionen und Aphorismen zur öster reichischen Architektur, Vienna 1984
7   Georg Simmel, Der Konflikt der modernen Kultur, Vienna 1918
8   Marshall Berman, All That Is Solid Melts Into Air: The Experience of Modernity, Penguin Books, New York 1988

Clinics for housing addicts
Chramosta

1   Walter Benjamin, Passagenwerk, Vol. 1, Frankfurt/Main 1972
2   Robert Musil, Man without Qualities, Vol. 1, (1930), Perigree Books New York 1980
3   Jose Ortega y Gasset, (Obras completas 1902-46) Gesammelte Werke, Stuttgart 1978

Interchange, Landscape, Limit, Navigation
Simeoforidis

1   Kostas Axelos, La question de la fin de l'art et la poéticité du monde, Le présent de l'art dans le monde contemporain, Centre d'art contemporain, Genève 1989, p. 187.
2   Ole Boumann/Roemer Van Toorn, The Invisible in Architecture (Academy, London 1994)
3   Y. Simeoforidis, 'On Landscape and Public Open Spaces', 'Architecture and Behaviour', vol. 9, no 3, 1993: 321-327
4   Anthony Vidler, The Architectural Uncanny. Essays in the modern unhomely, The MIT Press, Cambridge, Massachusetts, London, England, 1992 (part III: Spaces, p. 167)
5   Marcel Meili, 'Periphery. A letter from Zürich', 'Quaderns', 177/1988: 18-33.
6   Anthony Vidler, ibidem.
7   On this subject see, Quaderns, (Documents: Vall d'Hebron: A New Landscape), issue on 'Linked Images', n. 193, March/April 1992, p. 45.
8   Ignasi de Solà-Morales, 'Difference and limit. Individualism in contemporary architecture', 'Domus', 736, March 1993: 17-24.
9   Frame - Picture of use', Riegler & Riewe in discussion with Otto Kapfinger, in the catalogue Riegler/Riewe, Löcker Verlag 1994, p. 20.
10 'Architecture as an abstract concept', interview with PAUHOF, M. Küng, 'Archis' 7/95: 41
11 Friedrich Achleitner, "Constants and transformations in Viennese universalism", in Vienna Architecture Seminar, Verlag Ernst & Sohn, 1992, p. 37.
12 W.M. Chramosta, "From Graz to Utopia and back", in Zechner & Zechner, 18 dwellings in Graz, Neufeldweg, Europan Implementations 3, Untimely Books, 1994, p. 44.

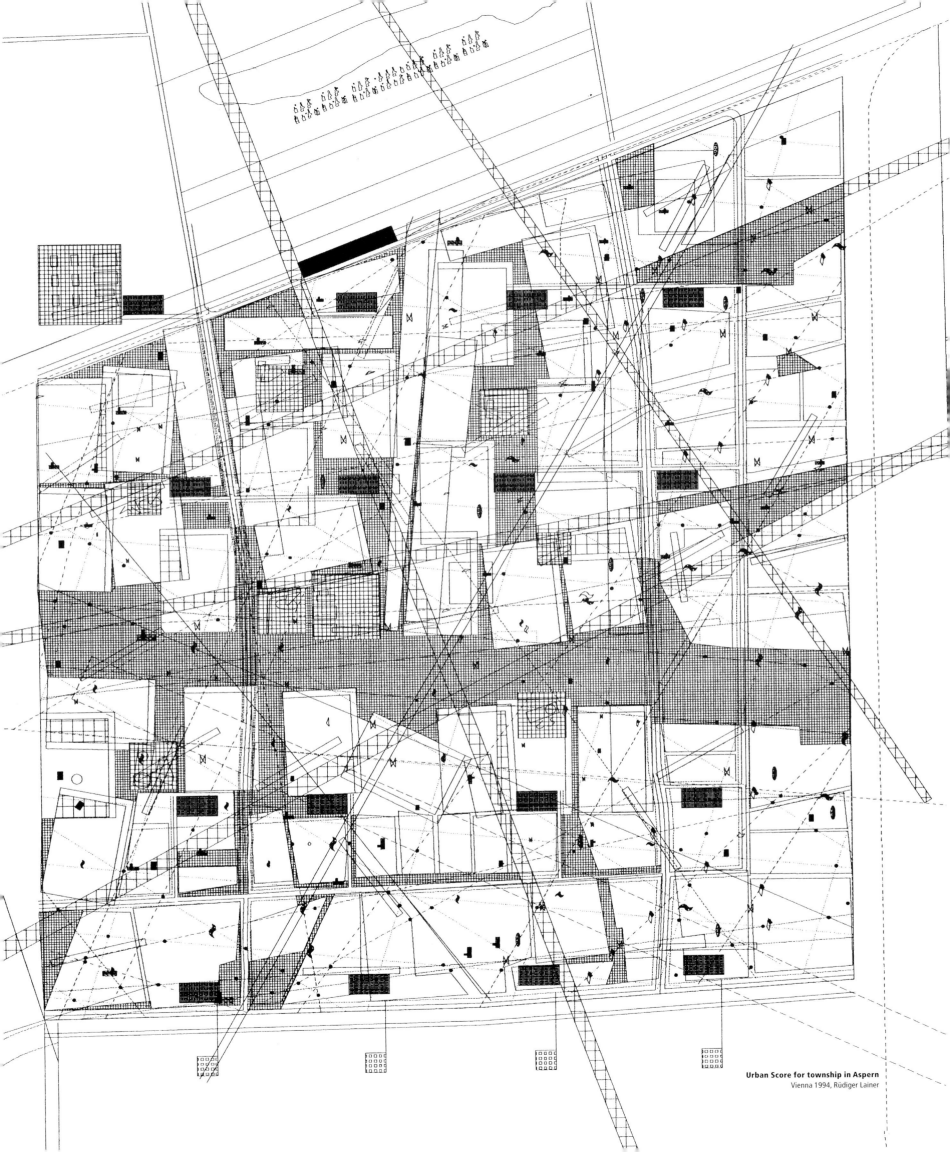

Urban Score for township in Aspern
Vienna 1994, Rüdiger Lainer

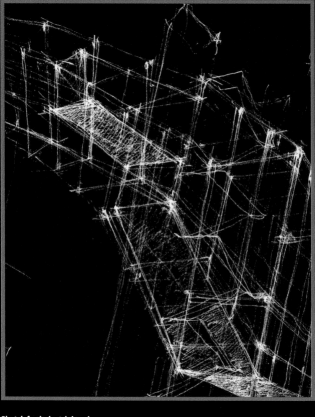

Sketch for industrial park,
Günther Domenig

Ramesh Kumar Biswas
Mommseng. 21/6, A-1040 Vienna
Fax: ++43-1-504 62 24

SpringerNews

Liesbeth Waechter-Böhm (ed.)

Heinz Tesar

With an Essay by Friedrich Achleitner

1995. 187 partly coloured figures. 152 pages.
Cloth DM 68,–, öS 476,–
Text: German/English
ISBN 3-211-82724-2
Portraits of Austrian Architects, Volume 1

Heinz Tesar has long belonged to the important and well-known representatives of that Austrian generation of architects which has made such startling advances and is already competing with the Holleins, Holzbauers and the Peichls. He also belongs to those for whom concentration on their work is more important than its coverage in the press. That is why there has up to now been no comprehensive book on Heinz Tesar published although examples of his architectural credo are to be seen in the architectural landscape stretching far beyond the confines of Vienna. In the capital itself there are residential buildings and a Kindergarten that he has planned but his representative building, the "Schömer House", is to be found in Klosterneuburg where another of his works, the Protestant church, has just been completed. Heinz Tesar has also left his architectural mark in Hallein, where, with the structural alterations to the city theatre and the extension to the Celt museum, two of the most notable buildings of this architect have been accomplished.

The volume documents the most important examples of Heinz Tesar's work using extensive plans and illustrations as well as short text analysis. An essay by Friedrich Achleitner introduces the reader to the work of the architect and in an interview with the same Liesbeth Waechter-Böhm looks for answers to the question as to what thoughts precede the architecture.

In preparation:

Carlo Baumschlager, Dietmar Eberle
1996. Approx. 200 partly coloured figures. Approx. 180 pages.
Cloth approx. DM 68,–, öS 476,–
ISBN 3-211-82725-0
Portraits of Austrian Architects, Volume 2

Robert Oerley
1996. Numerous partly coloured figures. Approx. 120 pages.
Cloth approx. DM 42,–, öS 298,–
ISBN 3-211-82776-5
Portraits of Austrian Architects, Volume 3

SpringerArchitecture

SpringerWienNewYork

P.O.Box 89, A-1201 Wien • New York, NY 10010, 175 Fifth Avenue
Heidelberger Platz 3, D-14197 Berlin • Tokyo 113, 3-13, Hongo 3-chome, Bunkyo-ku

Brigitte Groihofer (ed.)

Raimund Abraham

[Un]built

With an introductory essay by Norbert Miller.
With contributions by John Hejduk, Kenneth Frampton, P. Adams Sitney,
Lebbeus Woods, Wieland Schmied.

1996. 402 partly colored figures. 315 pages.
Cloth DM 148,–, öS 1036,–, US $ 95.00.
ISBN 3-211-82671-8

The book contains the complete work of the Architect Raimund Abraham. It is divided into three parts:
1) Imaginary Architecture
2) Projects
3) Realizations.
Texts are by Raimund Abraham, Kenneth Frampton, John Hejduk, P. Adams Sitney, Wieland Schmied and Lebbeus Woods. With an introductory essay by Norbert Miller.
The Austrian Architect Raimund Abraham, born in Tyrol, Austria, in 1933, lives, works and teaches in the USA since 1964. As an exponent of the Viennese Avantgarde of the early sixties his work was exhibited together with the works of Hans Hollein and Walter Pichler at the Museum of Modern Art in New York in 1967.
The drawing of architecture occupies a central position in the evolution of his work but challenges the predominant notion of built architecture. Drawing demands an autonomous reality, manifestation of his architectural concept. The drawings and projects as well as the notion of "collision" becomes a dialectical theorem as well as the ontological foundation of architecture.
Any architectural manifestation results either in the violation of the earth or the sky, while architecture is a reconciliation of these events, a transformation of the horizon: spatially, spiritually and psychologically. For Abraham architectural space is defined by the dialectical polarity of geometrical versus physiological space. The objective of a new architecture is to reject the regressive replica of historic vocabulary and to recognize the ontological limits of human existence in order to question it.

SpringerArchitecture

 **Springer**WienNewYork

P.O.Box 89, A-1201 Wien • New York, NY 10010, 175 Fifth Avenue
Heidelberger Platz 3, D-14197 Berlin • Tokyo 113, 3-13, Hongo 3-chome, Bunkyo-ku

To every age its **art**

Gate to the Ring, entrance to the bookshop, designed by James Wines/SITE

Romanesque, Gothic, Renaissance designed by Günther Förg

Historicism, Art Nouveau, designed by Barbara Bloom

At the beginning of the 'nineties the Austrian Museum of Applied Arts was remodelled under the supervision of Peter Noever, 120 years after its original completion by Heinrich von Ferstel. International artists and curators have placed the historical exhibits in a contemporary setting, thus making the Museum of Applied Arts a focus of tradition and experiment.

There's more to Vienna.

Vienna · Wien · Vienne · Viena · ウィーン

Vienna Tourist Board, fax +43-1-216 84 92. Vienna Representative Offices, Tokyo, fax +81-3-35 01 80 16, Hong Kong, fax +852-25 36 40 98.

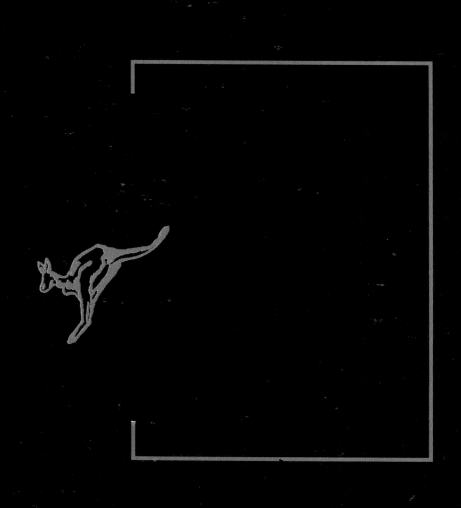